C000134029

DICK ISHERWOOD
MOUNTAINEER

An Anthology
Compiled by John Ashburner

An environmentally friendly book printed and bound in England by
www.printondemand-worldwide.com

Mixed Sources
Product group from well-managed
forests, and other controlled sources
www.fsc.org Cert no. TT-COC-002641
© 1996 Forest Stewardship Council
FSC

PEFC

PEFC/16-33-415

PEFC Certified
This product is
from sustainably
managed forests
and controlled
sources
www.pefc.org

This book is made entirely of chain-of-custody materials

www.fast-print.net/store.php

DICK ISHERWOOD MOUNTAINEER

ISBN 978-178035-010-2

Graphic design: Kevin Trent – *www.kevinatrent.com*

First published 2014 by
FASTPRINT PUBLISHING
Peterborough, England.

*Front Cover: Dick surveys the northern flank of Masherbrum (7821m) from
the confluence of the Mundu with the Baltoro Glacier, not far above Urdukas
Back Cover: Climbers approaching Dorje Lakpa (6966m) in the Jugal Himal*
Photos: John Cleare

"*We got through a long list of climbs that summer,*
climbs of all sorts; difficult struggles,
* light-hearted experiences, contemplative pleasures*
– but my longings were not yet satisfied.
Evidently such is my nature.
* Many of my wishes were fulfilled yet on each occasion,*
fulfilment gave birth to another wish."

Hermann Buhl, 1956
Nanga Parbat Pilgrimage

Dick Isherwood at Concordia (c.4700m), the remote confluence of the Baltoro and Godwin Austen glaciers. The southern flank of K2 rises in the distance. (June 1979)
Photo: John Cleare

DICK ISHERWOOD
MOUNTAINEER

An Anthology
Compiled by John Ashburner

CONTENTS

All articles by Dick Isherwood unless where otherwise stated

PREFACE	VII
ACKNOWLEDGEMENTS	IX
CLIMBS OF MY YOUTH	1
HOW TO BE A GREATER MOUNTAINEER	11
MORE CLIMBS IN SWAT	17
NIGHT CLIMBERS BEWARE! *Tony Greenbank*	26
CAMBRIDGE IN THE LATE SIXTIES *Rob Collister*	31
REFLECTIONS ON THE CUMC MINUTES *John Ashburner*	41
A GLIMPSE OF PRE-CAMBRIA *Bob Keates*	49
EXTOL	55
CARNMORE	59
A VISIT TO SCOTLAND	65
DIRETTISSIMA ON THE PIZ BADILE	68
PIZZO BADILE 3308M *"Popi" Miotti & Alessandro Sogna*	74
WEEKEND	79
HINDU RAJ 1969 *Colin Taylor*	84
ATTEMPT ON THUI II FROM SHETOR GLACIER	91
THE DUGUNDUGOO	96
PARBATI 1973	103
HIMALAYAN GRANDE-COURSE *Rob Collister*	109
LAMJUNG HIMAL	115
BIRDS OF SWAT AND GILGIT	123
A SUMMER IN GILGIT (1975) PT I *Rob Collister*	125

KANJIROBA 1976	133
BOOK KEEPING *John Ashburner*	141
ANNAPURNA II *Rob Collister*	144
BUNI ZOM	149
A YEAR OFF WORK	155
A FORTNIGHT IN GARHWAL *Geoff Cohen*	166
OF JIMMY AND THE TCHADOR	171
POKHARKAN SOUTH FACE, NEPAL *Dave Wynne-Jones*	177
BHAJE EXPEDITION	182
KING OF MOUNTAINS HAIZI SHAN 5833M, SICHUAN	188
A CAUTIONARY TALE	195
SHALULI SHAN, 2007 *Dave Wynne-Jones*	199
YANGMOLONG (6066M), ATTEMPT *Dave Wynne-Jones*	202
NO BLENDS!	204
BIFE DE CHORIZO	212
REFLECTIONS ON TREKKING IN NEPAL	218
THE CANOE DIARIES *Priscilla Kaufman*	222
RICHARD (DICK) ISHERWOOD 1943-2013 *Geoff Cohen*	226
APPENDICES	232
BIBLIOGRAPHY	233
CLIMBING EXPEDITIONS	236
NEW ROUTES	242
INDEX	246

ILLUSTRATIONS

Dick surveys the northern flank of Masherbrum (7821m)	FRONT COVER
Climbers approaching Dorje Lakpa (6966m)	BACK COVER
Dick Isherwood at Concordia (c.4700m) – K2 rises in the distance	FRONTISPIECE
Figure 1 John Peck on the upper long pitch of White Slab. Note the grass!	4
Figure 2 Bob Keates on the Big Groove, Craig Gogarth 1966	8
Figure 3 Jim Swallow prusiking up the initial overhang of Mynydd	10
Figure 4 The mountains of Siri Dara, Swat Kohistan	12
Figure 5 Mankial from the north-west	14
Figure 6 Siri Dara icefall and plateau from the north-west	19
Figure 7 Swat: Confusion (Left) and Batin peaks from the South	19
Figure 8 Peck's Dièdre (Pyramid Peak): just below the Crux	21
Figure 9 Mankial from the South	24
Figure 10 Starting the roof	26
Figure 11 The mountain and the expedition report	28
Figure 12 John Cardy on Llithrig, Clogwyn du'r Arddu.	32
Figure 13 Cardy – "shock of red hair and the enormous forehead of a boffin"	34
Figure 14 The bohemian John Peck at high camp on the North Kohistan expedition.	36
Figure 15 John Peck and Rob Collister with teachers from Bagral Primary School	36
Figure 16 Mount Ararat, Turkey, passed en route to North Kohistan, Swat in 1968	37
Figure 17 Dick Isherwood at the bivouac on Thui II, Chitral, August 1969	37
Figure 18 CUMC Sixties style: David Gundry at Chair Ladder, Cornwall, January 1968.	38
Figure 19 The Minute Book, now preserved in the University Library	43
Figure 20 Page 365 of the Minutes recording the visit of Dr Gurung	47
Figure 21 The Programme for 1963-64 as attached in the Minute book	48
Figure 22 The Big Groove, Gogarth North Stack	50
Figure 23 Dick on the crux pitch of Dwm, Castell Cidwm	51
Figure 24 Dick seconding The Grasper, Tremadoc	54
Figure 25 Dick leading the 1ˢᵗ pitch of The Crucible, Craig Yr Ogof, Cwm Silyn	58

Figure 26 Gritstone Buttress, A'Mhaighdean, Carnmore   63

Figure 27 Piz Badile, upper two-thirds of pillar on the North-east face   69

Figure 28 Approaching the steep final section of the Piz Badile   71

Figure 29 The monolithic north-east face of the Badile   74

Figure 30 The crack line clearly showing the direct nature of the route   76

Figure 31 The east face of the Badile - Via degli Inglesi   78

Figure 32 Isherwood on an early attempt on the line, later completed by Birtles as Deyco   80

Figure 33 Chris Wood, Dick Isherwood and Colin Taylor heading upwards   87

Figure 34 Thui II area, Hindu Raj showing the activities of the 1969 British party   92

Figure 35 Pachan Zom c. 19,588 ft to the north-west of Thui II   93

Figure 36 View south from the Summit of Pachan Zom   94

Figure 37 The ridge in the left foreground is the south-east ridge of Pachan Zom   95

Figure 38 Thui II from the east taken from the col between the Shetor and Qalandar glaciers   95

Figure 39 The face of Carstensz Pyramide from the Meren Glacier   98

Figure 40 The north face of Sunday Peak   101

Figure 41 Ridge Peak from the SW ridge of Parbati South   105

Figure 42 Parbati South (6128m) from Ridge Peak   106

Figure 43 John Cardy, Dick Isherwood and Geoff Cohen ready for the walk out from Base Camp   108

Figure 44 Parbati South from Advanced Base Camp   110

Figure 45 Dick on the SW face of Parbati South   111

Figure 46 Dick on Grade IV rock at 6000m on the summit slabs   112

Figure 47 The route of ascent.   115

Figure 48 Dick emerging up the E col   116

Figure 49 Carrying loads to the E col   118

Figure 50 Lamjung (6983m)   119

Figure 51 Load carrying on the E ridge, Lamjungspitze behind   121

Figure 52 John Scott on the final section   122

Figure 53 The N face of Rakaposhi from near Chalt   127

Figure 54 Gilgit, Chalt and lots of other places   130

Figure 55 The Kanjiroba Himal   134

Figure 56 Looking north up the Jagdula Khola towards the main peaks of the Kanjiroba Himal   135

Figure 57 Crossing the Jagdula Khola   136

Figure 58 Crossing the Jagdula Khola again   137

Figure 59 Camp 1 on Kanjiroba   139

Figure 60 Dick Isherwood observing pay-day for the porters, Lamjung 1974   142

Figure 61 Dick Isherwood on a recce for Annapurna I and II, Dec 1977   144

Figure 62 Machapuchare from high on Annapurna IV   145

Figure 63 Dick rehydrating on chang after descending, October 1978   146

Figure 64 Dick at almost 7000m on Annapurna IV just before their descent   148

Figure 65 En route to the Kachikani Pass   149

Figure 66 Dick approaching the West face of Buni Zom (right)   151

Figure 67 Buni Zom   153

Figure 68 Dick scrutinising Dorje Lakpa, Jugal Himal, showing the two camps on the West ridge   155

Figure 69 Dorje Lakpa (6966m) from the south   157

Figure 70 Dave Broadhead at the first ridge camp on Dorje Lakpa   158

Figure 71 K7 West, showing the high point reached   160

Figure 72 Des Rubens on Drifika, Karakoram   161

Figure 73 Geoff Cohen on K7 West   163

Figure 74 Geoff Cohen on the south-east ridge of Tsoboje, Rolwaling, Nepal   164

Figure 75 Dick resting below the NW face of Rataban   167

Figure 76 Dick on the NW face of Rataban   168

Figure 77 Dick below the NW face of Nilgiri Parbat   169

Figure 78 Dick moving round some ice cliffs on Nilgiri Parbat   170

Figure 79 A promising icefall in the Zanskar Gorge   173

Figure 80 The gompa at Tongde, Zanskar   175

Figure 81 A monk at Tongde with a heavily decorated conch shell   176

Figure 82 Dick with the friendly old Nepali yak herder   178

Figure 83 Kaji and Martin Scott on the summit of Pokharkan (6350m), Nepal   180

Figure 84 Descending through ice cliffs following the first ascent of Pokharkan's south face   181

Figure 85 "Far, far, the mountain peak". Pokharkan from the distance   186

Figure 86 Gatherers of the sought-after 'worm grass' below Haizi Shan   189

Figure 87 North face of Haizi Shan (5833m), western Sichuan   191

Figure 88 Dick Isherwood on the NE Ridge   192

Figure 89 Haizi Shan summit   194

Figure 90 The south face of the Gongkala peaks   196

Figure 91 Walking around the range on the south-eastern approach to Dangchezhengla   199

Figure 92 From the south-west, Dangchezhengla (5830m)   200

Figure 93 High on Dangchezhengla (5830m)   201

Figure 94 Yangmolong (6066m, left) and Makara (a.k.a. Central Peak, 6033m)   202

Figure 95 Broad summit ridge of Yangmolong (6066m) from north-east   203

Figure 96 The West Face of Jopuno, showing the route attempted   205

Figure 97 Paul Swienton climbing on Lama Lamani   207

Figure 98 Kabru (left) and Kangchenjunga (far right) from below   208

Figure 99 Simon Yates and Geoff Robb near the summit of Monte Bove   212

Figure 100 Camp on Monte Bove   213

Figure 101 Approaching Monte Bove across the Glacier Frances   214

Figure 102 High on Monte Bove   215

Figure 103 Lenticular cloud formation above Monte Bove   216

Figure 104 Dick "looking for orcas" in Johnstone Strait, NW Vancouver Island, May 2007   224

Figure 105 Dick sailing with Tim, his son-in-law and two grandchildren   225

Figure 106 Dick Isherwood in 1974 on a Joint Services expedition   227

Figure 107 Chulu East (6584m)   238

Figure 108 Dick and Sam Isherwood above Kamjung village on the Everest trek   240

PREFACE

"Sheltered completely from the weather, I uncoiled the rope on top of the rock bridge and tried to remember what I had read about solo artificial climbing. I tied on to both ends of the rope and made a big loop in the middle which I put over the high part of the bridge as a token belay.

Somehow I had only brought one étrier but I had a few slings to supplement it. I protected myself by tying loops into the two ropes alternately and remaining attached, as far as possible, to three pegs at once. The slanting fault in the overhang was loose and one peg popped out with me on it. Just below the chimney which led out of the overhanging band, I had difficulty placing a good peg, and I used a sling threaded round a flake as extra security. As I moved across I pulled on the sling and the flake fell off, hitting me in the face".

Dick describing a couple of close calls during his solo ascent of Sunday Peak, New Guinea

D ick Isherwood was a remarkable pioneer, explorer and naturalist and when he suddenly passed away in February 2013, his family and friends were left with a huge void. He had settled in the USA in 1999, soon after returning from some 30 years spent in various parts of South East Asia. His brother and sister-in-law, Mike and Chris, organised a wake in his memory at their country home in Cumbria in April 2013 where some fifty members of the family and friends congregated.

Prior to this, a call had been made to bring along any photographs, journals or expedition reports of interest to the gathering and a splendid collection could be placed on display. Someone remarked that the extensive material shown represented but a fraction of what had been produced by Dick, not to mention the many stories recounted by his friends and written up in various journals and letters. The Compiler of this book was then "volunteered" in an overnight discussion (and in his total absence from the proceedings) to put together this anthology. It was to comprise any available writings and anecdotes which could be traced.

The task would not have been possible without access to insider knowledge. Indeed, I hadn't myself seen Dick since 1968 and had been bitterly disappointed when he had telephoned me just recently in October 2012, proposing to visit me in a few days time in Southport, UK. I could not personally talk to him as I had just quite literally "lost my voice" due to having to undergo a total laryngectomy. But I also had to turn him down because the day proposed happened to coincide with that of my younger daughter's wedding. I was later to bitterly regret this unfortunate clash of dates.

So what awaits the reader and why put together these stories anyway?

Let's look at a typical observation of Dick concerning one of his companions:

"That afternoon we camped in a snowstorm a little way below the col. I was sharing a tent with Rob and witnessed a most impressive demonstration.

Antarctic Man was in his pit, with a brew on, and without a single snowflake inside the tent, while I was still trying to unfasten my boots. I realised I was in the right tent; the others were still putting theirs up. He was the only one whose boots didn't freeze in the night too."

Dick had a great ability to describe not only his companions but also the innermost thoughts passing through his mind. Take for instance his musings immediately upon reaching safety after an epic struggle on K7 West in the Karakoram:

"We had been five days on this climb and we were all very tired. I had slightly numb and tingling fingers and toes, and lay in the grass feeling as if I was in a shell. My body didn't want to do anything but my mind was very active, thinking of all the things I could do in the future provided I continued to survive experiences like this".

He loved a simplistic approach to his explorations with small, lightweight parties. Take for instance this plan sent to his intended companion regarding a peak which so happened to be 7885m:

One of the last communications he received was a card scribbled in an aeroplane and posted in Japan. It read:

"How about Distaghil Sar? Buy a goat in Hispar and drive it up the glacier. Dick."

He also delighted in ridiculing over-organisation. Here are his thoughts prior to his trip to Lamjung:

"We were, nominally, an Army expedition mounted from Hong Kong. We even had a military code name. However, as the number of experienced Army climbers in Hong Kong in 1974 was scarcely sufficient to mount an expedition to Llanberis, the original plan had to be modified along the way".

Dick had many experiences to recount during his rise to become one of the top UK rock climbers of the late 1960s and they are fully documented in this collection. Once he moved overseas, the stories inevitably changed but if anything their colour became even more vivid. Before releasing the reader to browse forwards, just glance at another episode which occurred during a bivouac on K7 West:

"The boots got passed to me at one end and I hung them all by their laces from a big chock placed in a crack - at least I thought I did. We had a surprisingly warm night, though it was all a bit cramped. In the morning I carefully passed the boots back and discovered that I'd failed to clip in one of Des's - it had spent the night merely wedged between two others.

I didn't dare confess to this and sat in silence as Geoff said speculatively:
'I wonder what would happen if you dropped your boots from here?'
Des replied:
'I doubt if you'd get down.'
I spent the rest of the climb wondering just what we would have done".

Now read on…

ACKNOWLEDGEMENTS

A t first glance it would appear simple to put together an anthology when such a range of material exists. But digging out the more concealed items or unpublished gems is more difficult. There were also some gaps which needed filling in and a number of pieces to be specially written in order to enhance the collection.

Apart from what Dick has written, the anthology also includes items which were originally penned or specially prepared for this anthology by Geoff Cohen, Rob Collister, Tony Greenbank, Bob Keates, Colin Taylor, Dave Wynne-Jones and my humble self. Bob Courtier gave me special orientation for the "Blurb" and the Foreword and even tracked down the Italian book by Giuseppe Miotti and Alessandro Gogna for which he led the translation of the vital chapter included in this book.

Most of the articles originally appeared in the journals of the Alpine Club, the Climbers Club, the Himalayan Club, the American Alpine Club or the Cambridge University Mountaineering Club, all of which have kindly granted permission for their reproduction.

Much of the preparation process used scanning and OCR techniques, either directly from the original journals or when uploaded to or downloaded from the Internet. It was thus important to cross-check that the reproduction was accurate and many assisted in this task. Apart from some of those already mentioned above, this proof reading was also assisted by Jeff Barker, Dave Broadhead, Simon Brown, Derek Buckle, John Cardy, Henry Day, Robin Devenish, Steve Hale, Jim Harding, Terence Lam, Anne Macintyre, Gordon Macnair, John McCormick, Phil Neame, Paul Newby, John Peck, Peter Rowat, Hugh Samuel, Patricia Wheeler, Mike Whelan and Chris Wood.

Retrieving the CUMC Minute Book from the University Library and photographing the records covering the two years 1963 to 1965 was kindly done by Paul Fox, whilst Henry Edmundson crept back in to redo a couple of key pages which were a bit blurred (had Paul suffered from vertigo whilst up in the library tower?).

John Cleare provided the illustration of Dick for the Frontispiece. He later very graciously also provided a light table of ideas for designing the covers together with some supplementary illustrations from his archives. Several of these have been incorporated into the book.

Additional photographs were provided by some of those already mentioned and also by Steve Kennedy, Sam Isherwood, Giuseppe (Popi) Miotti, Simone Porta, Paul Swienton and John Yates.

Background information, advice and other assistance came from many of the above and also from Dick's wife Janet, his son Sam and his brother Mike. Others giving a welcome hand were Vanda Agostino, Clare Courtier, Ron Giddy, Glyn Hughes, Mike Kosterlitz, Ted Maden, Steve Martin, Leo Murray, Richard Owen, Rupert Roschnik, Des Rubens, Veronica Sims, Martin Sinker, Unity Stack, Ken Wilson and Simon Yates.

Mark Paul kept my out-dated computer going, aided by my daughter Jennifer Paul whilst my elder daughter Wendy Clark did numerous encouraging things. As ever and without recourse to any complaint, my ever understanding wife Paty put up with all the clutter of electronic gear, books, papers, photographs, journals and empty coffee mugs occupying any available domestic space.

Final preparations were smoothed over by the understanding of the Graphic Designer, Kevin Trent whilst Paul Newby cast a baleful eye over proceedings, contributing significantly to the process. During eventual production, Marika Buttigieg provided careful guidance to enable full use of the services of Fast-Print Publishing. There will be inevitable errors or misinterpretations of events for which the editor apologises in advance – but it should be explained that it is too late for a second edition just yet.

CLIMBS OF MY YOUTH[1]

"With the rise of bouldering and easy access climbing, Cloggy can be an intimidating place to those without experience of large and remote crags, and the associated boldness required on some routes can make them feel relatively difficult to today's average climber".

Nick Dixon (2004) Guide to Clogwyn Du'r Arddu, Climbers Club

My old friend Jack Baines once tried to persuade me to write a book. When I protested that no publisher would touch it Jack told me that was no problem. I'd forgotten he was a partner in the Ernest Press. I set to scribbling but stalled around page 80. I stalled for so long that Jack died, and with him my literary prospects, but the CC Editor often seems a bit short of material so I've dug out a few passages.

I started rock climbing in 1961 when I went to Cambridge as a very young student, so young in fact that I couldn't even go into the pubs legally. I had been nothing more than a hill walker and I wondered for a while whether I really wanted to get into this apparently dangerous activity. My fears rose when I went to a CUMC slide show and the President, Terence Goodfellow, had difficulty limping onto the stage. "My God," I thought, "he must have fallen off a climb." I discovered he had been hit by a fast rolling barrel at the annual beer party.

I decided to give it a try anyway. We used to assemble at 6.30 on most Sunday mornings for a cold, cramped four-hour drive to Derbyshire where it was usually raining. The minibus driver was an enigmatic but dashing[2] Austrian research student, Rupert Roschnik who was the only one of us old enough to rent the van. My first attempts on the rock were in big clumsy hiking boots on green, slimy and chilly gritstone. Several people fell off, including Rupert who was climbing in leather ski boots, but somehow not myself. I'm surprised today that I even went a second time.

Friday evening lectures at the CUMC were a big event. In those days British climbers, however distinguished, hadn't realised they could charge for their slide shows, and Cambridge was known as a good place to visit. Even Don Whillans came for just his travel expenses and a good dinner and piss-up. (He learnt more quickly than most though.) Chris Bonington came twice in a year – first to tell us about the Central Freney Pillar, then again in early summer, at Terence's request, to lead a discussion on Alpine safety, as the club had recently had a few nasty accidents. It was great of him to do this and I for one learnt a lot before ever setting foot in the Alps.

That Christmas during a long bus journey I read Hermann Buhl's 'Nanga Parbat Pilgrimage'. I could not put it down, even for transport cafe food. Like many other climbers before and since, I was hooked from that day. The sheer enthusiasm, the risk taking for no material reward, and the progressive maturing of Buhl's understanding of the mountains made this something totally different from anything I had come across before. I have since reread it about every five years to help prevent the onset of middle age.

---

1 Dick Isherwood, *CCJ* 2008 pp 15-23
2 *Ed*. Bob Courtier remarked: *"dashing" was largely the result of Rupert's interpretation of the then recently introduced concept of 'Give Way' at road intersections. Rupert was convinced that the innate politeness of the British would always give way to him. Perhaps it was the downhill skier in him, but it worked.*

My own rock climbing progressed in fits and starts. I went to a Helyg meet in mid-December and was traumatized by a chimney on the Gribin Facet which was virtually a cold waterfall. Big hiking boots still. As the weather warmed up I started to get somewhere. I found I could lead the occasional Severe, and I started to understand gritstone climbing at a modest level. It was a great feeling. Confidence was beginning to build. I bought a pair of kletterschuhe – you weren't supposed to use PA's unless you did really hard climbs.

The next landmark, for me, was a knock on the door early in the summer of 1962. In trooped John McCormick, Nick Estcourt and Rupert.

"We need a fourth man to fill the car to Wales this weekend. Wrottesley's dropped out."

This was a big break for me as these guys climbed VS. The weather was fine and we did some good climbs – certainly by my standard. Phantom Rib and Brant were the highlights and I led one or two VS pitches. Rupert fell out of the V chimney of Brant and I led it feeling like a conquering hero.

The leading figures in the CUMC at this time were Nick and Rupert. Nick was very competitive and dying to lead a gritstone Extreme. He nearly did. He got hold of a car – not easy then – and went off to Stanage in midweek with John McCormick to do the Left Unconquerable, but ran out of steam near the top, fell off and was held head down, three feet off the ground. John was a big man even then.

Nick was also a prodigious farter, though less celebrated than Brian Chase, who could empty an entire hut with one quiet release. I once found myself running down from Stanage to the bus behind Nick in a late afternoon rain squall – he let one go and I almost bounced off it. The air really did become thicker.

Rupert was less overtly ambitious. He showed up in Courmayeur in 1962 with his seventeen-year-old brother in tow – a year younger than me – and sat in the campsite with a map and ruler, determining the longest route to the summit of Mont Blanc. The Peuterey Ridge!! They did it, over several days, narrowly surviving an avalanche on the descent, and I don't think his brother ever climbed again.

In my first summer the CUMC held an Alpine meet in the Bernina. We had a sufficient ratio of experience to lack of it, perfect weather and mountains of just the right size. We climbed more or less all of the good peaks, by routes including the Biancograt and the traverse of the Piz Palu, and I learnt a great deal. The meet was only marred by *Il Presidente* himself falling off the Piz Palu and needing a rescue. This apart, I thought it was the best introduction to Alpine climbing one could have. An attempt to repeat the experience in the Zillertal three years later ended in such a good party that the meet leader spent 24 hours in the custody of the Innsbruck police.

A certain amount of building climbing was practised. St John's Chapel was the classic, as its Victorian Gothic rock was much sounder than the real old thing. Tony Greenbank came along after a lecture and the Sunday Telegraph captured his leader bridging wide on the lower roof. Robin Devenish climbed it solo after a heavy night in the pub, forgot to go up the inside staircase and unlock the top door, and had to solo down the outside again. King's Chapel was done less frequently as it was heavily patrolled. One night a group was on the side chapel roof, about to climb the steel bars protecting the stained glass, when lights flashed. A young gentleman half way over the college boundary spikes in his dinner jacket began apologizing to the porters. "It's all right, Sir, don't worry, it's these night climbers we're after." We stayed very quiet before continuing. An old sling of mine stayed on top of one of the corner towers for the next four years. Nick had a closer call – he was spotted very low down, jumped off and ran, swam the Cam, then realised that the porter had crossed the bridge and was still coming. He swam another, very foul stream and ran all the way home to Magdalene.

The great prize of the time, for a few, was the University Library tower. It is a modern brick structure, singularly unsuited to free climbing, but Rupert had a plan. The square section drainpipes on the lower tier were too tight to the wall for us to free climb them but with a bit of wire and perseverance you could thread a piece of line and prusik up. This had to be redone at every bracket, so it took time. The sport plan for the tower was to bolt up to the long vertical windows, back and foot up them, and then bolt a bit more to the top. The plan foundered when we reached the foot of the tower and dawn was already breaking. I guess you could either bivouac up there or do it in the winter.

An annual ritual was the Ben Nevis Meet in March. Some of us had to hitch hike to get there. We carried a week's supply of basic food[3] up to the CIC hut, got the stove going, hoped the weather would improve, and tried to avoid using the appalling outhouse. It was still the age of step cutting, so most of us never got beyond Comb Gully, but Rupert did lead Point Five with one 85cm straight-pick ice axe, clearing another party's two-week old steps.

The CUMC Dinner was famous, or possibly notorious, depending on one's point of view. One year, as secretary, I had to make a speech and I wrote separately to Roger Chorley (the Alpine Club guest) and John Longland (representing the CC) asking each for scurrilous stories about the other. Of course they compared notes and I got nothing. I budgeted half a bottle of sherry a head for the warm-up, though many had been to pre-pre sherry parties starting around lunchtime. Ice cream with chocolate sauce and throwable biscuits was perhaps not a good idea for dessert, and we were banned from yet another college. Some of us made the most of the evening by traversing Trinity Great Court in the snow, still in dinner jackets.

In the summer of 1964 I discovered that Henry Day had a trip to Pakistan in the works and needed a fourth person. We drove from Cambridge to the Swat valley in a short wheelbase canvas top Land Rover, containing almost all our food (mostly donated) and the climbing gear. Much of the weight was on the roof rack which had to be re-welded to the roof frame now and then. Three of us sat in the front and one lay in the back on top of all the food and with minimal headroom under the canvas. It took four weeks to get there and it was the hottest and most uncomfortable journey I had ever been on. We all got galloping diarrhoea at times. When we got to Rawalpindi we found that a kitbag containing the ice axes had fallen off the roof somewhere.

Absolutely no climbing gear could be bought in Pakistan then, but we managed to borrow some axes from an Irish expedition who were coming home from Rakaposhi. Henry had various connections through which we had an audience with the Wali of Swat, who was still a genuine prince in a little whitewashed palace, dispensing justice to his subjects. The mountains were a bit smaller and less virgin than we had been led to expect, but we did a few modest first ascents and narrowly escaped destruction in

---

3 *Ed.* Bob Courtier remembers *"in Rupert's case, including a full-sized piano-accordion"*

a rockfall. The whole four-month trip cost £600, of which half was provided by the Mount Everest Foundation. For me it was a life changing experience, as they say.

In 1965 I really made some progress in my rock climbing. I broke through into what were then known as "the Extremes". An ascent of Cenotaph Corner with Peter Rowat, on a cold March day with a few snowflakes drifting around, gave me confidence and I never looked back. So much of rock climbing is in the mind. Later that year I did The Grooves on Cyrn Las with Ted Maden, then White Slab on Cloggy on a memorable summer's day with John Peck when we spent so long untangling our brand new double rope that we were almost benighted, and finally Vember. This last was by far the hardest rock climb I'd done to date and I can still clearly remember the feeling of insecurity in the shallow chimney high on the second pitch which is the crux. That summer I really came to appreciate the high crags of Snowdonia for their mossy cool recesses and splendid climbing situations.

In the same year I ceased to be a student and was forced to find work. I had very little idea what I wanted to do but the job market for agricultural scientists was amazingly good at that time – I had four interviews and was offered four jobs. I took the one that came with a company car. It was interesting enough work but most important at the time was that I could organise my life to be half way to North Wales on most Friday afternoons. My employers were very broad minded about the record high mileage on the car. They even let me take it to the Alps.

Figure 1 John Peck on the upper long pitch of White Slab. Note the grass!
Photo: Dick Isherwood

Around 1967 I started climbing regularly with Mike Kosterlitz. We had been at Cambridge together but for much of the time he was well ahead of me in rock climbing ability. I had closed the gap a bit by now and we did some good things together. Mike was smaller than me but very strong. One weekend I fell off a peg climb at Matlock, and dangled, barely in contact with the cliff. Mike just pulled me up hand over hand to the last peg.

One of our best climbs together in Wales was the Cloggy Pinnacle girdle traverse, of which I believe we did the third ascent (or crossing). I remember that we didn't get started until one pm – a bit late for one of the biggest climbs in Wales – and even so it was cold out on the front face of the Pinnacle. I got to lead Taurus and wore out my arms yo-yoing up and down around the small overhang above the big roof; it may have been the hardest pitch I ever managed to lead in Wales. I recently bought Nick Dixon's guidebook and was ever so pleased to see that this still rates E4. Mike climbed the short pitch round the top of the Pinnacle Arête so it was my turn to lead again when we reached the Hand Traverse. I got half way across this spectacular vertical wall and had to come back in disarray, arms and fingers not quite obeying commands. Mike stormed across it, tangling his runners and cursing wildly. It was now almost dark and we were worn out, so we decided to finish it the next day, and headed for the pub. Late in the evening Joe Brown, whom I hardly knew, approached me and actually initiated a conversation.

"I'm surprised you thought Taurus was hard – it's sooo well protected."

It was my proudest moment in the Padarn Lake. I later picked up the story that Whillans had had to give Joe a tight rope on it.

There was some more exciting steep climbing in the morning, between overhangs in a very exposed part of the cliff. Mike showed his Dolomite experience on the abseil (down what is now The Axe), which overhangs in two directions, sufficiently for you to lose all contact with the rock if you get it wrong. We had a massive knot in the end of the doubled rope in case of trouble. I galloped up the big vertical wall of Shrike to finish – it seemed so easy after what had gone before.

One weekend we went up to Cloggy at the end of a dry spell, and it started to rain. Most people headed down but it seemed a great opportunity to do the Black Cleft. If you didn't mind getting really wet all you had to do was stay in the back and work your way up clearing the watercress as you went.[4]

We did most of our rock climbing in North Wales, but we got to the Lake District and occasionally to Scotland also. One wonderful day on Dove Crag we did the three big climbs of the time, Dovedale Groove, Hiraeth and Extol. The weather was perfect and we had the cliff to ourselves. Lots of dark steep rock, dried up lichen and cool shady ledges.

A trip to Scotland one summer let us do the famous Carnivore on the Buachaille, once rated the hardest climb in Glencoe (though probably never so). Mike led the crux after I had failed dismally and had to let Geoff Cram's team through. After this section, which is very low down on the climb, only fifty feet off the ground, you

---

4 Ed. Bob Courtier recalls "Dick had a propensity for wet gully climbs. As early as 1962, on Buachaille Etive Mòr and following days of heavy rain, he had "swum" up Raven's Gully after having been repulsed from The Chasm's big waterfall pitch only by the deafening roar, the arm-length's visibility in the spray and the frightening vibration of the ground. That Richard did the Black Cleft, as he describes, in the rain when everyone else was going home, is very typical of him. I would not be surprised if this was also a very early 'numbered' ascent like many of his harder climbs."

traverse to and fro across some very steep and exposed country, and eventually emerge in a load of deep heather. Geoff and party tried unsuccessfully to do Whillans's direct finish, which cuts out some of the heather, but eventually had to abseil off. That evening one of them (a future Vice-President of the Climbers' Club, no less!) worked off his frustrations by getting very drunk and loudly insulting half the committee of the Scottish Mountaineering Club, in whose hut we were staying. I thought the Scots would arrest us at the border. The inter-club repercussions lasted most of the next year.

For a while my regular climbing partner was Bob Keates, perhaps better known for extraordinary eating and drinking feats than for climbing. Getting bored at one club dinner, he ate the daffodils off the table. Curry powder by the spoonful was commonplace. To my mind his most impressive achievement in this unusual area of life was to drink a quart of Daddy's Sauce non-stop from the bottle. This took place in a motorway cafe; the truck drivers stopped eating to watch him, forks in hand, and the entire kitchen staff came out to worry about his health. He moaned and clutched his stomach all the way home but was fine after three days or so. They didn't even charge him for the sauce.

Bob was a good climber too. He had a reputation as a crazy guy for a while, but settled down after one or two epics (e.g. getting caught above the overhangs on the Cima Ovest in a snowstorm wearing PA's[5]). One day we went to Craig Gogarth when it was still being opened up. We weren't into new climbs (that took an extra mental leap which I never quite made in weekend rock climbing) so we thought we'd look for marks of previous climbers and follow them. We found a promising line of flakes and grooves midway along the cliff which started out OK but half way up there was a choice of lines. I spotted a peg up in a corner, and struggled up to it to find it wasn't in very far at all. Going up further, I got very extended in a wide bridge between two flakes which diverged farther and farther. I pulled myself into a little niche and very nearly fell straight out of it again; it was a lot steeper and more sloping than I thought. I tried to put a peg in but it fell out and hit the sea after one bounce. Two pegs left. The next went in less than an inch and hitting it harder would send it the same way. I decided it would have to do, and went on. I could only make the next move, over a bulge to a very small ledge, by standing on the peg, it held. On the ledge I found a peg belay. Someone really had been here before. Bob led on to the top, scattering young cormorants on the bigger ledges. One, very panicked, lost its balance and tumbled over the edge. We watched as it fell, feeling a little guilty. Half way down it got its act together, learnt to fly just in time, and headed for Ireland. We met Pete Crew that evening and discovered we had done the second ascent of his Big Groove.

One Sunday on Cloggy, Bob and I were returning along the foot of the East Buttress from a climb I forget, and we stopped to watch Ed Drummond climbing the Great Wall[6] with Crew holding his rope and coaching. Drummond was wearing shorts – very non-traditional – and at the halfway ledge he pulled up a banana for a snack. He seemed a bit strange but he didn't make it look too hard, and we learnt lots from

5 *Ed.* I remember it well, being on the other end of the rope from Bob.
For the benefit of younger readers, perhaps it should be explained that Pierre Alain (PA) had invented this tight-fitting footwear used at the time for rock climbing – but certainly never intended for mixed climbing.
6 *Ed.* Steve Martin wrote to me in October 2013 and said "I'm sure you will have covered his early ascent of Master's Wall on Cloggy which was quite the best achievement on British rock by any of our lot in our (CUMC) era". When I queried the name he explained "Yes, you are quite right. It was Master's Wall until Joe Brown completed the first ascent, when it became Great Wall; a climb that we all dreamed of doing in my day".

Crew's commentary, so we stole a day from work and went to have a go ourselves on the Monday.

We had a 300-foot 7mm rope, and a 150-foot 9mm rope. This seemed just about good enough for a 200-foot pitch if you did the right things. Bob dug in at the bottom and I set off. It was not easy – we hadn't watched Drummond on the lower part and I struggled on the crux where you make a big move right on some very smooth rock and up to a peg – at least there was a peg there in 1967. A cunning lasso with a thin tape gave me some psychological protection but I swear I didn't pull on the sling – climbing ethics were peculiar but strong in those days.

I reached Joe Brown's retreat peg from around 1962, and it virtually fell apart in my fingers – just flakes of rust. I replaced it and put the remains in my back pocket as a souvenir. By the time I was at the half way ledge the mist had come in and I couldn't see Bob at the bottom. Since it was a Monday there was no one else on the cliff at all. It felt distinctly lonely. Geoff Cram had taken a stance here, but the ledge was awfully small and you really needed yet another peg, or even two, to make it at all secure, and that was surely cheating. I placed some mediocre jammed nuts and continued, up the part Drummond had made to look easy. All went fine for a while, then it steepened and I saw the shallow crack which Crew had cleaned from above to fit his chockstones. I placed a very small nut on a very thin sling and began to layback up the next bit of crack. I got my toe caught under the sling and it popped out. It was my only protection for a long way. I half panicked, scrambled for a peg, and hammered it a little way in before continuing. For really good security I clipped in the thick rope, which by this time was out of Bob's hands and snaking up the cliff. For some reason he hadn't bothered to tell me this. It took almost five hours for me to complete the climb, and Bob was frozen, but by the time he had come round to the top he was warm enough to abseil down and collect the gear. Yet another second who didn't follow, in the great tradition of the cliff. I stayed quiet about that extra peg for years – but I only used it for protection. It wasn't good enough to put your weight on.

I did several climbs in Wales with Jim Swallow. He was of an older generation and had what I thought was an interestingly antique set of gear. Jim preferred his slings unknotted so he could loop them round chockstones. He climbed in a venerable canvas anorak with lots of pockets from which, like a snake charmer, he would produce these bits of laid rope, then loop them around something, tie a loose overhand knot in the ends and clip in. This scheme was never put to the test while I was with him, but I didn't trust it at all. My own gear was very conventional for the period – nuts large and small, one or two from the Snowdon Railway but mostly scavenged from car repair shops and supplemented with a few Trolls and Moacs which were the cutting edge things then. Jim of course trusted my gear as little as I trusted his, so we climbed with two sets.

The most memorable route by far that we did together was Mynydd, Rowland Edwards' route up the widest part of the West Buttress overhang. I suspect this was the second ascent and I wonder how many more there have been. We identified the flake on the lip of the overhang which Rowland had lassoed, and took turns trying to repeat this feat. I thought I was good at lassoes after doing White Slab but this one required a different order of skill. Jim finally got it and had the privilege of prusiking up first.

Figure 2 Bob Keates on the Big Groove, Craig Gogarth 1966
Photo: Dick Isherwood

We were using old-style laid nylon ropes and as he spiralled up his back rope got all twisted around the prusik rope. I had to keep twirling him free. He finally got over the overhang and it was my turn. I at least had a rope from above beside the one on the flake but again I got all twisted up and had to wait for passers by to spin me out.

While we were doing this there was a cracking sound, I suddenly dropped a foot or two and something flew past me and hit the Western Terrace hard. Dr Swallow, the consultant physician, assumed his best bedside voice – quite different from his usual rather critical tone.

"Richard, I would be very careful if I were you."

I felt I was being told I had some terminal disease. When I got up to him I found that half the lasso flake had broken off. The rope had somehow stayed on the remains. Jim was standing on two very small footholds belayed to a peg that seemed to be beaten directly into the soft brown rock rather than into a crack. The rest of the route was relatively uneventful, though definitely not easy and on pretty ratty rock which all sloped the wrong way.

At times we were quite fit. Mick Guilliard and I drove up on a Friday night in midsummer, ran out of petrol somewhere between Llangollen and Betws, slept in the car, started rather late on Saturday and still managed to do Vember, Woubits and Slanting Slab in the day. We got down just before the pub closed. I fought my way through the crowd and bought six pints – three each. The first one went down without touching the sides. That, at least, I can still achieve.

Looking back on the Welsh scene from 40 years later, the thing that stands out the most to me is the achievement of the first generation Rock and Ice climbers, mainly but not only Joe Brown and Don Whillans. How many people in the years since then could have handled first ascents of Vember, Woubits or Taurus, on sight from the ground up, on vegetated and often wet rock, in gym shoes and with next to no protection? Not many, I suspect. Certainly not me. Is it coincidence that, although they went way beyond Snowdonia and did some impressive things in the Alps and bigger mountains, not one of them was killed climbing?

Figure 3 Jim Swallow prusiking up the initial overhang of Mynydd, Cloggy West Buttress c1968.
Photo: Dick Isherwood

HOW TO BE A GREATER MOUNTAINEER[7]
(THE CAMBRIDGE CHITRAL EXPEDITION, 1964)

It was no good. I simply had to have a rest. I leaned on my ice axe and contemplated my crampons as John steamed past and on up the gentle snow slope. Eventually I followed, envious of his even pace, morning and afternoon.

Half an hour later we made a dump. Four o'clock, and still not on top of the hump. It hadn't looked any distance from Camp One on the moraine. We radioed Hugh – just like Everest – and told him to put the supper on; then back. Without loads we were across the plateau, through the crevasse and down to the moraine in an hour and a half, after six hours going up. Crampons off, raucous yells to camp produced a reply, and we ran down the moraine to a steaming brew.

*   *   *   *

The mountains of Swat, which is a small state in North Pakistan, form part of a chain which runs south from the point of origin of the Pamirs, Hindu Kush and Karakoram. This chain has no name of its own and is not really assignable to any of its bigger relatives: but the ignorant English call it all the Himalayas anyway. The Siri Dara plateau, with which we were concerned, lies on this ridge, an irregular-shaped undulating snowfield approximately five miles by three, enclosed on three sides by a cirque of peaks and spilling out to the north-east as an impressive four thousand foot icefall overlooking the Kandia valley.

This valley had been visited in 1962 by Trevor Braham, an Englishman living in Pakistan, whose report in the *Alpine Journal* had attracted Henry's attention and formed the basis of all our plans. He had seen the whole plateau and gave glowing reports of virgin 21,000-foot peaks.

We had set up a Base Camp in the valley below the icefall, found by good fortune an easy way up its western flank, and put up a second camp below two long parallel moraines which led like a dual carriageway on to the plateau. The gods had been inconsiderate enough to give us a line of crevasses to cross, and just to make things difficult they had snatched our ice axes from the Land Rover's roof rack on the Grand Trunk Road – but we foiled them by borrowing some more from a Canadian Expedition, and eventually, belatedly, attacked the mountains, working from right to left around the cirque, because those on the left looked hard.

First attacks, with one axe and two ski-sticks, resulted in the ascents of Adam and Eve, two apparently superb granite spires which turned out to be puny piles of pebbles when seen from their bigger neighbours. Then we carried all our gear up to the moraine, then we festered to recover from this, then we found ourselves waiting for Hugh to bring the Canadian axes from Rawalpindi.

After two days we tired of food, drink and Mickey Spillane and went to do a rock climb on the Verte, a peak opposite Base. We reckoned 7,000 feet to the top and perhaps a bivvy on the descent. Fast time, but we had no bivouac to carry – it was all up on the moraine, the other side of the valley. Undaunted, we took an empty tin, a Tommy's cooker and lots of poly bags. We nearly got frostbite paddling the river, then

---

7 R.J. Isherwood, *Cambridge Mountaineering* (1965) pp. 20-25

vertical grass led to horizontal rock[8]. Eventually it steepened into icy cracks and slabs – just like Nevis but warm enough for shirt-sleeves – but in mid-afternoon we peeked over a ridge and saw the summit – miles away, aloof, icy and promising big thrills for an axeless party in the dark. We beat it – downwards. One section of the descent needed an abseil, partly free, and as we had no slings we went classical. The rope was wet, it wouldn't run, and John eventually came down hand over hand. It reminded one of Whymper descending the Matterhorn.

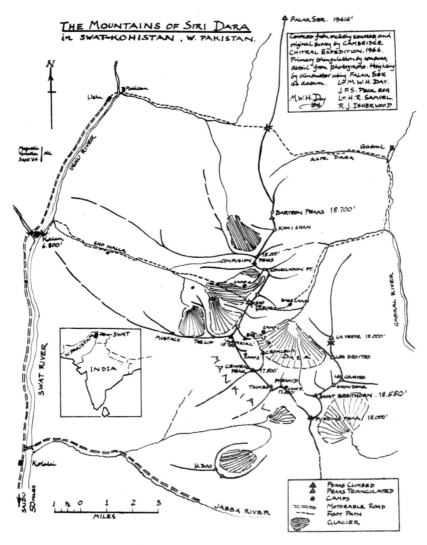

Figure 4 The mountains of Siri Dara, Swat Kohistan
Credits: The Cambridge Chitral Expedition 1964

8 *All angles are approximate*

We got down just before dark to find the wandering Samuel returned. Our first climb on the plateau proper was Central Peak – a fine hogsback named by Trevor Braham. This was a pleasant snow climb from the moraine camp – a typical Alpine P.D. made exciting by not knowing what was round the corner. For the first and last time we got up in the dark, and were early enough to see Nanga Parbat, fifty miles east, before the inevitable haze came up. Sunbathing and surveying on the summit – "Cor, look at those ice peaks!" Small, steep, distant, desperate – hankering for gritstone we called the biggest and fiercest the Indus Kohistan Eliminate.

On the descent Henry and I detoured to the Cromlech, a small rock peak that might have offered routes comparable to its Welsh namesake, but I'd left my nuts and threader at home so I went the easy side. Tracks in the snow revealed a difference of opinion in the Peck-Samuel cordée but Hugh, who had never climbed in Wales, prevailed, and they went straight back to camp.

Our next objective, the Watershed Peak, was considerably bigger so we carried up a tent and camped below it. This was our first big carry on the plateau and I nearly died from the effort. We camped in a beautiful hollow below a gendarme, thinking this would be sheltered. Later it struck us that it was formed by the wind, but fortunately the night was calm.

Two rock ridges came down towards us. One of these, or perhaps the broad snow couloir between? We chose the ridge directly above camp, hoping for good rock, but it soon degenerated into schist. Chossy, sometimes exciting scrambling on the sharp crest led to the junction of the two ridges, where manky rock gave way to manky snow. Surprised to find crevasses in a crest of snow five feet wide and little thicker, we floundered to the top just in time to take some survey photos before the cloud closed in and discover that this was probably the highest peak of the cirque.

Coming up the ridge we had seen two or three very regular piles of stones and I think the same thought had struck all of us – but no one said anything until just below the summit we found an empty tin. This took some explaining – we thought we were the first people to climb in the area at all. We later found that our Watershed Peak corresponded to Mankial, first climbed in 1940 by another ridge. We had thought this was several miles to the south. Who left the tin we don't know – but there are rumours of a Pakistani all-women's ascent. After a few speculative looks along the ridge to The Lip – a ferocious bit of scenery capped by a monstrous cornice – we descended the same way, a poor route on a fine mountain.

Food was short at camp: we ought to go down. But it was late: we ought to stay. As a compromise I stayed on alone and carried down the remaining gear next morning. My boots froze in the night and I thawed them over a candle, thinking hard thoughts.

We now headed for the left-hand part of the cirque and especially the most attractive peak of all, the Breithorn (again named by Trevor Braham). We had suddenly decided we were fit, and planned to set up camp for a week in one carry – but we would have had nearly a hundredweight each, so we thought again and set off with half of it. We never weighed our loads and competitive guesswork ran riot – I reckon I carried nearly seventy-five pounds once but the others wouldn't believe me. Henry was on skis that day but he spent more time on his backside, as the plateau was a bit more undulating than we expected. Consequently John and I got ahead and, as related above, made a dump, short of an elusive snow hump beyond which we hoped to find a campsite.

This failure led to a discussion about distances on the plateau. My estimate of three miles – and an average speed of less than half a mile per hour – between camps was quickly rejected and I was instructed in the first law of coarse surveying. According to this you double your estimates if you think there is any "hidden ground" about. Estimates were duly doubled and we prided selves on covering six to eight miles each way. When we eventually drew a map I had the laugh – three and a half miles.

Even eight miles in six hours was a bit slow, so we tore off next morning and did it in four. Another ten minutes took us over the hump, to the astonishment of the Chief Surveyors, and we pitched camp in another little snow hollow. "This one isn't a wind hollow" we thought: and it wasn't. Next day John walked round the tent and suddenly dropped in up to his thighs. The resulting hole seemed to be bottomless, endless and sideless, so we didn't walk that side any more.

Figure 5 Mankial from the north-west
Photo: The Cambridge Chitral Expedition, 1964

On our first day here we overslept, so the Breithorn was left in peace and John and I set off at the leisurely hour of 11.15 for the Pudding, a mound of uninspiring shape adjacent to it. A long plod was rewarded by a surprisingly good climb up a steep icy ridge. On top we celebrated the leader's absence by wasting all our panoramic photos on blank horizon and took lots of bearings on the puny snow dome that formed the other side of the dreaded Indus Kohistan Eliminate. Descent by another ridge scared me to death as the fearless Peck shambled down a narrow fragile crest, kicking bits of it into the abyss on either side.

Next day it had to be the Breithorn, so we got up early and were away by seven-thirty. We headed for a long blunt spur, approaching it diagonally from a break in the 'schrund. This entailed crossing a big shallow couloir in which we nearly met our end. We were wearing crampons on the first rocks of the spur when a thundering came down from above and we saw bits of mountain approaching fast. Henry and I crouched under a little bulge and the last I saw of John he was making a wall of death run across some slabs towards the rib. I had the best place and crouched for five minutes or so, listening to the crashing of boulders and watching the debris pile up round Henry. When it stopped I dug him out and counted his arms and legs and we all set off towards the crest of the ridge, fast. Chummy granite slabs, icy snow and a final manky ridge led pleasantly to the top. We had a superb view over to Chitral, where Tirich Mir stood out as a huge double snow dome – and north to Falak Ser[9] (19,400 feet) which, we were shattered to find, was higher than any of the Siri Dara peaks. Muttering rude things about Survey of Pakistan and its non-existent twenty-thousanders, we started down. Descent by the same route at noon seemed a bit risky, so we followed the backbone ridge of the mountain all the way, over lots of tedious gendarmes. John got ahead and we were honour-bound to solo after him in lots of places where I would have appreciated a rope. Eventually we reached the col and floundered campwards, collecting bits of rock-fall as souvenirs.

The reader may have wondered where the fourth expedition member was: he had regrettably been struck down with dysentery and spent a fortnight building cunning conveniences all round Base Camp. Thinking we had forgotten him, he rang up and demanded attention, so we retired for a fester. Hugh was duly impressed at our four peaks in eight days, and there was a lot to do – pancakes to cook, postcards to write, more pancakes, a brew, more pancakes…

After three days the pancake mix was running out, so we went up the hill again. Plans were hatched for a moonlight ice route, but then we saw something far more attractive. Above our camp was a little rock fluke – fully five hundred feet – and sitting near the top of it a superb granite corner. It was immediately christened "Peck's dièdre" and attacked next morning – or rather lunchtime. At its foot we realised it was a bit longer than the thirty feet we had expected – by about ten times in fact. Its discoverer must have the crux – so I led off up the lower part carrying our one rock peg and three prusik loops and wishing I'd brought my PA's.

After two pitches the crack got steeper and John retreated from a bulgelet that was clearly the crux. The middleman started looking for abseil points but the lure was too strong; I swapped ends with John and climbed up to his runner – a good old British thread. Just when it seemed to be getting hard, groping fingers fell into the mostest of jugs and I pulled up. Another big slot grinned at me so just to be fair I pulled on that too, and it was all over. John led on to the top and as we didn't know the easy way down we had to go to the summit and down the snow the other side.

Chuffed at this success, we started making plans for the harder peaks. These soon received a setback – it rained. They received another when Henry spilt the supper. Hot and cold in all bedrooms. We slept in a pond of vegetable soup and as the weather was still bad in the morning descent seemed prudent. We put everything on our backs – including most of the soup – and staggered down.

The next day was a triumph for Pye Telecommunications and the Royal Engineers. Two camps were moved simultaneously, under radio control – Camp One by Henry, John and I, and Base by Hugh, aided by five local goatherds and our policemen.

---

9 *Ed*. Perhaps spelt Falak Sher with a height of 5918m or 19,416 feet (Wikipedia)

(These last had been with us all the time – in twos, replaced at intervals – and supposedly protected us from brigands. They were good at washing up too). Collision courses were set and we duly met and continued over a pass of about 15,000 feet – this was the reverse of our approach route from the road head at Kalam. On the other side we camped in a fabulous meadow – a snow field only six weeks previously. Such a campsite could only be appreciated by a good fester; so we festered while the sun shone on our last objective – Confusion Peak. This name was given subsequently when we found it wasn't what we thought it was. It gave a sort of climb up two miles of horizontal moraine, half a mile of vertical moraine and a big snow-field and we couldn't see a thing from the top so we came down little wiser but I took a fantabulous photo of Henry jumping the bergschrund, so it wasn't all wasted effort.

Food was low so we ate the emergency rations, recruited porters from lower down the valley and set out for the fleshpots. These took some finding but after ten miles walking and eighty miles driving we hit the capital of Swat, Saidu Sharif, and clocked in at the five-star Swat Hotel. We even had a bath.

Four weeks later the Land Rover got home. Another week later I got home – hitching. John went to sea. All this – and the journey out – was as much fun as the climbing but there isn't space to describe it and it's not mountaineering anyway – though there was a good route on a Turkish lighthouse in the Black Sea...

NOTES

- If you really want to know what happened, buy an Expedition report from M.W.H. Day (Caius), H.R. Samuel (Trinity) or R.J. Isherwood (Queen's). Preferably from all three. John Peck (Magdalene) is now sculpting in New York – he wanted to go East but his ship took him the wrong way.
- Siri Dara and the adjacent area – north to Falak Sar – probably contain most of the climbing in Swat Kohistan. There is enough scope for another six-week expedition, though it might be largely filling in detail. There is some confusion over the geography and our activities were so localised that we probably created more than we solved. The Survey of Pakistan are (*sic*) now operating there.
- References to previous exploration in Swat are in Trevor Braham's article in the *Alpine Journal* 1963-2; the ascent of Mankial is described by R.L. Holdsworth in *AJ* 1942-2

MORE CLIMBS IN SWAT[10]

Ed.: This article may appear to be a repetition of the previous one but is included as Dick's style of writing for the Alpine Journal is very different from that in Mountaineering 1965. In later years, Dick was more relaxed when writing in the AJ. Anyway, there are some extra photos!

In the *Alpine Journal* for November, 1963 (*AJ* 68 251), Trevor Braham described his explorations in Swat and Indus Kohistan, that range of mountains in West Pakistan forming a watershed between the Indus and the Swat River to its west. In particular, he drew attention to a group of mountains surrounding a high plateau east of Kalam and known locally by the unfortunate name of Sira Dara ('Head of the Pass'). One of these, he thought, was that indicated by the Survey of Pakistan for many years and marked on its maps as 20,528 feet. Some of the peaks, he suggested, might even be higher than this.

Swat is sufficiently far west to escape the monsoon, and this area became the objective of the Cambridge Chitral Expedition, 1964, after it had suffered the same setback as several others and been refused permission to climb in Chitral. 'Cambridge Swat Expedition' did not roll off the tongue satisfactorily, and our headed notepaper was already printed, so the original title was retained.

The expedition was led by Henry Day, a member of the Alpine Club, and the other members were John Peck, Hugh Samuel and myself. All were members of the CUMC. With the help of Mr. Ian Stephens, CIE[11], we were put in touch with the Waliahad of Swat, who gave us a most encouraging welcome. Unlike the central government, the rulers of Swat seem to have no inhibitions at all about allowing climbers on their territory.

We received generous support from the Mount Everest Foundation, and other sources too numerous to list. Some, however, must be mentioned: the Army Mountaineering Association, who lent us a great deal of equipment (two of the party being lieutenants in the Royal Engineers); Trevor Braham, who put us up on our journey and gave us virtually all the information we had about the area; and Colonel Buster Goodwin, host to almost all expeditions passing through Rawalpindi[12], who averted a crisis when we found we had lost our ice-axes en route.

The party travelled overland both ways, and contrived to carry all its food and equipment in one short-wheelbase Land Rover. We left in mid-June in a chaotic rush - common, I suspect, to most expeditions - and arrived in Rawalpindi a month later. After a few days' travel, our organisation improved and accommodation for four in the vehicle was reasonably comfortable - three in front and one on top of the mountain of gear in the back. Little need be said about the route[13] - Germany, Jugoslavia (sic), Greece, Turkey, Iran - except that the southern route into Pakistan through Zahedan, Baluchistan and Quetta cannot be recommended in midsummer. The roads are bad and Baluchistan earns its title, 'the end of the world' - a name used, apparently, even by

---

10 R.J. Isherwood, *AJ* 1965 pp 205-212

11 *Ed.* Just to put this in context, time-wise, the last CIE was awarded in 1947. I'm not sure when Ian was awarded his but he was always incredibly interested in any "travels" to Pakistan, particularly if this involved Kingsmen – which in this case it did not!

12 *Ed.* Henry Day reminded me of Buster's very full Obituary in *HJ* XXXIX 1981-82 (Col. Eric Goodwin) which can now be read on-line.

13 *Ed.* I am not so sure that any of these routes would be advisable just at the moment.

the local inhabitants. Our return journey, by the southern road through Afghanistan, was considerably more pleasant; the Khyber presents few terrors, Afghan visas are free, and by 1965 the whole road between Peshawar and Herat may be tarmac. Another worthwhile variation is the Caspian coast road in Iran - considerably cooler and greener than the inland alternative.

In Rawalpindi we discovered that we had lost our axes from the roof of the Land Rover. This could have been disastrous, but Buster Goodwin immediately offered to borrow some replacements from a Canadian Karakoram expedition which was due to return shortly.

To avoid delay, we continued to Swat with one borrowed axe, driving over the Malakand Pass, and up the gradually narrowing and very attractive Swat valley – the 'Switzerland of the East', according to our brochure. After a night at Saidu Sharif, the capital, we continued to Kalam, the roadhead village, where we reorganised ourselves for the walk in. With the help of the English-speaking Tehsildar, the village headman, and a remarkable telephone service, we enlisted fifteen porters – militiamen from the fort at Matiltan, a short way up the valley – and arranged to meet them early the next morning, July 17.

The porters arrived only three hours late and the caravan set out in light rain. The first leg of the journey was one hour non-stop; but this was not to continue. Before the end of the day it was moving for five minutes and resting for ten – but we could hardly complain, as we were incapable of doing more ourselves. At this stage rumblings were heard against the Jamadar, a sort of shop steward among the porters, who was paid an extra rupee a day, carried nothing and initiated all the halts – but, two days later, at the top of the pass, he proved his worth.

Our route lay east from Kalam, up the Sho Nalla valley and over a pass, the Sho Ho Dara, crossed in the opposite direction by Trevor Braham. This appeared to be a regular trade route: we met several small parties carrying goatskins of maize, flour and *ghee* – a kind of fat – over to Kalam from the valleys of Kandia. On their return journey they carried principally rock salt.

About mid-day on the second day we reached the glacier snout, and in worsening weather began picking a way through the moraines. Prospects of crossing the pass that day were slight, and when a descending party suggested eight more hours to the top our porters gave us no chance to hesitate. They were off across the glacier immediately, heading for a grassy knoll on which was a group of small huts stocked with wood. The atmosphere inside these soon exceeded that in the C.I.C. hut on Ben Nevis. We preferred to camp. This was an impressive place, below a huge, icy wall which appeared periodically from the mist. Unknown to us at the time, this was the north-west face of Mankial (18,765 feet), one of the peaks of our group.

A short reconnaissance that night failed to reveal the pass: all we saw was a semicircle of rock walls shrouded in mist. Next morning, however, the weather had improved and our route was obvious – up a long moraine crest and a final snow-slope to the col, the only break in the rocks. Three of us were suffering slightly from altitude effects coupled with lack of exercise for the past month, and here the Jamadar came into his own, carrying a full load, kicking steps at the head of the party and returning at each halt to carry one of our packs.

Over the pass we were on rock and grass, and the porters stopped for prayers and a chilly siesta. Occasionally the cloud cleared, and we were pleased to see the plateau and icefall just as Trevor Braham had described them – though the icefall looked rather steep, and we wondered if we had enough fixed rope and ice pitons.

Descent into Kandia was long and steep, but fairly rapid, and we pitched Base Camp in the valley bottom about a mile from the snout of the glacier, at a height of about 10,000 feet. We paid off the porters with some difficulty, and they started their return the next morning.

Figure 6 Siri Dara icefall and plateau from the north-west.
Left to Right: Droites, Courtes, Snow Dome, Swat Breithorn
Photo: The Cambridge Chitral Expedition, 1964

Figure 7 Swat: Confusion (Left) and Batin peaks from the South.
Confusion was climbed up its right skyline.
Photo: The Cambridge Chitral Expedition, 1964

Although the only trees growing were extremely stunted junipers, wood was quite plentiful on the moraines; woodland must have been more extensive in the past. Later, firewood was collected from down the valley by our two policemen. These had been seconded to us from the fort at Ushu; they were full-time soldiers and wore a uniform of dark grey shirt and pantaloons, black beret and a bandolier of cartridges, ammunition for their elderly, home-made rifles. We hoped that they would stay with us the whole time, and intended to train them as high altitude porters, but their tour of duty comprised nine days on and five off, and every week they were replaced. Consequently, they served only as washers-up and guards. The first pair, Isakhan and Wazir, were the only ones to have pronounceable names; we knew their successors only as Boots and Ginger.

After a day spent organising Base Camp, Hugh returned to Rawalpindi to collect our replacement ice-axes, while John, Henry and I began prospecting a route up the icefall. We climbed a moraine ridge for a close view of the true right bank, recommended by Trevor Braham; but the view across the valley from here suggested strongly that the left bank would be easier. The next day we tried this and found a reasonable route at our first attempt. A steep moraine-covered rib, a gully and a rocky gangway decorated with wild chives and rhubarb led us up through the steep lower wall of the U-shaped valley, and we came out onto pleasant grass slopes, interrupted occasionally by sections of scrambling. I say 'pleasant' in retrospect, but at the time I was not nearly fit enough to enjoy it; and later, after four or five return trips, it became very monotonous.

Our next camp was established on a small platform a few hundred feet below the snowline, next to two long parallel moraines – a remarkable formation which, we had seen, gave access to the plateau at the only point on its lower edge free from séracs. After several carries to this camp, a journey taking about three hours from Base, we pitched a tent and stayed the night. The next day, we investigated the plateau, found the route to be as straightforward as expected, and climbed two small rock peaks, Adam and Eve. Eve lived up to expectations with some interesting scrambling, but Adam was a singularly insignificant, horizontal, loose ridge – not at all the fine summit it had appeared from below. From these we could see the whole plateau, and with rare imagination began naming the peaks – Verte, Droites, Courtes, Snow Dome. Central Peak had been named for us by Trevor Braham, as had the Swat Breithorn (indicating its resemblance to the Zermatt Breithorn). The big peak behind our aiguilles, whose far side, we realised, we had already seen, was also named, but it later became clear that this was in fact Mankial, first climbed by R. L. Holdsworth in 1940 (*AJ* 53 319). At the time we thought that Mankial was a considerable way to the south.

We returned to the valley, expecting to meet Hugh; but he was not back, so we marked time with a casual and rather abortive attempt on the Verte (18,000 feet) direct from Base Camp. This appeared to be purely a rock climb, but high up we saw that the last few hundred feet were on quite steep ice, so we retreated. When Hugh returned we went up to Camp 1 again and climbed Central Peak (17,500 feet). The approach to this lay through a line of large crevasses, first penetrated by an alarming route across the false floor of one of them. Later, we found a considerably simpler and safer way, feasible at all times of day. Beyond this obstacle, the undulating plateau led to the foot of our peak, which gave a pleasant snow climb of about 2,000 feet. The morning was memorable for our only view of Nanga Parbat, far to the east.

Figure 8 Peck's Dièdre (Pyramid Peak): just below the Crux.
Photo: The Cambridge Chitral Expedition, 1964

From the summit we had a superb view in all directions, and spent a couple of hours arguing over the relative heights of peaks and the relation of the valleys. Our rather elementary survey equipment provided further amusement—a hand clinometer and prismatic compass, and a gadget for taking panoramic photographs with an ice-axe as tripod. It is perhaps worth pointing out that the resulting map was constructed at Base Camp on the cardboard sleeve of a food-box, and is based on compass and clinometer readings. Most of the details were filled in at the time by eye—the panoramic photographs were not used very much. Bases for heights and distances were Falak Sar (19,415 ft.) and a baseline of nylon rope later measured by surveyor's tape.

Descent from Central Peak was uneventful, and we returned to Camp 1. The next day, John, Henry and I carried a camp up to below Mankial; Hugh, who was suffering again from a stomach upset, stayed behind. Unfortunately his condition deteriorated and it was later confirmed that he had dysentery. Thalazole tablets eventually cured him, but he was prevented from taking any further part in the climbing.

Camp below Mankial was pitched in a snow hollow apparently sheltered by a gendarme. Later, in our sleeping bags, we realised that the hollow was wind-formed; but fortunately the night was calm. Next morning we rose early, by our standards, and were away before eight o'clock. We had already found that afternoon snow conditions were quite reasonable, better than is usual in the Alps, and very early rising seemed unnecessary.

The ridge we had selected gave some interesting climbing, but on very poor rock and, later, on rather treacherous snow. At several points we found small, regular piles of stones, and the same thought must have occurred to all of us; but nothing was said until we found an old tin bearing a label 'Made in Peshawar'. From here to the top was only two or three hundred feet; our peak must have been climbed before. As mentioned above, we later found that this was Mankial, and that we had climbed the next ridge south of that ascended by Holdsworth. The tin must have been left by a more recent party, whom we have not been able to trace. We found no sign of them on the other peaks. It is possible that they approached the plateau directly from the west, as did Holdsworth.

On the summit we discovered – now to our horror – that this was marginally the highest peak in the group. A short way west, along a ridge, was a subsidiary peak, the Lip, a fantastic sight as its sharp summit bore an enormous cornice. The weather was not too good, so after a few minutes we descended by the same route.

Next morning, we dismantled the camp, carried it down and dumped it on the plateau, and the following morning we set out for the further parts of the cirque, collecting our dump on the way. Progress was much slower than we expected – especially for Henry, who was on skis and found the deceptive undulations of the plateau difficult to move over. Mid-afternoon saw John and myself moving slowly up a long, gentle rise which seemed to go on for ever. At four o'clock we made a dump and radioed to Hugh at Camp 1. From this stage onward, the expedition's two-way radio sets (loaned by Pye Telecommunications, Ltd.) were invaluable in co-ordinating two distant camps.

Without loads the long walk back passed very quickly, and we were soon removing crampons at the top of the moraines and shouting down to the others in camp. Next day we carried up the rest of the gear; and ten minutes' further walking, to our joy and surprise, took us over the hump and down to another depression. This was clearly not a wind hollow, so we pitched our tent in its bottom. We later discovered a crevasse three feet to one side, but there were fortunately no mishaps.

Our main objective from this camp was the Swat Breithorn, a splendid peak which formed the gable-end of a long ridge. However, two days' heavy work caused us to lie in late, and at eleven o'clock John and I set out to climb Pudding Peak (18,000 feet), a rather unimposing mass in a corner of the plateau. This gave a much more interesting climb than we expected, and we were able to traverse the mountain over two sharp snow and ice ridges. The return to camp was enlivened by leaping a bergschrund and landing up to our thighs in the only really soft snow that we encountered.

Our camp was superbly situated on the edge of the plateau, at a point where it was contained by a low, rocky rim. A gap in the rim behind our tent was known as the Window, and provided a beautifully framed view of some lower peaks to the west. In the morning and evening, these were often the only projections from a huge sea of cloud, covering the plains and extending far up the valleys. On the very edge of the rim, above a long drop, was a niche in the granite which became a favourite haunt at sunset.

The next morning we climbed the Breithorn. Our route followed a broad spur on the west face, and to reach this from the best crossing-point on the bergschrund involved traversing a steep snow couloir. We had just crossed this when a rumbling from above announced a rock fall. We crouched under a small, conveniently placed overhang, and for several minutes rock debris and large blocks flew all around us. Fortunately no one was hurt; we were just across the couloir in time. The rock fall was a surprising occurrence, as the sun had not yet touched the west face, and everything seemed well frozen: later, we found that a portion of the summit ridge had come away, probably loosened by sun from the opposite side.

After this, the rest of the climb hardly seemed exciting, but again we had pleasant scrambling on faultless, yellow and grey granite, finishing up a snowfield and a final, narrow snow arête. We were able to see Falak Sar from the summit and were disturbed to find it higher than any of our peaks. The peak of 20,528 feet was simply not there, and how the legend arose we do not know. Descent by the same route seemed to be tempting fate, so we took a long route down the South ridge, over innumerable gendarmes, to the col below the Pudding.

That night, our regular radio conversation with Hugh, now in Base Camp, was more significant than usual. He was feeling very ill and needed attention. Next morning we descended and did what we could to rouse his spirits. After a day or two he improved considerably, and eventually his course of pills produced a temporary cure.

After these idle days, sun-bathing and cooking pancakes, we returned to our top camp, to find it sitting on a 2-foot pedestal of ice – an instance of the speed of ablation. We re-pitched the tent, and next day climbed Pyramid Peak (17,000 feet), a small aiguille directly above the camp site. The summit was no more than 800 feet above us, and its easiest route scarcely merited attention; so we looked for a hard way. This was supplied by 'Peck's Dièdre', a superb granite corner 300 feet high, named after its discoverer. The crucial pitch was at least grade IV by alpine standards, and excellent climbing above and below this made for a pleasant day. The easy route, in descent, took less time than those from some Welsh crags.

Our eyes now moved further left round the cirque: in particular to the Snow Dome, which offered a very interesting climb up a snow and ice ridge rising from a heavily crevassed part of the plateau. Plans were laid for a moonlight ascent, but nothing resulted, as the weather, which had been perfect for almost four weeks, promptly broke up. Rain began in the early evening, and continued – as rain – for most of the night; with three in a two-man tent, we regretted having no fly-sheet. Crisis point came when we spilled the supper inside the tent: vegetable soup everywhere. After a miserable night in wet sleeping bags, the weather was no better, and the visibility poor; so we decided to pack up camp. We had food for a further two days, but were apprehensive that, if the weather deteriorated further, we should have difficulty finding our way back over the plateau.

After a long, tiring day, carrying wet gear down to Camp 1, we radioed to Hugh, and organised a combined move of both camps. He had recruited several local goatherds, led by one Peroz whose ambition, it seemed, was to come to London with us; and these and the policemen moved Base Camp, while we traversed round the rocky hillside to meet them. The route out lay back over the same pass and down Sho Nalla to Kalam— but, a short way over the pass, we camped in a glorious meadow of buttercups and edelweiss, and prepared to climb a last peak, which at the time we thought was one of the Batin peaks, climbed by two New Zealanders in 1957. We paid off the goatherd; and Peroz seemed to forget entirely about London, rushing off to Kalam to spend his newly found wealth.

We wasted another brief spell of good weather in this idyllic camp, cooking pancakes and contemplating the huge face of Mankial and the Lip, now fully exposed before us. The face is about 5,000 feet high and offers no obvious line of attack in its mile and a half length. After two days the bad weather returned, and consequently our climb, which was rather uninspiring, told us less about the geography of the area than we had hoped. We also planned to climb a peak further north, which was a little higher than any of the Siri Dara peaks, but saw that it was separated from us by a deep valley, leading into Kandia. Later observation from the Swat valley suggested that this, in fact, was one of the Batin peaks; so our peak was re-named Confusion, perhaps a fitting commentary on the cartography of the area even now.

Figure 9 Mankial from the South. The route lay up the ridge directly facing the camera.
Photo: The Cambridge Chitral Expedition, 1964

Lack of food now drove us down to the valley, assisted by more local goatherds. The move took one long day, and in the late evening of August 23 we reached Kalam, civilisation and six weeks' mail.

Further scope for mountaineering expeditions in Swat is limited. Falak Sar, almost certainly the highest peak in the state, has been climbed; and we saw little outside our area to merit the attention of an expedition from this country. Exploration and mapping, however, are far from complete, and another expedition on a similar scale to ours, devoted mainly to survey work, might be very rewarding.

To end on a financial note: the total cost of the expedition, after re-sale of the Land Rover, was £650, for four people for thirteen weeks. This included all our food, film, petrol and what little equipment was bought, and should encourage other expeditions on a similar scale.

NIGHT CLIMBERS BEWARE![14]

Tony Greenbank

Night climbing is forbidden in Cambridge, and it is extremely perilous. But – like mountains – those spires and towers are there. As Mandrake's man on the Cam saw last week, there will also be night climbers, risking life, limb and the wrath of the authorities. Witness the picture on the right (Ed. below).

Figure 10 Starting the roof
Photo: Tony Greenbank (*Mandrake's man*)

14 *Sunday Telegraph*, 28 February 1965 (following his lecture to the CUMC on 24 February 1965)

This towering wall would scarcely have suited Mr. Walter Bonatti, eminent Italian mountaineer, recently down from his Matterhorn North Wall trip[15]. Not on his own, as he often prefers to climb, at least. He knots a rucksack to the far end of his rope – part of an ingenious anchor-technique if he falls. Imagine his fate *here* in Cambridge, after midnight.

A figure hunches up the great white tower – "Most sensational climb I should think in the U.K." (says a whisper). And from the lodge comes the cry, "There!" How does one explain to a rucksack that the proctors of Cambridge are after you?

Not that this highly illegal sport of climbing college chapels (John's or King's or Trinity or Pembroke, or any other for that matter) is really *"diretissima"* But it seems alarmingly direct: 150ft of cold stone sober verticality.

"Sssh! – keep bloody quiet," says the whisper. "It's the chop if we're heard." We freeze a full minute.

Every sound on a night climb explodes. Loose change, when you climb in over the pointed gates, a belch crossing the grass. And that stone tub below the first drainpipe which rocks on to the pipe as you leave the ground. So you play it by ear … softly.

"No need to rope-up till the chapel roof … just up the drainpipes." An anorak scrapes upwards. "Sssh!"

A tile splinters off, is fielded and stuffed in a pocket. "This is it – the chapel roof." The tower leaps up in the pale darkness.

White. Huge. On goes the rope. For the most conspicuous landmark in town …

"These climbers from away – like you – were going to do it, and they couldn't find the chapel, and climbed into and out of three colleges looking for it. And this black Zodiac stopped as they were walking down the street with ropes and slings. Well, two men in macs got out, police, and asked this chap his tutor's name. 'J. Brown,' he said. And then they ran…"

The tower is noisy; rope scrapes across slates. Higher, with the leader's silhouette lengthening and shortening up the white wall; snap-links clank, clank on drainpipes. Then, three tugs – the "Go" signal.

"Up the tiles, then up the drainpipe," the whisper had said, so softly. "Mantleshelf into the recesses, chimney up these – then swing up left onto this ledge and heave, over the top overhang."

The sky seems nearer, the drop below is appalling. Presently, with both hands cupped round the top of a little cross, there is one last pull to be made. The stonework slots on your fingers like knuckledusters.

At the top, looking across: "King's is the real classic. Harder than this. This is predictable climbing: you know how many inches the next hold should be away."

"So few night climbers. Virtually no mountaineers do it. One chap did really fabulous night climbs, and never went near a mountain."

Going down the easy spiral stairs – the torch is used for the first time[16]. But this passage is much too narrow for a rucksack. Not really a climb for a lone epic by Mr. Bonatti.

---

15 It should be recalled that Walter Bonatti completed the first solo and winter ascent of the North Face of the Matterhorn on 23 February 1965, only a few days before the present article appeared (see below)
16 Dick Isherwood recalls in "Climbs of my youth": *Robin Devenish climbed it solo after a heavy night in the pub, forgot to go up the inside staircase and unlock the top door, and had to solo down the outside again.*
In Sept 2013, Robin himself has further elaborated that it occurred after the Annual Dinner

NDAY TELEGRAPH   FEBRUARY 28,

Night Climbers Beware!

NIGHT climbing is forbidden in Cambridge; and it is extremely perilous. But—like mountains—all those spires and towers are there. And while they remain there, as Mandrake's man on the Cam saw last week, there will also be night climbers, risking life, limb, and the wrath of the authorities. Witness the picture on the right.

THIS towering wall would scarcely have suited Mr. Walter Bonatti, eminent Italian mountaineer, recently down from his Matterhorn North Wall trip. Not on his own, as he often prefers to climb, at least. He knots a rucksack to the far end of his rope—part of an ingenious anchor technique if he falls. Imagine his fate *here*, in Cambridge, after midnight.

A figure hunches up the great white tower—"Most sensational climb I should think in the U.K." (says a whisper). And from the lodge comes the cry, "There!" How does one explain to a rucksack that the proctors of Cambridge are after you?

Not that this highly illegal sport of climbing college chapels (John's or King's or Trinity or Pembroke, or any other for that matter) is really *"direttissima."* But it seems alarmingly direct; 150ft. of cold stone sober verticality.

"Sssh!—keep bloody quiet," says the whisper. "It's the chop, if we're heard." We freeze a full minute.

EVERY sound on a night climb explodes. Loose change, when you climb in over the pointed gates, a belch crossing the grass. And that stone tub below the first drainpipe which rocks on to the pipe as you leave the ground. So you play it by ear . . . softly.

"No need to rope-up till the chapel roof . . . just up the drainpipes." An anorak scrapes upwards. "Sssh!"

A glance between both feet—near the top—reveals a glass dome below, a bubble about to burst. "Sssh!" again. A tile splinters off, is fielded and stuffed in a pocket. "This is it—the chapel roof."

The tower leaps up in the pale darkness. White. Huge. On goes the rope. For the most conspicuous landmark in town. . . .

"These climbers from away—like you—were going to do it, and they couldn't find the chapel, and climbed into and out of three colleges looking for it. And this black Zodiac stopped as they were walking down the street with ropes and slings. Well, two men in macs got out, police, and asked this chap his tutor's name. 'J. Brown,' he said. And then they ran. . . ."

The tower is noisy; rope scrapes across slates. Higher, with the leader's silhouette lengthening and shortening up the white wall, snap-links clank, clank on drainpipes. Then, three tugs—the "Go" signal.

UP the tiles, then up the drainpipe," the whisper had said, so softly. "Mantleshelf into the recesses, chimney up these—then swing up left onto this tiny ledge and heave over the top overhang."

The sky seems nearer, the drop below is appalling. Presently, with both hands cupped round the top of a little cross, there is one last pull to be made. The stonework slots on your fingers like knuckle-dusters.

At the top, looking across: "King's is the real classic. Harder than this. This is predictable climbing; you know how many inches the next hold should be away.

"So few night climbers. Virtually no mountaineers do it. One chap did really fabulous night-climbs, and never went near a mountain."

Going down the easy way—spiral stairs—the torch is used for the first time. But this passage is much too narrow for a big rucksack. Not really a climb for a lone epic by Mr. Bonatti.

Figure 11 The mountain and the expedition report
Photo of Chapel: John Ashburner
Article: *Mandrake's man* **(Tony Greenbank)**

Ed. Tony Greenbank was asked by John McCormick in June 2013 if this was his photo. He replied, later adding further recollections to the Editor:

"That's my photo. The action pic, as sharp as anything. Yes, John's Chapel. I was gripped by the article.

Secondly, is it too late to add one or two of my comments to a highly memorable evening despite the copious number of pints supped and which kept arriving as if on a conveyor belt?

First memory is of a gale of laughter at the start of the proceedings. The projector was set up and I was positioned to stand near the door in the corner at the front of the full-house seating – pointer in hand.

I tapped it on the screen and tapped again, the supposed signal that I was ready for the next photo. Nothing happened. Can we have a picture? I asked the guy working the slides. "Look behind you," he said. There, projected on a screen across the angle of the corner overhead was a picture already projected and awaiting my elaboration.

It was of world champion heavyweight contender Sonny Liston extending his Cumberland sausage-like fingers – like sports page pictures of goalkeepers with big hands. He was training for his second fight with (the then) Cassius Clay; anyone who paid five dollars could watch him do his daily workout in a Denver gym, hence my photo opportunity and his gracious "OK" when told by his handlers there was a "limey in the crowd" who would like an interview for a Brit newspaper.

After a sleep of the dead that was interrupted by the alarm far too soon, we began the climb at 0400 hrs. I noted this momentous evening in my diary as: "Also did John's Chapel, Cambridge, with Richard Isherwood. Cold and clear. Did it the quickest Dick had ever done it".

Then back once more to the sleep of the dead, waking at 0900 again interrupted by the alarm to face reality.

My deadline was 1100. With my copy then to be phoned in – as you did in those days long pre-internet – to a copy taker at the Sunday Telegraph.

It was a big time for me as a humble freelance hack, just starting out in the world of full time journalism – and on my first "national" assignment. And my mind was blank and dreadfully hung-over. Arrrgh.

The place was deserted, not a soul about. I brewed some coffee and sat with a blank foolscap pad on the table and a pencil which I sharpened – putting off the inevitable moment of trying to write something coherent.

Nothing rational came. What a load of shite. Panic! Was I going to have to plead illness? I scribbled several first attempts, despairing at the only gibberish I could muster.

10.00 hrs came – mind still frozen. I despaired; the points of the clock ticking inexorably round, doomed.

I flicked through a copy of a newspaper someone had left on the table. And there …Salvation.

It was the mention of Walter Bonatti soloing great climbs by tying on the rope, and clipping into pegs as he ascended – with just his sack tied on the other end of the rope.

At last! I was able to make a start as you then read, and the remainder of the piece just flowed as writing something for money (usually) does.
Hugely relieved, I wrote the final full stop after four scrawled pages. I can still see it in the mind's eye in all its glory, and rushed out to find a phone box.
What an epic evening...

CAMBRIDGE IN THE LATE SIXTIES[17]

Rob Collister

Whether the Cambridge University Mountaineering Club in the late sixties was more or less active than at other times I do not know. There was no one as well known as Nick Estcourt, who was just before my time, or Alan Rouse, who was just after. On the other hand, Ken Wilson's anthology *Games Climbers Play* (Diadem, 1978) contains no less than four articles culled from *Cambridge Mountaineering* of that era. Talks in the Downing Site lecture theatre could attract audiences of up to a hundred and we had the chance to listen to the wise, or more often irreverent, words of speakers like Eric Shipton, Tom Patey and a clean-cut young P.E. teacher called Doug Scott. The Freshers' meet in Derbyshire easily filled a coach, but the six o'clock start on a Sunday morning and a three-hour drive each way ensured that a minibus was normally sufficient for outings to gritstone. The active membership in climbing terms was about twenty, though when I organised a weekend in Wales specifically to walk the Fourteen Threes, a totally different set of people emerged. For the demographically-minded, the majority of the club's keenest members were on the Science side rather than the Arts, most came from the North, and women were conspicuous by their absence.

Twenty-five years later, Olly Overstall organised a reunion in North Wales. It was surprisingly well attended. For some, it transpired, climbing at Cambridge had been a hugely enjoyable but brief interlude before embarking on a career. But for many, mountaineering in one form or another continues to fill their leisure time and for Bob Barton and me, Cambridge proved to be an apprenticeship leading to the *Métier de Guide*. For all of us, however, it was an inherently dangerous period in which we learned many lessons the hard way and accidents did occur. The atmosphere was sombre at the first Tuesday tea-time gathering one Lent term. Roger Wilson had been killed during the holiday period, when his gear ripped on the first pitch of Haste Not on White Ghyll. I remember all too clearly reading in a Swiss newspaper of the *chute mortelle* of Rollo Davidson and Michael Latham on the Biancograt. There but for the grace of God … We were ambitious, competitive and climbing "not wisely but too well," we had more than our fair share of near-misses.

Of my immediate contemporaries, the leading personality was undoubtedly Mick Guilliard, a good-natured extrovert from Leek, hard by the Roches, with an infectious laugh and an astonishing appetite for beer. We were in the same college and shared digs for a year so I knew him well and put him to bed more than once. As a climber, I was never in the same league but I remember leading through, with trepidation, on an early ascent of Dream of White Horses when a fierce wind was blowing spume from the waves and the ropes billowed out in an arc on the final pitch; and again, on White Slab on a grey day with no one else around and wreaths of mist drifting in and out behind the Far Far East buttress, adding to the menace of the Black Cliff. And then there was our disastrous first Alpine season along with John Hamilton and Pete Hughes, when two of our three routes involved a forced bivouac and I nearly died when an abseil anchor failed. Although the most accomplished and enthusiastic of us all, once he had qualified as a vet, Mick took up skiing and fell-running and hung his rock-shoes up for good.

---

17 R. Collister, *AJ* 2008 pp 181-190

Figure 12 John Cardy on Llithrig, Clogwyn du'r Arddu.
Photo: Rob Collister

John Cardy, with his shock of red hair and the enormous forehead of a boffin, was another distinctive figure. Neither of us was particularly strong in the arms and when we climbed together we usually chose our routes accordingly. We were in our element on the never-ending girdle of the West on Cloggy and tip-toed up Bloody Slab in good style; but when it came to Cemetery Gates, my hands were actually on the belay ledge when my fingers opened and I fell off. I was not to own a harness for another 10 years, but I came to no harm and still have the garage-nut that held me. Adrenalin propelled me back up onto the stance but I was less than pleased when Cardy announced on arrival that he was too pumped to lead the top pitch. With John, too, I spent several dank, autumnal days dangling nervously beneath ludicrous overhangs on limestone aid routes like Castellan, Twilight, Hubris and The Prow, all long since freed. John was something of an aficionado. I did not care for aid one bit but felt it was a necessary part of my education.

Rob Ferguson was a geographer whose keen interest in mountains was not just recreational. Unusual in his dislike of technical rock, Rob was a very confident snow and ice climber and became my mentor on early visits to Scotland and the Alps. When a large party was marooned on Tower Ridge at dusk, it was Rob who was dispatched into the infamous gap while the rest of us sang mournful dirges and yelled obscenities into the night to keep the cold at bay. It was Rob who led me up my first ice-climb, Three Gully Buttress, cutting steps expertly with a straight-picked axe (though it was Bob Jones and Gordon Macnair who saved my life, calmly fielding me when I tripped over my crampons on the descent to the Carn Mor Dearg arête). And it was Rob who had the audacity to suggest attempting first the Fletschhorn and then the Grosshorn north faces at a time when, the Triolet excepted, Brits just did not climb alpine ice. Rob was always very organized. He was the only one of us properly shod when we bivvied on the crest of the Cuillin ridge, one March, prior to a traverse of the main ridge. I was wearing Hush Puppies because of an Achilles tendon problem. Denis Mollison was wearing baseball boots because they were all he had, and during the night it snowed...

Geoff Cohen was another more experienced mountaineer who initially took me under his wing. Geoff was, and is, a delightful person, famous for his inability to make decisions except, fortunately, when climbing. During my first long vac we visited the northern highlands, cheekily knocking on Tom Patey's door in Ullapool and spending a few nights in the bothy at the bottom of his garden. The doctor took us in person to the obscure Alladale Slabs and pointed us at the second ascent of The Fiddler on Ben Mor Coigach. One night we joined him in the pub at Inveroykel where closing time was unheard of. Patey was singing and playing his squeeze-box into the wee small hours and beyond, and while we crashed out in a barn nearby he was driving back across Scotland for morning surgery. The following winter Geoff and I teamed up again on Ben Nevis. The week in the CIC hut had started badly when Gordon Macnair, the President, was avalanched by a collapsing cornice while soloing an easy gully. As we struggled to splint his leg and put him on a stretcher brought up from the hut, we were all hit by another avalanche and swept further down Coire na Ciste in a tangled mess of bodies and equipment. In retrospect, we were extraordinarily ignorant to have been launching ourselves up snow gullies in semi-tropical conditions. By the end of the week, it was at least colder, but otherwise the weather was atrocious and everyone else was heading downwards as we set off for the North East Buttress. This was regarded as a long, serious climb rather than a hard one, but it felt quite hard enough for me, chipping steps in earnest for the first time. The sense of commitment at the foot of the Mantrap in thick mist and a howling gale, the exhilaration of fighting our way over the summit, and the state of contented exhaustion in which we squelched our way down the boggy path in the dark to Fort William, were all new but were to become quite addictive for a few years. It may have been the same occasion when the police moved us on from a comfortable bivouac in a bus shelter. The night being dreadful and the cells full, they found a railway carriage for us instead, first class at that, with the stipulation that we vanish by seven in the morning.

Figure 13 Cardy – "shock of red hair and the enormous forehead of a boffin"
– tip-toeing up the Bloody Slab, West Buttress, Clogwyn du'r Arddu, June 1970.
Photo: Rob Collister

While my friends were pushing their grades in Wales and the Lakes, the whole of my second long vac was taken up by an expedition to the Hindu Kush. I was recruited by a group of ex-CUMC members – Alan Cormack, Dick Metcalfe and John Peck.

Peck was a colourful figure with shoulder length blond hair and an enormous beard, who lived in a garret in Spittalfields, producing what he called 'semi-pornographic' etchings. The overland journey to Pakistan in an old army truck was a six-week epic in which personal relations broke down almost as frequently as the vehicle. The mountains, when we finally reached them, felt like a rest cure by comparison. Before we could climb anything, however, we first had to rendezvous with Henry Day, who we had last seen in the Officers' Mess of the Royal Engineers in Osnabrueck. We had arranged to meet at our proposed base camp beside a lake near Sor Laspur in Chitral, but plans changed when we learned that a party of Austrians were at the same site. Having no permit, it seemed tactful to go elsewhere and we ended up on the other side of the watershed in Swat. Unfortunately, there was no way of letting Henry know. In the event, Alan and I missed him by a day, after a week's journey over untrodden glaciers involving rock-fall, an almost fatal crevasse incident and some scary river crossings. I was learning all the time and discovering that mountain travel could be just as rewarding, and as hazardous, as actual climbing. However, my most vivid memory is of meeting, near the lake, a dignified but courteous Chitrali horseman, a falcon on his wrist, a spaniel running to heel and a retainer walking behind carrying a musket and a bag of provisions. Subsequently we climbed a number of peaks just under 6000 metres and I acquired a taste for that sort of exploratory mountaineering which has never left me.

When Dick Isherwood asked me to join a small team going to Chitral the next year, I jumped at the chance. At the time, Dick was one of the best rock climbers in the country as well as a formidable powerhouse in big mountains. In his company, an awestruck youth, I found myself rubbing shoulders in Wales and the Peak with god-like figures such as Crew, Boysen and the wonderfully voluble Holliwell brothers. On that trip I learned a great deal about alpinism from Dick, and from Colin Taylor too, but above all I learned that in the mountains you must seize your chances with both hands. We oh-so-nearly climbed Thui II, a beautiful peak at the head of the Yarkhun valley, but we bivouacked early and the weather broke during the night. We were prevented from making a second attempt by our liaison officer, an extremely unpleasant man who later had us turned back at the Khyber Pass because of "currency irregularities" and did his best to have me thrown in jail.

Skiing was not a sport that appealed to climbers in those days, but I had been on a couple of school ski trips and I was inspired by a picture in Alan Blackshaw's *Mountaineering* (Penguin Books, 1965) of a mountain tent guyed down with skis in a blizzard. Chris Barry was equipped with my Mum's edgeless skis from the thirties, given a day's tuition in Coire Cas and then dragged off over the Cairngorm plateau to Ben Macdui. I was hooked even if Chris was not, and the next winter a Land Rover-full of us, including Tim Nulty, an American economist who had been enormously helpful in Pakistan the previous summer, the bohemian Peck and David Gundry, companion on many an escapade before and after, set off on a three-day marathon drive to the Bernese Oberland. Christof Lehrner, a guide in the Loetschental, lent us a straw-filled barn to stay in, warmed from below by cattle and sheep, and a day tour in his company taught us a lot about skins and kick-turns, though not, alas, how to ski difficult snow. Even snapping my brand-new skis, four days stormbound in the unguarded Hollandia hut and a sightless descent in total whiteout did not diminish my enthusiasm for ski-mountaineering.

Figure 14 The bohemian John Peck at high camp on the North Kohistan expedition.
Photo: Rob Collister

*Figure 15 John Peck and Rob Collister with teachers from
Bagral Primary School, North Kohistan, 1968*
Photo: Rob Collister

Figure 16 Mount Ararat, Turkey, passed en route to North Kohistan, Swat in 1968 – a six-week epic drive on which "personal relationships broke down almost as frequently as the vehicle."
Photo: Rob Collister

Figure 17 Dick Isherwood at the bivouac on Thui II, Chitral, August 1969.
"We oh-so-nearly climbed it."
Photo: Rob Collister

Figure 18 CUMC Sixties style: David Gundry at Chair Ladder, Cornwall, January 1968.
Photo: Rob Collister

Times change but topography does not and Cambridge has never been the ideal location for a climber. Purpose-built climbing walls were still in the future, but the notion of training for performance must have been gaining ground, for no sooner had the old lime-kiln at Cherry Hinton, with its carefully chipped if rather slippery holds, been blown up on safety grounds, than the energetic development of disused railway bridges began. The arrival of Harold Gillespie and Mick Geddes from Edinburgh with tales of the Currie Walls must have had something to do with it.

Of course, generations of Cambridge climbers had found adventure aplenty on their doorstep, at night. Geoffrey Winthrop Young with his pre-First World War *Roof Climbers Guide to Trinity* was only perpetuating a tradition which found its finest expression in the thirties with Whipplesnaith's *Night Climbers of Cambridge*. The sixties' contribution to the genre by Hederatus did not match the whimsy and humour of that classic, but it reflects the secretive nature of the activity that I never knew who wrote it. For myself, I loved the heightened awareness created by the dark and the illicit, the sense of being privy to a totally different night-time world when the only other signs of life in the silent town were perhaps a solitary light high up in a tower window or the hooting of an owl. Most of the keenest climbers of my time, though, did not much care for night climbing, with its need for stealth and silence. The metallic clink of a karabiner or the briefest flash of a head torch could be enough to betray one to a prowling bulldog and the authorities suffered from a sense of humour failure when it came to night climbing, especially on King's.

King's is the most famous route in Cambridge and it certainly has some unique situations, but John's is the better climb. It offers lay backing, bridging, a delicate slab, and a final strenuous overhang in a superb position; there is even an easy descent if you have played your cards right. Dick Isherwood described it as "the finest Severe in England" and he was probably right. One ambition I never achieved was the Senate House Leap. Chris Barry had a room ideally situated high up in Caius. One night we used a plank to measure the distance and practised standing jumps in the corridor. Neither of us could ever quite make the chalk mark on the floor and discretion proved the better part of valour; though on another occasion, after a dinner, Chris used the same plank to walk across.

Night climbing skills could be deployed in other contexts, too. During the Europe-wide student unrest of 1968 there was a sit-in at the Old Schools which I was able to drop in and out of as I chose. It was good fun though I cannot for the life of me remember what we were protesting about. During my final year my wife-to-be, Netti, was at Newnham. Visitors had to be out of the college by 10 pm which seemed unduly restrictive so we kept a rope under her bed. Abseiling out of the window into the garden was given an added frisson by a don occupying the room below.

I suppose I had a rather cavalier attitude towards my degree. Hours spent gazing out of the UL at clouds and trees along with subversive texts by Thoreau, Richard Jeffries and Henry Williamson convinced me that whatever I did in the future was going to be out of doors. In my fourth, final year, the university careers department, mystified by this attitude, arranged only one interview for me, with a firm of rubber traders in Malaysia. Fortunately help was at hand in the form of Noel Odell. Odell was in his eighties then, but still very fit and spry. He had a weakness for crumpets and used to call round at tea-time, usually on a Monday, to compare notes about the weekend. On one occasion, staying at the Pen y Gwryd hotel for a C.C. dinner, he had walked over the Glyders on Saturday and up Snowdon on the Sunday and was full of it when we met. Mick Guilliard, who had also been up to Wales, had already told me at breakfast that the weather had been so vile that they had spent the entire weekend in Wendy's cafe and the Padarn ... It was Odell who introduced me to the Alpine Club, driving me up to London in his Mini a number of times and later proposing me for membership. Like many of his generation, it seemed, he was a great raconteur, and I loved listening to his stories of Everest and Nanda Devi.

From Odell I learned that the British Antarctic Survey employed mountaineers for its fieldwork and that Sir Vivien Fuchs was giving a public lecture the following week. One thing led to another and a year "on the ice" with a dog-team made it even less likely that I could settle into an office job or endure the rigours of the chalk-face. Eventually, I drifted into instructing and guiding almost by default, but I have never regretted it, the boundary between work and play often blurring. Looking back, I can see that my years at Cambridge (Selwyn 1966-70) were not just enormous fun, but they gave me a profession, a spouse and some life-long friends. What more could one ask of a university education?

The year 2006 was the centenary of the Cambridge University Mountaineering Club. The Club committee organised a special dinner, which was well attended, and solicited past members for contributions to a commemorative book. This piece was one of those contributions, although the book itself has so far – August 2008 – not materialised.

(*Ed.* No change yet in January 2014!)

REFLECTIONS ON THE CUMC MINUTES[18]
John Ashburner

"*Friday evening lectures at the CUMC were a big event. In those days British climbers, however distinguished, hadn't realised they could charge for their slide shows, and Cambridge was known as a good place to visit*"[19].

The lectures of the Cambridge Mountaineering Club (CUMC) were all faithfully recorded in the Minute Book, the previous meeting's account being read out just before the next lecturer was introduced. I was very impressed by the first meeting I ever attended of the CUMC when Mike Dixon gave a talk on October 11 1963. The then Secretary Rupert Roschnik recorded the following in the Minute Book:
" ... *Mike Dixon began by apologising for his title* "More climbs in Britain and the Alps" *because he had not in fact done any more climbs since his last visit*".
And so each meeting was opened by the reading of ever more memorable records. Ian Clough's lecture included a number of slides featuring brewing up at a bivvy:
"*Ably assisted by his companion, Mr Blank (Chris Bonington), he carried a Bluet gas stove up two of the major north faces of the Alps and succeeded in photographing it many times on the way*".
The list of lecturers enticed onto the stage in Cambridge was indeed impressive. During the "reign" of Nick Estcourt (President) and Rupert Roschnik, these also included John Clements, Bill Tilman, Pete Crew, Don Roscoe, Chris Bonington and Ian Howell. The latter had been hosted by the Club the previous evening...
"*The minutes of the previous meeting were read, approved and signed by the Journal Editor (Dick Isherwood).* The Secretary then invited Ian Howell, who was still visibly and audibly suffering from the after-effects of the Annual Dinner.*"
*A note in the margin elaborates...
"*The President having been gated as a result of events following the Annual Dinner*"
Dick Isherwood entered the fray as Secretary with vigour and I tried to use his own minutes as a yardstick in order to ensure that my own efforts the following year when I also became the Secretary kept up this long-establshed tradition. Below are some classics penned by Dick following meetings during the year 1964-65.
On October 16th 1964
"*The President then introduced the speaker, Mr David Cox, Senior Tutor of University College, Oxford and Senior Member of the OUMC. After locating in turn the platform, the audience and the screen Mr Cox showed a fine set of slides of Machapuchare.*
... *And it is not only the mountains which are holy in this part of Nepal: we were shown slides of several monkeys making a girdle traverse of a sacred temple and depositing their sacred excrement on the ledges from which mere mortals were not permitted to remove it.*"

18 Compiled by John Ashburner
The Minute book is now kept in the University Library (Ref SOC.XXI.1.4) and the relevant pages were kindly photographed by Paul Fox, Senior Treasurer of the CUMC. A couple of pages were a bit blurred and so Henry Edmundson was persuaded to creep back to retake them.
19 R.J. Isherwood. *Climbs of my youth. CCJ* 2008 pp 15-23

On October 22nd

"The President introduced Alf Bridge, a regular lecturer to the CUMC since 1929[20], who read a short paper "On Falling Off". Although it was only 32 years since his last talk to the Club on this subject, this maestro on (sic) the 1930's showed no sign of staleness and entertained us well – though he cunningly avoided giving away the secrets of his craft.

He began with a short exposition of gravitational theory as proposed by Newton, and proceeded to a detailed analysis of the proposition "The leader shall not fall". This, he concluded, was far from a universal truth – a fact well known to some of the audience. Traversing delicately past the crux of the matter – namely how to avoid getting hurt – Alf went on to describe some of his deliberate peels, in particular one made during the first girdle traverse of Pillar. "I shall fall off half way up this wall" he said, and sure enough he did. A less substantial peel on the Flake Crack of Scafell Central Buttress was arrested by grabbing the chockstone with one hand in passing."

Denise Evans addressed the Club on 30th October.

"The six members, led by Countess Gravina, called themselves the "Jagdula" Expedition to confuse John Tyson who had led an expedition to Jagdula and called it the Kanjiroba Expedition.

With a few wild swipes at the map of India, Denise showed us how the various members travelled out to meet in Delhi. Many slides of the approach march showed that they were attracted by the landscapes and plant life, and also by the hairy men of the hills. They attempted to pass through a steep grotty gorge but, like Tyson's Expedition the year before, they met defeat. This is already one of the last great problems of Himalayan climbing...

The President said Ta and the meeting adjourned to coffee."

On 6th November, current member Henry Day described the 1964 Cambridge Chitral Expedition

"which of course didn't go to Chitral at all but to the State of Swat, by personal invitation of the Wali and Waliahad thereof...

It soon became clear who was the photogenic member of the party – pictures of John Peck smoking, John Peck sleeping, John Peck making mud pies and little boys making faces at John Peck took us rapidly from contact to contact through the Middle East... Nevertheless Base Camp was established and the formidable Seri Dara icefall attacked with an umbrella and two ski sticks – the party's ice axes having inconsiderately dropped off the vehicle en route..."

For the next meeting, another current member:

"Twas a dark and stormy night as eight hard men moved swiftly towards the Sedgwick Museum to begin the 433rd Meeting of the Mountaineering Club, on Wednesday November 11th at 8.30 p.m.

...and the President introduced that well-known Casanova of Kashmir and Cambridge, Suman Dubey who spoke on the Second Indian Everest Expedition. The members of the party had difficulty in distinguishing themselves from their 900 local porters but eventually these were paid off and then began the formidable

---

20 The entry on page 357 regarding the Committee Meeting held on January 21st 1965 records *"It was agreed that Alf Bridge be offered Hon. Membership in view of his long-term friendship with and affection for the Club and his many visits as speaker."*

task of eating 18 yaks, 90 goats and 500 chickens which had been brought alive
to the Base Camp..."
The Secretary was a bit savage in his assessment following the meeting on
November 20th
"...Trevor Jones, hanger-on to several generations of hard men, who described a
variety of Welsh and Gritstone (sic) climbs, most of which he had himself seconded.
We were first introduced to the speaker's rear end, Jim Swallow's head, and most
of Joe Brown, and then saw slides of British highways and the screes below Cloggy,
occasionally interrupted by blurred foreground images of men climbing cliffs...
When after 45 hysterical minutes Mr Jones ran out of both breath and beer, the President
thanked him for his riotous lecture and the meeting adjourned to the Bun Shop."

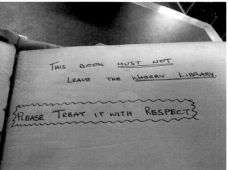

Figure 19 The Minute Book, now preserved in the University Library
Photo: Paul Fox

On November 27th,
"...the President introduced John Hartley who delivered the most sober talk the
Club had heard for some weeks...
After a bivouac on the descent a decrepit van just about took them back to a
glorious sunset.
The President thanked the speaker and the meeting adjourned to the Bun Shop
and more sacred places[21]."
Don Whillans was the guest on January 22nd, speaking about the British Nepalese
Expedition to Gauri Sankar.
"Like all successful expeditions they had the material blessing of Arthur Guinness:
their ultimate failure may be attributable to the fact that Ian Howell left it all at
home by mistake.

---

21 *Ed.* If I recall correctly, a circuit of Trinity Great Court was completed later in the evening

Tearing themselves away from the harems of Lancashire, the expedition drove out backwards over snow-covered deserts and arrived in Nepal in time to catch the end of the monsoon.

…Next stop was at a snake charmer's where pictures of a small boy about to lose his manhood to a malevolent cobra were but a portent of things to come when the leeches struck. Their mail runner broke a world record with forty leeches on each foot and an unspecified number in his more private places. Other hazards of the long approach march were the monkeys who got mixed up with the expedition members and a leaking cow which purged the sleeping Clough of his many sins. When after an hour's lecturing the speaker still had not reached his mountain, we feared disaster: would they reach their goal before the pubs closed? Eventually Gauri Sankar was found and they looked for a way up. Several hundred interesting grassy ridges were crossed before Camp 8 was established just below the snowline. The West ridge which they had planned to climb was found to be desperate, so they trespassed across the Tibetan border to cross the NW face and reach the easier N ridge. By now winter had come, but being hard men and members of the ACG they pressed on to the respectable height of 22,000' before avalanches made any further progress dangerous. They retreated just in time to rescue Dennis Gray from a horde of Tibetan brigands and headed for home and Guinness."

The Secretary was impressed by the visitor on January 29th

"…The President then introduced Barnsley's greatest gift to mankind, Peter Crew, who showed an exciting series of slides of recent climbing on Clogwyn du'r Arddu. ….Contrary to expectations, only one of the pictures was of himself – on the Pinnacle Girdle – and then he was invisible – so the audience was given little idea of his own contribution. However his brief comments about such heroes of the Sedgwick Museum platform as Trevor Jones and Colin Mortlock made his position very clear. Obviously not wishing to boast, he described how Banner had seen seventeen possibilities on Cloggy in 1958, climbed the Troach which he thought would be the hardest, but failed to get up any more. The rest have since been climbed by Crew.

A superb photograph of the cliff taken by a drunken camera was followed by a systematic dissection of its buttresses into cracks, walls and walls between walls. The next generation was recommended to try the walls between the walls between the walls."

On February 5th,

"The minutes of the previous meeting were read and objected to but nevertheless signed.

The President introduced Peter Biven, at one time the leading top-roper on gritstone and more recently the champion of climbing in Cornwall….

To the accompaniment of pathetic squeaks from an elderly record player, we saw film of various climbs at Bosigran and Chair Ladder, and heard the latest reports on the new never-never guide to the Cornish cliffs. All these climbs starred the speaker and his sixty-year-old second, the Stanley Mathews of British climbing, Trevor Peck. His attitude to peg protection produced hisses from those unable to do the climbs he described.

Of great interest to millionaires in the audience was the Peck two-ton van, equipped with four double bunks and a deep freeze large enough to hold all their food for the Alps. Consuming only two gallons per mile, this seems likely to supersede the Centurion tank as a general transport for mountaineers."

There was another Member's Night on Tuesday[22], February 9th and

"The President introduced Brian Chase, liaison officer to several CUMC bus meets, who described some of his recent expeditions to the Peak District. It soon became clear that on the infrequent occasions when our speaker disengaged himself from the bazaars and belly-dancing of Derby, he had in fact done a number of good climbs.

...he showed some good slides of limestone peg routes, including Mecca on Ravenstor, the White Edge in Dovedale and the tenth and first successful Cambridge Expedition to Nemesis in Water-Cum-Jolly.

Continuing to Wales, Brian described in great detail his 12 ascents of Shadow Wall, and... he moved on to the Lake District and Thirlmere Eliminate on Castle Rock, with the President (Mike Kosterlitz) leading the desperate Original Finish clutching a misleading Fell and Rock Journal in his hand.

...But the highlight of the evening was the speaker's heroic traverse of the Colorado Grand Canyon unroped and wearing only shorts and a ten-gallon hat."

The Club must have run out of speakers in February as on the 18th, there was yet another Member's Night with Suman Dubey, the Secretary (Dick) and Brian Chase (for the second week running!).

"The first of these showed some slides of the last Alpine Meet... Base Camp was established in the hamlet of Chamonix and several climbs were made on Mont Blanc and its subsidiaries, including the Old Brenva route by the speaker and a maiden of flawless virtue, Miss Gurythia[23] Petersen.

The Secretary then showed a series of slides of present members of the Club failing on gritstone V.Diffs, a nocturnal ascent of the Big Plum, and the first Magog assault on Goliath's Groove, which was defeated by exhaustion eighteen inches off the ground[24].

Brian Chase... Showed some pictures of his climbs in the Alps, this time taken by Bob Courtier. These included forty shots of the Aiguille du Plan from slightly differing positions, clearly designed to illustrate some profound but unexplained thesis about the steepness of its walls. A fine shot of the President's feet somewhere in Wales concluded the evening."

At last a "proper" speaker was attracted back to the Sedgwick Museum again and on February 24th,

"The President introduced the speaker Sir Anthony Greenbank who spoke about his visit to America in 1964. Besides a brief attempt to win the heavyweight championship of the world[25], he spent some time at an American Outward Bound Centre in the Rockies and gained a remarkable picture of American climbing psychology and methods. The principal attraction around the centre was a virtually horizontal slab of rock down which pupils were taught to abseil – but to do so they had first to ascend it, wearing crash hats in case they fell over forwards.

---

22 *Ed.* The Dinner was on the Friday, hence the Tuesday meeting
23 *Ed.* Name indecipherable and I forget!
24 The Magogs (the female equivalent of the CUMC) was (were?) absorbed into the Club in 1962 when Terry Goodfellow was President and Mike Gravina Secretary. (See the Note in *Cambridge Mountaineering* [1962], p.42 by Unity Stack)
25 For further details of this incident see Tony's description on page 28

The speaker soon discovered that the power even of the bong-bong was limited and introduced the American people to the use of jammed nuts on a first ascent on the local crags. Sliding across a valley on a mile length of nylon rope provided further amusement but when this disappeared overnight, Tony decided he ought to go too. Escape was affected by catching a near-lethal disease from a sheep tick, and he went to recuperate in the company of Mrs Royal Robbins. Recovery was swift and he then climbed with her husband, discovering that some Americans at least could free climb."

On March 5th,

"The President introduced Tony Smythe to speak on The Moose's Tooth"…

Detailed plans were made over two cups of coffee in Bristol and the Expedition split into two groups who travelled out separately and both arrived broke. Six months later, by which time Tony was a T.V. star and an experienced miner and Barrie Biven an ace duck-shooter, they set forth again in a derelict car and drove up the Alaska Highway to Anchorage.

…After four weeks the expedition reached its climax – the journey out on foot. Feet became ineffective after a time when water cut them off all round, so they took to rafts. Raft no.1 sank rapidly with most of their gear,: Raft no.2 nearly drowned them. The heroic pair were rescued from small sandbank by an amphibious plane and made their way home with another demonstration of how to live for nothing in North America."

After the Easter break on April 29th,

"The President introduced Dr Harka Gurung, a geographer from Nepal who showed slides of the country and peoples of central Nepal, including occasionally the mountains. An interesting though possibly incomprehensible map showed the area concerned – centering on Pokhara and including the Annapurna massif. The latter figured on most of the slides which followed – nearly always photographed from the same direction, and providing a background for cattle grazing on the airstrip, the central Nepal cup final, and the other delights of the streets of Pokhara. We were then taken up-country and closer to Annapurna – which, however was no longer visible. Interest was sustained though by Pleistocene lake deposits, specimens of Bombex (sic) ficifolia and forests rumoured to be full of yetis. Dr Gurung showed photographs of vertical grass to put Derbyshire limestone in the shade and ended by horrifying the outcrop climbers in the audience with the story of a farmer who had to walk 30 miles to work because a river intervened between his house and his field."

The Club year was rounded off on May 5th when…

"The President attempted to introduce Mike Banks but was rapidly outshot by Major Banks who obviously preferred to look after his own publicity. A few shots of Rakaposhi took care of this and he continued to his main subject, a joint services expedition to Mt. McKinley. The purpose of this was not clear at first as McKinley is climbed quite regularly, but his real motive emerged when the hand-picked Army and Air Force representatives went down with gut rot and it was left to the Marines to uphold the British flag. The climb was only eventful for the soft snow which at times reached up to their – er – thighs.

…The expedition then ended but Mike remained in America, making his contribution to the Defence estimates with a tour of all the US military installations which were near some climbing."

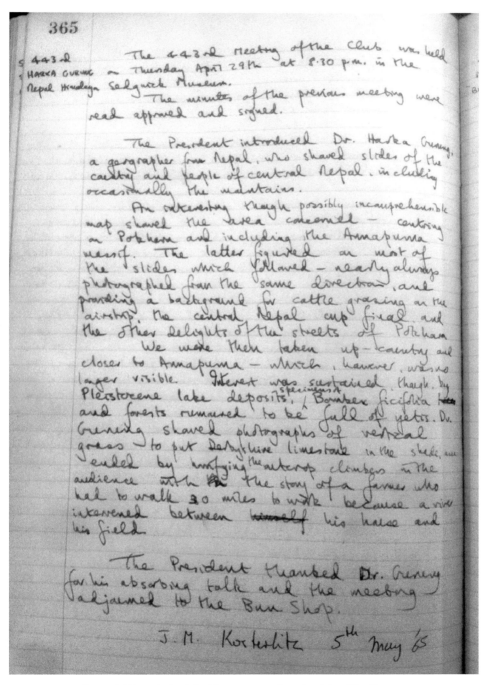

Figure 20 Page 365 of the Minutes recording the visit of Dr Gurung
Photo: Henry Edmundson

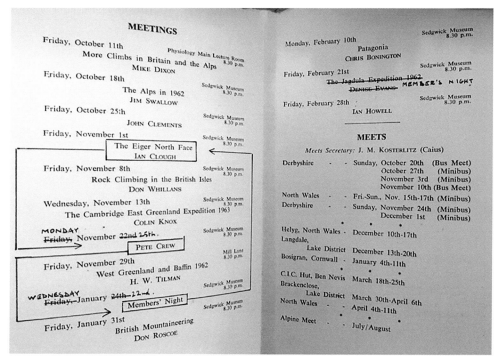

Figure 21 The Programme for 1963-64 as attached in the Minute book
Photo: Paul Fox

A GLIMPSE OF PRE-CAMBRIA[26]

Bob Keates

Jim Harding writes "This I believe to be a brilliant article, redolent of climbing attitudes during the mid-1960s. It is also an accurate depiction of Dick as a climber at that time, at least as I saw him. Bob Keates was a one-off, so his statements should not always be taken as authoritative. A Peterhouse scholar, climber and photographer he pursued an idiosyncratic course as an undergraduate. He had a gift for communication but no gift for grammatical expression.

The article has accordingly been heavily edited by Jim both back in 1967 and just now

The first whispers of the big cliffs on Anglesey filtered down to the masses in March. In April the television film almost gave the game away, but the Red Wall was a red herring. The Big Cliff, over a mile away, was still secure from mass invasion. However the secret could not be kept much longer, and by May *everyone* knew about Craig Gogarth, the fantastic cliff which plunges almost 400 feet into the sea. By May almost all the good lines had been climbed and what was left looked desperate, so the 'in-crowd' could safely allow 'the rest' a glimpse of the crag.

Before launching out into the unknown the cautious climber asks the usual tentative questions. If he can gain any sense from the answers he will stay in Wendy's, but fools press on…

"Well, the VS's go up to Cenotaph standard, the Hard VS's to Vector standard, and the Extremes are harder than that." A very matter of fact statement from the Manchester Sherpa[27], slit eyed and grinning. "Three twenties and forty scored".

Next, the Television Star[28], paunch in one hand, pint in the other. The Photographer[29] introduces us, then the question is put.

"There are some good routes there, but all hard – try Diogenes – and you ought to be capable of Mild Extreme before setting foot on rock there. By the way, are you any relation of the poet?"

Now it's the turn of the Photographer, the London Lips strike again. "It's so fantastic: if you're going to do anything good you *must* tell me first."

It appears that the place is quite hard. It is also photogenic – must be steep. So, set about finding a safe, easy route to start with.

"What's a good, ordinary V.S. at Gogarth?"

"Go for 15s and 10s." This explicit answer comes from a tall individual[30] distinguished from the crowd by his southern accent. Peering over his glasses in schoolmasterly fashion he pronounces, "Traverse at sea level for some way then go up some grooves. It's about V.S."

A freckled face appears out of a mug of mild. It is the Oxford Voice[31]. He is triumphant; today he has actually *led* a climb, unprecedented behaviour in one who

---

26 R.A.B. (Bob) Keates, *Cambridge Mountaineering* (1967) pp 18-22
27 Joe Brown
28 Ian McNaught Davis
29 Ken Wilson
30 Martin Boysen
31 Tim Lewis

is reckoned as one of the best seconds in the business. "We did Gogarth: it's as hard as Vector but loose and more serious, and it's committing, once you get started you just have to go."

His partner, would be Conquistador of the King Street Irish[32] confirms, "The rock is made out of potato crisps."

So that's it! Loose rock. Suspicions are aroused.

"If you want to climb at Gogarth go this year before it all falls into the sea" asserts the Sceptic.

(These were early days of course. Now it seems everyone is revelling in the looseness. "Better than the Dolomites", they all say. Starting with Dinosaur people are now looking for the loosest route yet).

"It's better when you get used to it". Back to the Manchester Sherpa, who is lighting a fat cigar. There must be good money in the equipment trade, whatever he may say.

"We did this route last weekend where the best rock was as bad as the worst on Doppelgangen."... (This love of looseness is a new discovery; any fool can climb on solid rock, but it takes a real idiot to get anywhere on South Stack).

Figure 22 The Big Groove, Gogarth North Stack
Photo: Bob Keates

---

32 Dick Isherwood.
According to Jim Harding "*There were rumours at the time that an obstreperous undergraduate was subdued by the simple expedient of being pinned beneath an upturned table by some basically pacific Irishmen who then sat on the table for a while*"

Undaunted the quest is continued, and finally the Oracle[33] is consulted. The blond Demi-God of Welsh climbing is sitting in Ynys having his hair cut. In the course of conversation he lets drop this plum. "Traverse at sea level to a V-shaped niche and go up the obvious line of holds to the right. Then go back left and up a groove, or you might try going straight up."

I have a bad day on Saturday, unable to lead the final pitch of Dwm, and later, worse, a failure on the final pitch of Diagonal. (Why does Dick have to say, "that's where Terray fell off"?) After this last fiasco we just arrive back in the Padarn in the last minutes of serving time.

Figure 23 Dick on the crux pitch of Dwm, Castell Cidwm
Photo: Bob Keates (not in the original *Cambridge Mountaineering* article)

Sunday dawns, and it's still raining in a spasmodic way. Good... maybe we can fester all day instead of climbing... But it's Sunday and there's nowhere to go except Wendy's.

Wendy's looks much as it always does. Papers are read and Sunday begins to drag. Dick suggests we should look at Anglesey – it might not be raining there. Nick[34] and Peter[35] agree; they want to do Gogarth. I agree to go along and watch; there might be some good photos to take.

An hour later we are having tea in the South Stack Café. At least this is better than staying in Wendy's all day. Suddenly the sun appears and we are stirred into action.

33 Peter Crew
34 Nick Estcourt
35 Peter Rowat

For some reason we change into breeches, and ropes and gear are taken 'just in case'.

Over the hill, and suddenly the crag appears. It's just as everyone has described it; steep, even overhanging, not just in little bulges but also in vast areas of blank wall. Cameras come out, and much film is burned off.

Soon we come to the steep little gully that leads to the cliff bottom. Dick tells us to put our PA's on and leave our sacs here. Not realising the full implications of what I am doing, I comply. I swing two cameras over my shoulders. Dick adds the ropes and picks out a great pile of slings.

We reach the bottom of the cliff. Dick is leaping around over barnacled rocks. I find the slings which he has put down and hide them.

Relief for the moment. Dick is absorbed taking photos. Nick and Peter are scrambling to the foot of Gogarth.

Dick has now realised that the tide is down and the traverse below the main cliff accessible. He cannot find the slings so he picks up the ropes and disappears behind Gogarth Pinnacle. I retreat to the safety of the big island, just accessible at low tide, whilst Nick ensconces himself on top of the Pinnacle.

Suddenly peace is shattered. There is a great yell from Dick who wants me to join him. He is using that compelling tone of voice, so I retrieve the slings and round the corner of the Pinnacle. On the other side there is a small cove with vertical walls rearing to overhangs 80 feet above. The steepness of the place is deceptive. From the roofs dangles a string, actually part of a full weight rope, testifying to someone's epic hereabouts. It seems to grow out of the rock at an angle instead of hanging down in the normal way, but it is the rock that really leans over and the mind which cannot grasp its overhang.

Dick has the rope uncoiled and is already tied on. While he sorts the slings I belay in a V niche. To our right it's just as described; a line of jugs and a narrow gangway leading rightwards across an overhanging wall. Dick starts up.

Dick stops. There is an awkward move onto the gangway. The jugs are rounded off and he cannot get high enough to put a foot on the gangway. "Fail," I say to him mentally. I try to will him to fail so that we can get out of this place and go back to safety to watch Peter and Nick, now making good progress on Gogarth. At first it seems to work – there is an obvious move which he cannot see so close up – deliberately I don't tell him. Then he comes down to rest and spots it.

Up he goes, no trouble this time, and he is up the ramp. Back left, then out of sight. Soon it is my turn to follow. This is the point of no return; the tide will soon be up and escape cut off, the only way upwards. Once I start to climb the tense, sick feeling goes; the rock is good and solid and the climbing interesting without being desperate.

Soon I am in front, and I reach a ledge about twenty feet from Dick's stance. There are two pegs in a corner, so I bring Dick up as he is grumbling about his stance. He reckons I have not done my share of the leading, so he takes my place by the pegs.

There is a short overhanging wall, about head high but without holds above it. I try it with little success, so I look round the corner behind Dick and come back appalled. Dick takes a turn, with equal success. Then it is my turn again. Meanwhile there are great splashes coming from the right; obviously Peter is having fun with Gogarth. Suddenly there are two loud splashes close together and we look down to the sea half expecting to see two bodies swimming.

Again I do not feel I have the go in me to make the move over the bulge, so Dick tries. He is more pokey and, with a lurch, he is up. The line obviously enters a groove on the right which seems to continue to the top of the cliff. There is an awkward move in and this causes delay. Finally he is in the groove and finds a peg. Obviously Crew was not giving anything away when he talked about going straight up. The sound of hammering floats down and a peg sails down to the sea below. Another goes in its place; the rope moves in little jerks, then he shouts that he is up.

With a rope from above the first move over the bulge becomes easy, but the stride right stops me for a while. Instructions come from above, and finally the move is made. Then up the groove to a niche where I can rest. There is a peg in the niche, about half an inch in, but (*it's*) vital to get out of the niche and back into a wide bridge across the groove. The bridge gets wider and wider; I am splitting. A thrash upwards and I join Dick on his foothold.

From here everything looks easy and I make the mistake of saying so. But I am deceived by the excess of verticality which has made steep rock lie back at an apparently easy angle – until I am established on it. The cracks are choked, the groove blank. What holds there are lie hidden under a carpet of green hair. Progress upwards becomes slow. We are using Dick's nuts and they are the wrong size. I am gripped.

I poke a hole in the crack and manage to place a nut. Just as well; the next moves are hard. Then, suddenly, dead stop. Something has caught. I am on poor holds, out of balance, and my hammer which I took out of my pocket so I could semi-back and foot across the groove has caught in the runner. More grip. I try to shake it free, but it now tangles with the rope. If I go up the runner comes out, and if I try to reverse I might fall off. I go down.

PA's shaking violently, I sort out the mess. Then up again. More hard moves, and just one line runner. I find myself standing on inadequate footholds, with inadequate handholds. I am sweating. Experience at Cherry Hinton has taught me that the only way out is a quick move up before sweat greases the handholds and you are off. I go up. It is thin. I don't believe my foot will stay on the wrinkle on which I place it. The tiny fingernail flake for my left hand looks like breaking off. Slowly I move, then a jug comes within reach and I am over the worst.

A mere ten feet above is an obvious stance, but like a mirage it disappears as I approach. On to another stance, but this too is a mirage. The groove here is huge and steepens. I place good nuts and start up the steep bit. Thirty feet to the top, then suddenly a block I am pulling up on levers out. I swing into a layback on my right hand and rebalance the block. Back down to the nuts, nerves taut.

Down at the nuts I find a foothold and liberal imagination makes it into a stance. I bring Dick up. As he arrives, the sun sets. He too finds difficulties on the way and is impressed by the thin move. However he is very scornful about the stance. He takes the lead, watchful for the loose block, and soon reaches a proper stance.

I join him and take the final easy pitch up a V-groove above a cormorant's nest. Two baby cormorants eye me suspiciously from the nest. As I approach they leap up the groove, wings flapping and claws scrabbling. First one then the other falls off. Tumbling over and over they hurtle down seawards. Halfway, wings spread in astonishment, they suddenly learn how to fly, peel out of their dive, and head towards Ireland. So we get to the top.

Back to the South Stack Café, which is closed. We beat on the door. It is half past nine and we have a raging thirst. After a few cans of orange we hit the road back to Llanberis, hunting for a meal. It is too late to go back home so we stop at Ynys for an early start next morning. Here we meet the instigator of our excursion, who is pleasingly surprised at our success. He had only put up the Big Groove a month previously

Figure 24 Dick seconding The Grasper, Tremadoc
Photo: Bob Keates (also not in the original Cambridge Mountaineering article).

EXTOL[36]

Some way north of the Carnedds there is a place called the Lake District which has a few outcrops and a cliff called Dove Crag This is even further from the road than Cloggy and it doesn't have a cafe on the way up. Nevertheless it's worth a visit as it's big and black and steep just to look at. Most people have heard of the routes there but not many have done them which, of course is a good reason for doing them yourself.

Dove Crag is a compact dome-shaped lump, about three hundred feet high in the middle, overhanging on the right and vaguely vertical in other places. In the middle is a sort of black hole, and the classic route of the crag. Hangover climbs into this up some slabs and schemes out to the right above all the overhangs. Further left are three other routes of the sort known as "modern classics".

Farthest to the left is Dovedale Groove, all overhanging and thrutchy and reputedly desperate. It was ten years before it had a second ascent. Next to it is Crew and Ingle's route, Hiraeth, which is Welsh and means "Wish I'd stayed in Wales." The third, though, is the one to do. It goes right up the middle of the cliff and it was first done by a small square man with an impressionable second. They were so gripped that they couldn't decide what to call it, so it featured in the books first as Entity, then as Extol, then as a bit of both, until another route was born called Entity so it had to settle for Extol.

Anyway it was clear that this was the big line of the crag, and when we walked past it one evening it was even clearer. As I had nothing better to think about it became a big ambition of mine to do this thing. Unfortunately it was hard – much harder than me. So, when I had exhausted all sources of grants to climb from Cambridge. I got a job teaching climbing at a sort of freelance Borstal in the Eastern Fells with a view to training up for it and maybe taking it by surprise one weekday when no one was looking. But I got no time off, and the only rock I saw was Shepherds Crag which is about as big as Cherry Hinton Wall and not as good, and all the good weather came and went, and November came and I went, and that was that for the winter.

When I returned I was better set up. I had a real job and a Motor Car and a bit more strength in my fingernails, and, most important, someone for the sharp end. This time the weather fixed us. It waited until we were halfway up to the crag, then it surrounded us with wet clag so thick that we couldn't even find even find the thing. Keates got his hush puppies soaked and we cleared off to Keswick and the pubs and a night of hazy memories in a nasty wet shed; and on Sunday we went to Kilnsey and he got arrested in étriers and so another fiasco was complete.

Only a month later we were back again. Saturday afternoon dawned fine at Bawd Hall in the wilds of Newlands, revealing Peter Rowat walking stolidly uphill. He denied walking all the way from Manchester – just from Langdale. Ten minutes later he was wittering about Dove Crag and tugging at his lead so hard that Estcourt got interested too. I was sure I'd thought of Extol long before they had so a second was needed quickly. "I'll do any route in the Lakes except those three," said the old man of Cherry Hinton, so that was him opted out. The only other candidate was Steve Martin. He claimed he was unfit but I didn't believe him, so like the splendid guy he is he came along to prove it.

36 R.J. Isherwood, *Cambridge Mountaineering* (1967) pp.32-35

We drove round as near as you can, which isn't near at all, and Rowat, being loosened up by his night walk, set off at a run. But the opposition hadn't been there before so they lost the path and went the steep way and we caught them and all arrived together – except Caroline that is. Now came the crunch as we all remembered that all the others wanted Extol too. Finally we tossed and Steve and I won. Nick was sick, and he was a lot sicker when he found he had no PA's for Hiraeth.

The bottom of Extol is a nasty chimney, all loose and full of dead trees and moribund cabbages. All it lacks is snakes – and runners. I nearly killed Steve with a big rock but otherwise it went alright. It will all fall down some day, then you'll have to go the easy way up Hangover. We swapped slings in the big hole in the middle of the crag and he got about twelve belays and I was just setting off when the monsoon broke. I should have been angry but I was so scared I was glad instead, so we went up Hangover which sidles off to the right. Before we got to the top the rain had stopped and we felt a bit foolish, especially as the Hiraeth team were still in action.

Down we went and round to the bottom. Coaxing was needed as Steve had proved his unfitness already and he was far from keen. Being a gentleman he said he'd go it if I really wanted to, so I said I did and got started before we had time to change either of our minds. We went up Hangover this time and it was great – real rock. Again we swapped slings and Steve tied onto all the belays within reach, and I looked at the sky and this time it wasn't going to rain.

To get into the big corner from the stance you have to swing across on a jug, but first you have to catch it, and trying to do this I pulled off a huge block and nearly fell off. Squawking came round the corner as it had just missed the future Mrs. Estcourt. Next time I found a real hold and leapt across onto some grass in the corner and went up for miles without runners because it was easy and I had to save the gear for the top where it might not be easy.

Eventually all the loose jugs and the lettuces fizzled out and it was all steep and hopeless above so I went left into the dreaded smooth groove that some said was the crux. Lots of cunning runners were fiddled into the bottom of it and I crept up on little holds and bits of moss. Not too bad I thought, nearly there, one more move... Then when I thought I was up all the holds ran out and a sort of hopeful wriggle had to be made with as much clothing in contact with the rock as possible. This led to an infant spike for a runner and some grass to stand on.

From here you were supposed to launch out of the corner and climb a wall on the right, but it looked hopeless and besides straight above was a piton with a real alloy karabiner for the taking so I went that way. I soon regretted it as the peg was lousy and things were now hopeless in all directions at once. You had to go right and climb the wall now, but someone had turned this wall upside down so that all the jugs were undercuts and the ledges were roofs – two or three little ones at first, and then daddy at the top, all black and nasty with bits of evil plant leering out from under him.

Well at least I'd better try I thought, so I started groping onto this horrid wall. There was a spike on it and after a bit I found a crafty side-pull and crabwised across on to a foothold and put a sling on the spike and somehow wedged myself and felt happier. The next section was very weird. Being wedged by the spike was alright if you didn't think about it, but as soon as I tried to move up I swung out, so I had to come back and rewedge very quickly. Eventually I got mad with myself and swung out properly and up and scrabbled a bit and popped into another funny hole. At this moment Estcourt appeared across the comer and wanted photogenic positions, so I got hold of a sort of fang on the big daddy roof and leapt out of my hole like a real Bcrgsteigcr. Holding this for the camera scared me to death so I went back in again and started searching for runners. I found a bad one and eventually courage returned.

I saw a great nutting crack round the roof so I made the big move on the fang again and got my feet right up and stuck my head round the roof. I nearly had a stroke as there was no crack for nuts at all, but there in the bottom of the groove was a rusty old haken (sic). Quick as a flash I stuck a finger into it, and equally quickly regretted it as I had to get the finger out and a sling in. Then the slings knotted up and I nearly strangled myself and it was ages before I clipped in and sagged on the peg, which bent. The position here was too harrowing for Homo Sapiens so I pulled up and tried to stand in the sling. I tried so hard that before I knew it I was in the bottom of the groove above the peg, standing on nothing much but clutching a big fat jug and back in balance at last.

Here the world was right way up again – the grass grew upwards – and it was only thirty feet to the top. It looked easy but it wasn't and it had no runners either, and when you thought you were there it all gave out into moss. I nearly had a top-rope from the two grinning faces above, but eventually made it unaided, without enough rope or energy to get a belay. The faithful Rowat tied me to the cliff and Steve came up. He demanded a "fishing line" with a loop on the end so he could grab it if he was gripped, but it hung so far out that it made him more gripped, so he just kept going.

It rained, we fled, and the ale at Brotherswater was terrific.

Ed. I managed to track down Steve Martin …
 "I'm sorry but I cannot help you with photos of "Extol", which I remember was quite a challenge. I'm sure you will have covered his early ascent of "Masters Wall" on Cloggy, which was quite the best achievement on British rock by any of our lot in our era……Dick was a wonderfully understated character who just went out and did great things without making a song and dance about them."

Ed. Master's Wall is now known as Great Wall and Dick describes it above (see p.6).
 As there were no photos of "Extol" I have included one of The Crucible – Bob Keates informed me in January 2014 that on that occasion, Ted Maden was "the 3rd Man" on the rope.

Figure 25 Dick leading the 1ˢᵗ pitch of The Crucible, Craig Yr Ogof, Cwm Silyn
Photo: Bob Keates (neither was this in the original *Cambridge Mountaineering* article)

CARNMORE[37]

It was pouring down on the M5, as it nearly always does everywhere on Friday nights. My windscreen wipers didn't work. I pulled onto the hard shoulder and sat swearing until the AA man knocked on the window.

He was very helpful but, as he explained, he couldn't do anything without taking the dashboard completely to pieces.

"You'll have to manage without. Are you going far?"

"Inverness"

From the look on his face I guessed that I must be the first person ever to go from Worcestershire to Northern Scotland.

The rain eventually stopped and I got to Manchester only about three hours late. Gordon, Bob and Eddie were on their fifth or sixth pints. Peter Rowat, frustrated from going to Carnmore again himself, was telling them what lines to climb – and how, and what to call them and why but no-one was listening. I bought his pack frame and gradually moved the others out of the Guild. Happily it didn't rain again until we arrived.

Inverness was bought out of porridge and sticky milk and sausages and other goodies, and we reached Poolewe at opening time. It was drizzling and the mist was down over the sea.

"What are we waiting for?" asked Bob.

"Tomorrow", we told him.

So we cooked ourselves a midge risotto and slept in a horrible shed and miraculously tomorrow was dry. We drove inland up a road labelled "No Entry" and came after a couple of miles to a locked gate and nasty man. Regrettably we had no permits.

"You can't park here."

Just like London. We unloaded the sacks and I took the car back onto the next estate where no-one was watching.

The walk into Carnmore is about seven miles, reasonably level and furnished with bits of path. The views of the Loch Maree hills, close up on one side, and countless lochans spread out on the other, are excellent. It would make a very pleasant afternoon, if you had nothing to carry – or, I suppose, if you were fit. For us it was hard work. Eddie was sure his sack was the heaviest. It was certainly the smallest, but then we had given him all the tins, so he might just have been right.

After about two hours, when my knees were beginning to sag, we came down to the Fionn Loch by the "Little Crag". This, the first real cliff we'd seen, was impressively steep, but it didn't quite live up to Bob Keates' four hundred feet. I wondered momentarily whether we could divide all his other figures by two.

Fortunately the Ghost Slabs round the corner were no disappointment, a thousand feet high at least. And by now we could see across the loch to the real thing, Carnmore Crag. Along the sandy shore, across the causeway, a last desperate uphill section – all of fifty feet – and we were at the barn.

Col. Whitbread's shooting lodge looked attractive but as uninvited guests we felt we could only use the stable. This, however, was very comfortable. Two feet of dry

37 R.J. Isherwood, Queen's. *Cambridge Mountaineering* (1968) pp 13-19

manure made a good mattress and there was even a table. We brewed up and looked at the crag. Almost five o'clock – just about time for a quick route, we thought. Gordon and Bob chose Dragon, and Eddie and I went to do Gob, as these looked to be the best of the existing routes that we knew of.

We rather forgot that the cliff was in two tiers and that both these routes were at the top. We had to do something to get up there, and just what Eddie and I did I'm not sure. It was a rather nondescript bit of rock which may well have been unclimbed and it was quite pleasant. Steep granity rock, but none of the nasty featurelessness of Cornwall or Chamonix – lines of lovely pockets appeared at just the right moments. The crag was almost perfectly dry, the sun was still full on it, and the ledges were full of blue and yellow flowers – a change from plain Welsh grass.

Three pitches took us to the big bay in the middle of the crag. The top two were quite steep in places: not dramatic climbing, but it gave us some idea of what could be done on this accommodating rock.

Gob took a very satisfying geometric line: out along a big slot, up in a groove, left for a long pitch under the big roof, then through it by another corner groove and up to the top. The rock confirmed our first impressions: pockets again, just as you needed them; otherwise mostly incut or sharp flat holds; lots of little runners, threads and spillikins and nut-holes; and a steepness that was enough but not uncivilised.

This, at any rate, was true of the middle of the upper wall. On either side, it was clear, things were a bit different. Out on the left, beyond Dragon, were some very steep grooves, the line of Abomination, a Creag Dhu route which looked decidedly uncivilised. Dragon too had its awkward bits we were informed as we waited at the top of the crag at ten o'clock.

On the right-hand side of the upper crag was the dreaded Red Corner – clearly the last great problem of the cliff, and the focus of Peter Rowat's daydreams for a whole year. He had abseiled down it the summer before and despite losing all contact with both walls after the first ten feet, he was sure it would go free.

"It only overhangs twenty feet, and there's a good fist-jamming crack – in the middle."

When Peter found he was unable to come with us, his enthusiasm reached even greater levels. He drew us a diagram indicating a "stance" in the middle where a spidery creature crouched in a faint depression in the overhanging wall, attached by forces that were difficult to imagine. Geoff Cram, who had been up a few weeks earlier, had actually tried the corner and had soon formed his own opinion. Peter, however, was undaunted – on our behalf. He thought we might need a peg.

Faced by all this encouragement, we felt we had to try. Fortunately the corner was still wet, so we reckoned we had a couple of days' grace.

But this is digressing. To return to the top of the crag at ten p.m., the striking thing was that we were still in shirtsleeves – and sunshine. Eddie and I just sat and looked – at the grass, the sky, the lochans, the colours, the crags. Rock everywhere. The slabs across the Dubh loch, in two big fans coming down from a black bulging upper tier, at least a thousand feet in all though some parts were a bit jungly. To their left in the shadows, a Big Black Wall, very steep, totally unclimbed and intriguing. On the near side, across the descent gully, was Torr na h'Iolaire with about four Grochans, one on top of the other, or so it appeared to a casual glance. (Looking up the old guide, we found that they were fairly gentle Grochans.) Further up the valley were more cliffs again, so we understood from Bob and Peter. It seemed that a week would not go very far.

When we had finished eating it was just too dark to read. We sat around, expecting it to get fully dark. When the half-light was still there at half past one we realised that it just wouldn't, so we went to bed. For me one of the best things about Carnmore was being able to stay in bed till lunchtime and still get a full day's climbing.

New routes were the form next day. I had a line on the upper crag, right up the middle, starting out of a cave between Dragon and Gob, crossing the Gob traverse and taking a slightly hopeful line through the big overhang. Gordon and Bob had schemes away on the left.

Again it seemed a pity not to climb on the lower tier, so Eddie and I found a nice little line there – to warm up on, we thought. On the right of the lower tier was a set of overlapping slabs, the site of another of Peter's good ideas. His drawing showed an eight foot roof, split by a hairline crack and labelled "crux, may need a peg". Fortunately we found a cunning traverse, above this roof and below the next, which solved things very neatly. It led off along a steep flake, whose edge formed monstrous jugs, then a peculiar wall where the pockets only just sufficed and gave some superb moves: great fingery swings alternating with delicate balancy foot-shufflings. A peculiar step round a minor overlap led onto the lip of the big lower roof, which had appeared from the start to be a pretty thin slab. When I reached it the benevolent pockets were so big that it was no more than an exposed walk.

I belayed on a tongue of flowery grass in the central groove and Eddie came up and led through. Thirty feet above was another overlap with a groove above it. The slabs between looked a bit bare but again the pockets kept turning up. A good move over the overlap and out right onto the top slabs in sunshine and flowers; it was good to be alive. We called the route Penny Lane: it had a sort of dreamy quality.

We had expected to go straight on from here to the upper tier, but now another crag, which we hadn't even noticed, forced itself upon us: the Grey Wall. A little line was found up a cracked arête – very steep, this one, but so well supplied with jugs that it was quite reasonable. Eddie's pitch was really steep with some peculiar flakes that were not obviously attached to anything but still perfectly solid. Again the cliff was accommodating.

This brought us out below the Red Corner, still wet, so we traversed across into the lush shadowy grass below my line. By now it was five o'clock – but what did it matter?

The crack started as a cave, twenty feet high and with no obvious big holds to get you out at the top. As a first approach, we thought we'd traverse in from the left just above the cave, so we climbed up a dirty groove to reach a stance on a heather ledge next to Dragon. Eddie took a belay and I looked at the options.

The lowest traverse line was reasonable at first, but it soon gave out into steep blankness where the wall heeled over into the cave. Ten feet higher was another line and this looked much better. Again the rock was perfect: just on balance, little sharp flinty holds, and still in sunshine.

I moved out onto a rib, but here for once Carnmore let me down. I wanted to step down, then across right to a ledge, but there were no handholds, and it was a very big step. It was such a pity – two moves, and I was sure it would be reasonable again. I could see spikes and nice ledges.

On such a helpful crag there had to be a solution. I looked around and saw a big natural thread, just sticking out of the wall about twenty feet above me. If I can fix a runner there, I thought, a little tension might do it. I climbed up a vague crack to the higher level and got hold of the thread. Half of it broke off in my hand but the other half made a spike and seemed quite solid. I went down again and further down on the rope to the vital foothold. Moving right to the ledges was very odd. Tension had to be supplemented by fingernail-sized underpulls behind a little roof to prevent me swinging out. Eddie juggled the ropes very expertly and I reached a resting place.

The next section was easier, then a short awkward wall led to the main break and I found myself bridged across the top of the cave, contorted to avoid some unsupported blocks. Coming straight up did look hard.

From here to the traverse line of Gob was about eighty feet. The crack was never desperate but it stayed interesting all the way. I passed one enormous loose block, narrowly escaped pulling it off in my arms, and then resisted temptation – one of the ropes was directly below it, and it was mine. The stance at the top was two footholds and a peg crack, and there was about six feet of rope left.

At this point I remembered that Eddie had no hammer. (In fact he had no gear at all, except a sort of suspender belt full of loops and rings to hold all the pegs and karabiners he hadn't got. He had no PA's either – he regretted that.) He tried knocking out the belay peg with stones, but he could only find little ones, so he had to leave it.

It seemed a good idea for him to put the rope directly round the spike to avoid leaving a sling. Unfortunately it stuck, and he found himself in mid-traverse, unable to move and being sworn at. His reply was short and to the point. He had to go back and leave a sling, but when he came across again he was so shattered he swung off altogether and a big pull just averted disaster. He shifted the loose block, leaving a crater in the grass and a smell of burning whatsit in the air. It nearly hit the barn.

By the time Eddie reached the stance it was half past eight. Bob and Gordon, out of sight round the corner, had already finished. I was feeling pretty tired but I was sure that, if we didn't finish the route that night, the weather or some other fate would prevent us coming back. So we looked at the next pitch, a short corner, continuing the crack line and splitting the big roof, which here was offset a few feet.

From the stance I could step up a couple of moves. Out to the right was a niche, in the back of the corner, which seemed to be a good resting place. Its floor was formed by a block and if I could reach that, I was halfway there. A tape sling on a spikelet gained me a couple of feet – I was almost level with the block but too far to the left. Five or six times I came down, re-knotted the sling to a slightly different length, and tried again. Really this was pointless as there was nothing at all to go for. But I was tired in mind as well as fingers and I hadn't any other ideas.

Finally the crucial handhold broke as I was moving up, and I very nearly fell off. The shock woke me up and I came down to the stance for a think. I could still see no way of progressing free, so I tried to place a peg, in a crack below the block and miles to the right of my sling. Frantic leanings-over brought this just within reach, and, in peril of turning upside down, I clawed away a mass of green hair – reminiscent of Anglesey – and poked the peg in. Attempts to hold it and hit it at the same time were almost disastrous, but eventually it went right in.

Figure 26 Gritstone Buttress, A'Mhaighdean, Carnmore
Photo: Eddie Birch

As I hadn't been able to see the peg crack at all I just had to move across on hope. Fortunately the crack was good, and I reached the block. The promised resting place was useless so I moved on towards the arête on very small footholds.

Just before the arête the holds became a bit too small but by then I was committed, mentally at least. I pulled out on some indifferent things and stepped onto a very poor hold on the edge. Calves were quivering, and I groped urgently for a big jug. The cliff didn't fail me a third time – my hand fell into a beauty, and I was up.

This time I could lower the hammer to Eddie, so we lost no more gear. I hauled the sack up before he came so he didn't find this pitch too bad. He'd compared the previous pitch to Vector, but wearing boots and carrying the sack (which contained my boots) may have influenced him.

The top pitch was easy, even for cramped arms, and we emerged at ten-thirty to see a Brocken spectre on a patch of mist in the gully. We coiled the ropes and screeched down through the mist to supper and endless brews and competitive exaggerations.

After a day like this we couldn't help an anticlimax. Again we got up at lunchtime and again we looked at the Red Corner. But it was still wet and, besides, the day was cold and windy. Bob and Gordon went up again and found two more lines near to our first two of the day before. (It is rumoured that their route on the Grey Wall is impossible if you're shorter than six feet three.) We went to look for the Gritstone Buttresses of A'Mhaighdean and found them, after a long search, situated at the top of an almighty grass slope. We, of course, were at the bottom.

The line we tried was a good one – a corner leading up to a bit of a roof and continuing above, but here, although the geometry of the cliff was again satisfying, the rock was nasty: brittle conglomerate like perverted inedible treacle toffee. We were foiled by the roof – there just wasn't quite enough over the top – and we had to be content with a big bottleneck chimney in the middle of the crag, into which we cunningly traversed avoiding the bottle part. We didn't fancy any more and it was freezing cold, so we went for a walk.

When we returned to the barn the clans were gathering. One kilted hairy Scotsman had lit a fire out in the open, in scorn of our primuses. It transpired that he was no less than a full member of the S.M.C.

As we cooked our supper the big guns appeared: John Cunningham, Ronnie Marshall and two apprentices. You could almost see the Red Corner shaking as they looked at it. We made plans to start at dawn, but the weather beat everyone. It rained steadily for three days. When it stopped alcohol starvation drove us all home. I read "A Town Like Alice" at least twice before it was needed for more urgent purposes.

Those three days were by no means wasted. There was some interesting verbal fencing over the merits and grades of Wales and Glencoe (if you're interested, the Bat is "a wee bit harder than Sickle") and first hand accounts of great steigs in the Coe. I've been trying ever since to imitate Cunningham imitating Whillans.

And it isn't every week that you get the chance to lie undisturbed in a dung-heap for three days.

A VISIT TO SCOTLAND[38]

Whitsun was always fine until the Labour government meddled with the calendar, two or three years ago. Now, as the state spring holiday, its date may be more predictable but its weather is definitely not.

Failing to realise this important fact in time, we went to Scotland last Whit weekend. Mike (Kosterlitz), Berit [39] and I all took Friday off work and we roared off into Thursday night. Our original plan had been to climb in Glencoe, but since it had been fine all week we thought we'd just have a day there to warm up, and move on to the Ben and perhaps the Bat.

The bank of cloud began near Coventry. It built up gradually as we went north and over the border it was beginning to look ominous, but Radio Luxembourg went off the air promising another week's sunshine for the whole country so we pressed on. An hour or so later it was drizzling in that silent effortless way it does in Scotland. All the urgency to get there was suddenly gone and just after dawn we camped by Loch Lomond. The Bat was obviously out.

Before we had the tent up the little bastards were on us. Rain and midges together seemed a bit unreasonable. Mike and Berit persevered in erecting their tent, but I just laid mine down and crawled into it. After twenty minutes I was both damp and badly bitten. I slept in the car instead.

In the afternoon, after we'd set up house in Lagangarbh, the rain stopped. Eager to salvage something, we rushed up the hill and started climbing. We did a thing called Whortleberry Wall which was one of the first VS climbs that I ever saw anyone do, the first time I came to Glencoe. It takes the best, highest part of the once-famous Rannoch Wall and in my memory it looked appalling, but now it just seemed a nice, fairly steep climb. It started up a red slab, then zigzagged left and right to reach a big steep corner full of jugs, from which there was a huge move rightwards, round an exposed arête onto clean white rock and through funny patches of moss to the top. We ran down through the mist to supper feeling pleased because one of the best things about the climbing in Scotland is the graded lists, and this climb was very near the top of its list, and we thought it was easy.

The climb at the very top of that graded list was Carnivore, and since it was also the nearest climb to the hut it seemed a good choice. That night we went up the hill to look at it. The cliff was tremendous, huge and long and overhanging and apparently blood red in the fading light. We knew that the climb was a monster rightward traverse, and we could see bits of traverse line, but all the starts we could find were impossible. Still it was dry, and very little else was.

Next morning when we set out we found we had competition. Geoff Cram, John Jones and another had come in the night and were living in a hole next door. They too realised that this was the only dry climb for miles, but they let us go first because we were a two, and didn't try to burn us off on the walk up to the cliff.

38 R.J. Isherwood, Queen's. *Cambridge Mountaineering* 1969 pp. 22-25
39 *Ed.* I could not remember a climbing partner of either Mike or Dick called "Berit" so I asked Mike in September 2013 for the surname and e-mail. He couldn't understand my cryptic question and told me the only one he knew was the one he had eventually married. I apologised profusely and sent my regards – I had, of course first met her back in '63 - '66 during my days at Cambridge.

Mike was the clever one who found the proper start, miles away on the left hand edge of the crag, so I let him try first. He climbed up twenty feet and stuck, without runners, below a bulge. He tried all possible ways of surmounting this, but eventually he came down, swearing. By now a foursome had appeared too, spearheaded by Little Nick. I had a go, and I found three good runners that Mike had missed – but none of them was close enough for a handhold so I couldn't do it either. We hung our heads and moved down the queue.

Disturbingly, Geoff did it first time. He was up so fast I didn't see how to do it, but we picked it up from the other two. As soon as John Jones had done the hard move – it was only one – Mike was at it, jumping the queue and clawing at the rock in a fury of two point climbing. He went over the crux at twice the speed of Cram and set out to chase them across the huge traverse.

In no time he was at the stance – a long grass ledge right in the middle of the wall – and I had to go. The little bulge wasn't too bad on this end of the rope – a funny fingery move – and just above this was a resting place and a peg runner. From here it really looked exciting. The rope went diagonally downwards for about a hundred feet, with two sad little runners clinging to it, before coming up sharply to the near end of the grass ledge. The first part of the traverse was very fingery and the nearest runner was nearer to the ground than it was to me.

I was so impressed that I arranged a back rope. This was almost a disaster as the drag was so great I had to climb with one hand and move the rope with the other – difficult on a steep wall. At the first resting place I untied from this rope and sorted it out. The rest of the traverse was easier, but there was a horrid little wall at the end, still far to the left of the belay. I struggled into the spongy grass and crawled along it looking for bilberries but they weren't ripe.

The next pitch was comparatively easy. It led up and right to another spongy ledge, more useless bilberries, and a second belay from which the rope hung totally free. Some clown had done a bolt route up to here – we admired his perseverance on the hard volcanic rock, if nothing else. He will obviously go a long way in life – but I hope he gives up climbing.

Above us there was a minor traffic jam. This stance is tiny, John was saying, let's abseil off, it's going to rain. The other two agreed, so he came down and they started fixing an abseil. Seizing the opportunity to regain some prestige, we said we were going on, although the sky did look bad, and below us Nick and his team were retreating too.

The next stance in fact was quite adequate – provided you stood on one foot. The rock leading up to it was odd – very smooth and black with white specks. It looked like tasty liquorice toffee, but we didn't try it. Obviously it would be unpleasant to climb down in the wet, and this might be necessary for we were now too high to abseil off.

Above was a nasty groove that looked as if it was steeper than it looked – if you know what I mean. This was Whillans' direct finish, the villain's revenge. We didn't try that – we went the crafty original way of Cunningham and Noon, even further along to the right following a break that was both overhung and undercut and by now enormously exposed.

Up to this point, we knew, the route had been largely pioneered by Whillans, and it had much in common with Extol, Woubits, and especially Slanting Slab. Like Slanting, it is a fantastic intricate line up an improbable crag, and particularly on the first pitch, not too well protected. Now we were at the place from which he and Cunningham had retreated each, according to legend, leaving the other's pegs behind.

When I started the next pitch I was very glad that the small square man hadn't found the line. The break was very steep and even with six pegs in thirty feet it was hard enough. Whillans might have done it all free. The traverse led to another small stance, in a little cave with some peculiar thread belays in the back. For the fourth time in succession all the rope hung free.

One more pitch to the right, along a difficult sloping ledge, protected midway by an old sling at foot level, whose attachment to the rock we could only guess at, took us to a huge heather ledge more or less off the end of the cliff. Already the rain was beginning. You could finish here and go down through the vegetables, but it might take several days, so we followed the rock back to the left as we were meant to do. Cram and Jones meanwhile, having jettisoned their middleman down the abseil rope, had returned to the struggle and were trying to leapfrog by doing the direct finish.

This pitch was easy. This was lucky because when I was half way across – returning to the left above our previous traverse line – Armageddon arrived in the shape of a big hailstorm. The little jugs I had my hands on got flatter and smaller as the deluge continued and I distracted myself trying to put knife blades into blind cracks for a bit of security. When the hail stopped the pitch had changed its diameter. All the holds were flat where before they had been incut, and the steep little wall just above had started to overhang. This presented some difficulties, as did the waist deep moss and heather which dominated the last hundred feet. We paddled down to the hut to find that we were the only ones to finish, which put us in a delicate position.

That night we had a few beers and then a few more. Half Manchester was in the Kingshouse and most of them came back to Lagangarbh for a brew. The hut, which had been empty when we left, was now full of very senior Scottish mountaineers. The story cannot be told in print – suffice to say that a difference of views arose. Next morning it was still wet, so it seemed a very good idea to leave. We drove to the Lakes where it hadn't rained at all, and we did the three big routes on Dove Crag, all in the same day. But that is another story.

DIRETTISSIMA ON THE PIZ BADILE[40]

When you have only three weeks holiday, you have to make the most of it. Mike Kosterlitz, Richard Stewardson and I left England on Friday evening 28 June 1968, and reached the Val Bregaglia at dusk on Saturday. For three days the weather was perfect, and on Wednesday Mike and I were prostrate by Lake Como after doing the North-west ridge of the Sciora di Fuori and the North ridge of the Piz Cengalo (the latter a superb slab and groove climb on perfect rock). We had also reconnoitred the route which was my main ambition for the summer, the unrepeated Corti-Battaglia route on the Piz Badile.

This climb lies on the big pillar forming the left hand part of the Badile's familiar North-east face. It was first climbed in 1953 and the only facts on record are that the climbing was largely artificial and the unfortunate Battaglia was struck by lightning on the summit and killed. The face has several cracks and from the Sciora hut it is not clear which is the best line of weakness. But we had had a grandstand view of the upper two-thirds of the face from the Cengalo's North ridge (see Figure 27) and we were in no doubt what must be the line.

It was a beautiful S-bend crack, slanting slightly to the right, steep at the bottom, easing in the middle, and rearing up at the top to end in a long, straight groove capped by a roof. It reminded us of the Great Wall on Clogwyn du'r Arddu.

However, unlike Cloggy's East Buttress, this face is guarded by a steep snow and ice couloir with an obviously difficult bergschrund. During our day on the Cengalo nothing fell down the couloir; nevertheless its lower section looked unpleasant. In contrast the upper part was quite amiable and we thought of approaching from the Italian side and descending from the col between the Badile and Cengalo. This would probably be as long as the approach from the Sciora hut though less difficult, but its chief advantage was brought home to us late that same afternoon, as after descending from the Cengalo, we waded through knee-deep snow to the Passo di Bondo on our return to Switzerland. Neither of us wanted to repeat that.

So when the joys of Como began to pall and our wallets to grow thin, instead of returning to Bondo, we drove up the Val Masino to the road end and tackled the 1400 m of ascent to the Gianetti hut. The guardian, Fiorelli, was suitably impressed when we mentioned the Corti route and told us that it was "estremamente difficile", "tutto chiodi", and that it needed lots of "cunei di legno". Privately, we thought we knew better – after all, it was less than vertical, so some of it must be free. We never thought to ask him where it went.

Bad weather compelled us to wait for two days, though on the second day, a Sunday, the black clouds cleared a little and several routes were done by weekend parties. Despite our ascent of a 400 ft *Via Inglese*[41] on an outcrop below the hut, we were a bit demoralised that night. We decided to give it one more day and go on to Chamonix.

That night the sky cleared and the morning was fine. We reached the col by an easy snow slope and looking down the couloir we thought how clever we'd been. It was fairly steep, but obviously it was only 500 feet or so to the foot of the crack line.

---

40 Dick Isherwood, *AJ* 1969 pp 1-6
41 *Ed.* Interesting – the route they were about to put up later became known as the "via degli Inglesi" – see p.249. Of course the spelling divergencies will be easily explained and confirmed by any linguist.

Figure 27 Piz Badile, upper two-thirds of pillar on the North-east face; from the North ridge of the Piz Cengalo. "We were in no doubt what must be the line. It was a beautiful S-bend crack". In fact the Corti-Battaglia route probably goes to the left up a different crack system.

Photo: Dick Isherwood

We went down one at a time, kicking big steps in the hard snow. After 1,000 feet we realised we'd underestimated a little, and only after 1,500 feet of descent and two hours' effort did we reach the start. It was now a quarter to nine. Still, it was midsummer, so we hoped to get away without a bivouac.

Mike led off up the first pitch, a steep, wide crack. He had a fair amount of difficulty and had to use a few pegs though he found an old ring peg in place, which was encouraging. By the time I followed, I was very cold, and the rock here was wet. A pile of curious jammed flakes supported us both, but a small block which I dislodged higher up sent them all tumbling into the couloir. Hands were numb and the climbing was hard. I grasped the old peg and almost came on the rope – he hadn't told me he'd taken it out and stuck it into a clump of moss. I struggled up to the stance wondering how many days the good weather would last.

We exchanged loads and I went on. The lighter sack was a relief but our thirty pegs and karabiners made the leader's load as heavy and at least as awkward as the second's. Fortunately the climbing eased, and the next three pitches were largely scrambling. This was more encouraging – our initial impressions that the lower half would be free were now being confirmed.

In fact, we found only two more difficult pitches before the steep final section. The one I led was a pleasant corner crack, but Mike's pitch, just below the recess in the middle of the face, was a nasty loose chimney, slanting to the right. Just above my stance he climbed over three blocks jammed abreast, then over a frightening projecting flake, and with considerable skill avoided sending down any rock until he was well out of my line. Then a barrage started – boulders, gravel and Scottish oaths flew down the cliff for minutes on end. The sack seemed to be annoying him particularly. When I followed I saw his point – the chimney was fine if you had nothing to carry. He hauled the big sack as he'd cleverly hauled his own, so I was able to enjoy it, using the rubbish at the back of the chimney as a sort of treadmill.

Two easy pitches took us to the pedestal at the foot of the steep top wall. The three parallel cracks leading up from here were thin and obviously it would be pegging at first. Higher up, the right-hand crack ran into a big dièdre where we hoped to find free climbing. The roof at the top was about 200 feet away, we thought – this proved to be our second underestimate of the day. We ate some chocolate and thought about big spaghettis for supper.

Half-past-one; my lead first. The pegs had come to seem a reasonable load by now, and it was good to use them after carrying them so far. We were able to free-climb bits of the pitch and we used several jammed nuts to save time and effort. There was no ledge so I took a stance in étriers and Mike led on. Oddly, the roof seemed no closer.

After 90 feet of rather loose pegging he stopped at the foot of the dièdre. Above was a huge flake, apparently poised across the crack, and for a few minutes we thought of swinging across into one of the other cracks – but these were equally loose and ledgeless. I came up, impressed by the instability of some of the pegs and the general looseness of the area where Mike was belayed, but gratified to hear that this compared to A3 climbing in Yosemite. Very cautiously I approached the big flake. From close range I could see that it was part of a really enormous block – half the face – and that there was no danger. It was a remarkable formation, a tongue of rock four feet deep, a foot thick at its centre, and fifteen feet long, extending across the dièdre with daylight behind it all the way. I mantelshelfed onto it and continued.

Figure 28 Approaching the steep final section of the Piz Badile
Photo: Dick Isherwood

Sadly, there was no chimney in the dièdre as we had hoped, and not even a hand-jamming crack, so it was pegs all the way, supplemented by nuts. Again the stance was in étriers but the roof did seem closer – 40 feet, I suggested to Mike. Eighty at least was his estimate, and by now daylight was getting short. He ran out 130 feet at best

Californian speed and he still wasn't there. He found a ledge, the first since lunch, and suggested we'd have to bivouac there. "Is it big enough to cook on?" "Wait till you see it".

I still had hopes of reaching the shoulder, but darkness came when I was half way up the pitch. In a way it was a relief – tension was reduced, we knew we'd have to bivouac there – and suddenly I felt really tired. I left three expensive pegs – the first we'd had to leave – and Mike hauled me bodily onto the ledge, which seemed to be made of wet clay.

It was already very dark, but he'd spied out the ground, such as it was. There was a long flake crack, pointing comfortingly down into the mountain and we put several pegs into this. The "ledge" was useless, since it was too small for two, and it was under continuous drip from the roof. We stood partly on a tiny, sloping gangway below the flake but mostly in étriers. I was struggling to stay awake, but the fun was only beginning. We dressed up in duvets, cagoules and gloves, but long johns seemed to be out of the question. Then we decided to move further along the flake since Mike was under a big drip. I banged another peg in and it sounded so good that I transferred both étriers to it. We retied the belays, hung out a pan to catch the biggest drip, and settled down under the bivouac sack.

After a few minutes we both felt very thirsty and peered out to see how much water we'd collected. Unfortunately we both took off the sack simultaneously and it vanished, slithering wetly down the crag into the night. Suddenly it felt cold. We looked at one another, drank the water and tried to sleep again.

Although the position was very uncomfortable, I at least was so tired I could sleep. I woke to find myself falling – the "good" peg had come out. I never came onto the belays, for after slipping only a couple of feet I was held, mostly by Mike's hand on the back of my neck but partly, I swear, by will-power. We put a few more pegs in, doubled the belays and tried again. There were no more incidents, but the morning took a very long time to come. I slept a little, but my legs, pressed against the wet rock, were very cold. Mike was less fortunate; his anorak was less waterproof, he was still under a bigger drip, and he didn't sleep at all.

At first light we began to organise ourselves, but it was a good hour before I started climbing. For one awful moment we were both entirely on one peg, which wasn't even fully in, but soon I was close under the roof. Swinging on pegs placed vertically upwards is not my strongest point, so I took a lot of trouble and clipped the ropes into everything. I regretted this when I moved round the very sharp lip and found myself jammed, 15 feet short of a big ledge, in a spectacular position. I had to untie one rope and still needed all my strength to move the other. When Mike came up we saw that one of the ropes was partly severed – it was proving to be an expensive route. He led the last 15 feet to the shoulder and we took off our wet duvets and lay in the sun, delighting in an almost-horizontal world.

Two big brews made from a snow patch used up our tea and sugar and reluctantly we began to climb again. There was one difficult pitch on the shoulder where a thin slab led into a bank of steep, soggy snow, but otherwise the climbing was easy. Far below we could see a party on the Cassin route, already approaching the central snow patch.

The descent was rapid although our hands, which had been wet all night, were now very painful. When we reached the hut we met Richard and Chris Wood who had climbed the North ridge the day before. They told us that we had done a new route – something we'd suspected, since we'd seen no trace of Corti after the first couple of pitches of our climb. Fiorelli was engaged on his two-way radio and we gathered from snatches overheard that he was talking about us. He had been up on the Cengalo that morning and had seen us finish. On the best photo he had, he indicated that the Corti route started up our line but branched to the left fairly low down and joined a parallel crack system several hundred feet away. The reason for this was not clear to us – perhaps Corti and Battaglia were put off by the loose chimney pitch.

We paid our bills, and set off for the valley where, it seemed, the whole world was waiting for us. We were very pleased not to have to face the Passo di Bondo again, and grateful to the builders of the excellent Gianetti hut path. When we reached the valley there wasn't the battery of microphones and TV cameras we had been led to expect, but the local correspondent of *Il Giorno* did us proud. We had free baths in the hotel at Bagni del Masino, where the water was apparently not only medicinal but radioactive, and dined in style as guests of the management. Before eating we were shown a plaster model of a mountain, recognisable as the Piz Badile only by its labels. We were asked to mark our route with a dotted line like the others. No features could be made out so we put a straight line directly up the centre of the space between the Corti route and the Cassin route. The little group that had gathered was obviously impressed by this, and then someone said the magic word –*Direttissima*. We went in to dinner feeling very pleased with ourselves.

SUMMARY

Bregaglia. Piz Badile, North-east face by new route. 8-9 July 1968.
R. J. Isherwood and M. J. Kosterlitz. Standard: ED. Length: *c.* 2000 ft.
Technical description in *AJ* 73 254.

PIZZO BADILE 3308M[42]
EAST FACE (VIA DEGLI INGLESI)

"Popi" Miotti & Alessandro Sogna

Figure 29 The monolithic north-east face of the Badile
Photo: Giuseppi (Popi) Miotti

42 "Miotti, Giuseppi and Alessandro Gogna (1986) *Dal Pizzo Badile al Bernina. Le 100 più belle ascensioni ed escursioni in Val Masino e Bregalia, Disgrazia, Bernina*" Engadina Perfect Paperback. January1986. Translated by Bob Courtier with assistance from several others.

Ed. This description is based on that for Route No. 100 in (Miotti and Gogna, 1986). However the entire description was updated by Giuseppi (Popi) Miotti in September 2013 and the original photographs have been replaced by more recent ones.

The East Face of Piz Badile is the most impressive structural feature of the peak. A crack line starts from where a stretch of more compact and monolithic rock forms a beautiful little pillar, bounded to the left by the gloomy Cengalo couloir. This line then runs up through the true east wall itself. One of the most striking features of these large cracks is their continuity and linearity. No one seems to have taken much notice of the large wall in the past, perhaps because it was overshadowed by the nearby and famous North East Face (*Ed. w*here the popular Cassin route lies). It was not until 1953 that Claudio Corti and Felice Battaglia tried to solve this last big problem, only succeeding after two days of hard climbing. Tragically and after their tremendous achievement, Battaglia was struck by lightning on reaching the summit and killed.

The 'via Corti' was not subsequently repeated in its entirety until Corti himself completed the second ascent in 1975. In 1968, a British team who were little known within the local alpine climbing fraternity, attempted to repeat the Corti route. A route finding error meant that they climbed straight upwards at the point where the original route traversed left (*Ed.* about 250m up from the start). And so it was that Mike Kosterlitz and Dick Isherwood found themselves forced to proceed up the beautiful crack line that runs without deviation, leading up to the eastern edge of the large funnel basin at the summit of the Badile. The climb took two days and this stretch of the wall required extensive use of artificial aid. It was some years before either Corti's or the British route was attempted again. Meanwhile the name of Kosterlitz became famous in Italy, mainly because of the difficulty of some of the routes opened up by him in the Orco Valley of the Piemonte. The second ascent of the British route was made by the Swiss team of Ruedi Homberger and Hans Jörg Wellenzohn. Unlike the Brits who had first descended from the Cengalo col, the Swiss went up to the base of the cracks from the steep couloir. The Swiss completed the route after two days of climbing and used about twice as many pegs as on the first ascent (which had included a lot of nuts). It was then considered to be the most difficult route on the Badile.

Several more repetitions occurred over the years and today the 'via degli Inglesi' is as popular as other major routes on the Badile, such as the 'via del Fratello' (*Ed.* a TD sup first climbed by the Rusconi brothers in 1970 on the edge of the east face, right of the 'Via degli Inglesi').

The rock is always good and better than on the Rusconi brothers' route. Route finding is straightforward as it just follows the crack line. Some pegs are in place but it is more practical to use nuts and friends. The recent great changes in climate mean that a safer approach when the Cengalo couloir is completely free of snow is from the Italian side. You can then easily find the abseil anchors. It is preferable to make this approach at night, and then to start climbing at first light. The descent from the Cengalo Col (as on the first ascent) requires four to six abseils depending on the conditions.

Whilst describing this beautiful climb the names of the two great Czechoslovak climbers should not be forgotten, Zuzana Hofmannová and Alena Stehlikova, who made the first winter ascent in 1982.

It is a beautiful route, which deserves to be better known and probably, could be completely freed of aid to perfect its purity.

Figure 30 The crack line clearly showing the direct nature of the route
Photo: Simone Porta (taken in 2009)

First ascent: Mike Kosterlitz and Richard (Dick) Isherwood 8-9 July 1968.

Vertical height: the wall itself is about 600m in height (from 2700 m to 3308m); you then climb into the funnel basin for the last 100m up to the summit.

Difficulty: a full length route with the main difficulties on rock and with some mixed sections. Overall, TD + or ED-, pitches of VI and Al

Duration: from the base of the wall to the summit 10-15 hours.

Equipment: 2 full sets of friends and at least one Camalot No.4; 1 or 2 sets of nuts/stoppers; 2 to 3 angle pegs; étriers. If early in the season and if approaching from the Swiss side, ice axe and crampons.

Starting point: Rifugio Gianetti 2534m (Italian side) or Sasc Fourà hut 1904m (Swiss side)

Route: *Approach:* From the Gianetti hut easily reach the Cengalo col between the Badile and Cengalo (1½ hrs). Here there is a fixed rope to help crossing left horizontally for about 120m. At the end of the rope is the first anchor point of the recent "Via Panoramica" route. Make 4 to 6 abseils. This approach does not require axe or crampons.

Alternatively, from the Sasc Fourà hut follow the approach route up the Cengalo Glacier, which is the same as that for the north east face routes (including the Cassin and the 'via de Fratello'). Climb the glacier aiming towards the couloir between the Badile and Cengalo; surmount the bergschrund (preferably on the left side) and gain the slope above. Climb the couloir (45°) up at the base of the obvious crack where the route starts (3 hours from the refuge)

Climb: Start at an obvious groove with two parallel cracks and follow them for four rope-lengths with pitches of IV and V (sections of V+ and Al on the second pitch). Continue up the obvious and logical wide crack line that opens up to a chimney and then overcome the bottleneck above which leads into a gully and the top of this vertical section of the wall (passages of IV and V and one of Al).

Climb across to the right-hand crack of the three that run up the stretch of wall above. The next section consists of three rope-lengths with a stance in étriers, mostly pitches of V and Al, where the use of nuts is very effective in making for faster climbing. Follow up the last corner, which leads to the big roof closing the line of ascent, until you are about fifty metres below it. Take a small crack to exit along the left wall of the corner and reach a niche (V, Al).

Beyond the niche you go left to gain a beautiful wide crack that follows on up to emerge after about 45m. Go to the right and stop at some blocks (V, Al). The last pitch leads to the shoulder of the great funnel basin of the north east wall. The route then goes to the brink of the basin following a spur of broken rocks, after which you turn right onto the north east wall and climb on easy terrain (some snow patches and ice, particularly early in the season) to the summit (four rope-lengths, IV, IV + and then III, some loose rock).

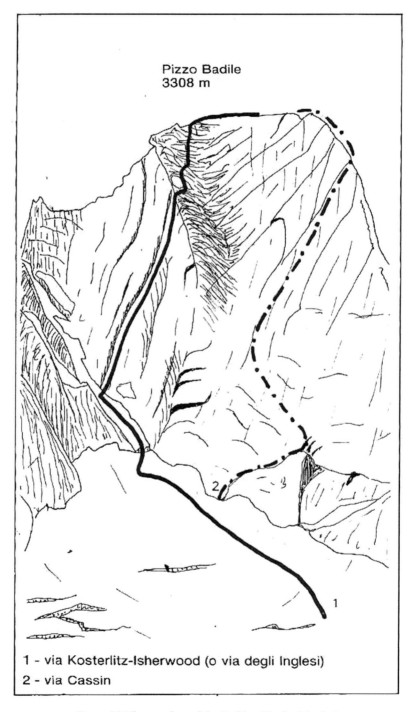

Pizzo Badile
3308 m

1 - via Kosterlitz-Isherwood (o via degli Inglesi)
2 - via Cassin

Figure 31 The east face of the Badile - Via degli Inglesi

WEEKEND[43]

I hadn't climbed with the Kosterlitz for months. He'd been operating here and there with Dave Potts, scratching at Anglesey and the Carnedds and returning out of breath and usually unsatisfied. One day they had conquered two pitches of the Skull – the lower jaw, you might say – but they hadn't managed to return for the big pitch. It seemed that he wasn't interested in that any more, so we went up to Cloggy and thought about things.

I don't recall exactly, but I think he got the ropes that day because he was in front for a bit. I remember we were both half-naked and hideous in the pale sunshine and all the trippers moved quickly out of our way. At the Half-way House we met Howells and Whybrow, bound for Woubits.

"What's this team going to do?"

We didn't answer much – we didn't know. As we walked into the shadows we started to debate it. He'd done all I wanted to do and I'd done most of what he wanted. But you tend to forget girdles – I do, anyway. So as we walked past many an obvious unclimbed scratch on the lower reaches of the Far East, we were still arguing abstractly about Haemogoblins and West Buttress Eliminates that were sure to be still wet.

At the foot of the East Gully the obvious dawned on me. It was early – only twelve.

"What about the Pinnacle Girdle?"

"Well, we could, I suppose. It's very strenuous. Are you fit?"

"Well, no. Are you?"

"Well, no"

"We could try, though."

"I can't think of anything else,"

So we trogged up the terrace and left the sack and slithered desperately down the ledges to the foot of Pinnacle Flake. By now it was one o'clock.

"I'm scared of Taurus, I'm doing this pitch."

Thus the fearless Scot. He was so quick with the ends of the rope that I couldn't really argue. I belayed to pegs and nuts and off he went. He couldn't get off the deck at first so he said it was cold. He did it at his second attempt and vanished scrabbling round the comer.

He didn't progress very quickly and it was almost an hour before he had a belay. He was right about the cold – I was frozen. Everything at the start was sloping except the very tiny things – the grain of the rock, no more – and my fingers were too cold for tinies. I tried a couple of times and retreated with screams for slack. You can do the Guinevere start instead but I've tried that – it's even worse. Hats off to C. T. Jones. So I tried the Pinnacle Flake way again with a great hopelessness and got up by the skin of my teeth to find that all his runners had floated off.

Going across the front was easy really – I don't know why he took so long – but there was a minor thrill at the end with a rope move from a peglet.

Taurus leered at me round the corner and he leered at me too. Frying pans and fires. I took all the slings and pegs and, trying to plan some excuses, I ventured out. Getting to the roof was reasonable, in a loose sort of way, and I put a nut in a little hole at the

Figure 32 Isherwood on an early attempt on the line, later completed by Birtles as Deyco
Photo: Ken Wilson

back of the great overhang. This was it – the dreaded Taurus. Unrepeated for years, loose and overhanging and unprotected and desperate. I felt to be at the centre of all the black steep rock in Wales,

Still returning to reality, it did have holds. I fixed some nominal runners and all the previous ones fell out. A sort of slither out leftwards into a "layback on underpulls", just like the legends, and there was the peg sticking out and beckoning. I gave it a token waggle before committing body and soul to it – surprisingly it didn't move.

Above the peg were more underpulls but the higher the fewer and the smaller. I went up quick and returned quicker. Little runners were fixed and many more attempts were made until I got my feet right, contorted round the little upper roof and popped my hand, blind, into the vital pocket. Over onto a stance to end all airy stances, in Wales at least, and the spare rope hung very free.

The creature came up fast despite his illnesses and frozen hands – but he did get gripped trying to take out a little nut. I had to pull him – it made my day. He leapt on upwards and instantly he was pressed again.

"Put your foot there, Mike."

"*** off."

He reached a ledge and his eyes gleamed, for down leftwards was a peg. Being small, he needed fantastic contortions to reach it. We later learned that it took half a day to put it in. He swung down into a sling, up out of it, down again and out leftwards. Round the arête life was clearly easier – rope went out rapidly. He put lots of runners on – to protect me, as he told me – but before he took the rope in they were all off. I got into the sling on the peg and, like him, I tried all the wrong ways first. It was a peculiar move and it led you to a very airy spot on the Pinnacle Arête, especially so when the belay was thirty runnerless sideways feet away. I arrived, shattered, to find that we were at the top of the cliff

"Can we stop here?"

Who said that? It cannot be revealed. We both thought it, but really it was too early to give up. So he found a belay just out of Octo, a respectable three feet below the top, and I inspected the Hand Traverse.

The Hand Traverse may have inspected me too but it didn't say anything. It just sat there like a long, straight permanent grin, just wide enough for your finger ends but sadly not continuous, and slanting upwards too. The wall below it was impressive. As a first move I climbed a bit of a jamming crack and fixed a runner so high that I was on a top rope.

Then I looked for some footholds and to my amazement there were some. For two moves. I did these and attempted to start hand-traversing. All the upping and downing on Taurus showed its effects now, as one swing was almost too much and I lurched back to the last foothold. Suddenly inspired, I tried putting my feet in the traverse line ("Perhaps nobody's thought of that.") but like many good ideas it didn't work. After a few more spasms I decided it wasn't for me so I came back to the stance and we swapped ends.

His blood was up now and he swarmed across first time. He was just as gripped as I was, but he's brave – I have to admit it. He stood in a sling and fixed lots of runners and tangled his ropes to hell and it's good that he didn't fall off because I was taking photos all the time. I came across in one big swing, half on the rope and half on hope with odd bits touching the rock.

"Let's come back tomorrow."

He said it this time. It was six o'clock, so fair enough, I thought, to the pub, but before I said so I held out for a minute,

"Let's just look at this next pitch, Mike. It might be easy."

Of course I couldn't do it but I think I scored a point for trying. We marked the spot on the top of the crag and fled.

*   *   *   *

In the pub we met a man called Brown,

"I'm surprised you thought Taurus was hard. It's sooo well protected."

I bought some more pints.

*   *   *   *

We reckoned we'd done most of it so we didn't get there any earlier on Sunday. We abseiled down the upper mossinesses of the Hand Traverse and I tried the next pitch again. There was a ring peg on the arête and I was six inches short of it. I knew that the pitch had been climbed backwards but didn't at first realise the significance of this. Desperate lurches for five-year-old pegs are not my best line so I laced the area with runners before I tried seriously. It was still a hard move and round the corner things remained awkward for a move or two – steep and creaky.

Down and across, the pitch went now, on an amazing hanging wall, undercut and overhung, isolated from the world, straight above the lush greenery of the East Gully. Down and across was fine, but up at the end was a peculiar move and it was some minutes before I dug out a new jug and pulled up into the chimney of Gargoyle.

I belayed in a dewy hole and watched Davey Jones losing himself in the fields below the Orb and the Sceptre. Mike seemed quite impressed, especially when I pulled the wrong rope.

He went down Gargoyle, putting on lots of runners as I instructed, and belayed in the hanging gardens on the next buttress. The slings made it easy for me and I featured off onto the Croak. Up a crack to a traverse line and some hopeful moves left to a peg on a ledge in a really great position. The next bit was problematical – a very strenuous heave and mantelshelf onto a flake, or commit yourself to a bilberry bush. I chose the bush.

The belay, a few feet higher, was in a cave, full of huge potential trundles. Must go back mid-week. I found a solid spike or two and realised that my last objective was achieved – he'd got the diagonal abseil.

To my surprise he wasn't worried by this. In fact he was unusually organised. He'd been counting the pitches too, I guess. He vanished over the edge and in no time he was there. I unbelayed and came round.

"Christ."

As I stepped round the arête the verticals suddenly went mad and I saw Alan Heppenstall on a wall which just didn't relate to anything I understood. After a bit I adjusted, but East Gully Wall still looked pretty impressive from this viewpoint. Of course I had no film left.

I frizzled down to the half-way thread runner – getting a little old – and further down until I was barely in contact with the arête and tending to swing into space in two directions at once.

"Ya run across an' grab this thing."

Oh, yes. So I did as I was told and grabbed the thing which was a monumental creaky spike. I was glad I was number two.

One more pitch. Off again on the sharp end. This was mostly Shrike and therefore known country. Actually I very nearly fell off the last move.

He was very happy when he came over the top – until he realised that I'd had all the pitches that day. Then he was a bit fed up but we'd brought a huge bottle of cider and that cheered him up. We still had time to do Ghecko and he was welcome to the crux of that.

I'm glad he came. I wouldn't have enjoyed it much on my own.

HINDU RAJ 1969[44]

Colin Taylor

Last summer, four of us drove to Pakistan to climb in the Hindu Raj. Dick Isherwood led the party and he will write the definitive article on the expedition for the *AJ*[45]. This is an informal account of a four-month holiday with a little time spent climbing. It was a splendid experience marred only by a problem in the shape of our very expensive liaison officer. For those not well up in expedition lore, I should explain that expeditions visiting Pakistan have the choice of registering themselves as Official Expeditions or of taking a chance that they will not be turned back by the ubiquitous military. For a sensitive area, such as ours on the Kashmir border, there is no real choice to make. Although permission to climb will perhaps be forthcoming in six months or so you probably won't hear definitely one way or the other until you reach Pakistan. You are also allotted a Liaison Officer from one of the Pakistan Armed Services for whom equipment and food has to be provided. This man may make or mar your trip as he wishes. Some are an asset to their expedition – some are not.

Dick Isherwood planned to climb in the Hindu Raj with Rob Collister in the summer of 1969. Looking for a third man, Dick wrote simultaneously to Chris Wood and myself in Manchester, and then we both said we would go. I changed my job. Chris changed his job, got married and bought a house, and Dick found himself a job in Bangkok. Rob being still at Cambridge wrote begging letters. On 12th of June we left Cambridge in a brand new Ford Transit. I, for one, had spent much of the previous month being injected against T.B., Polio, Cholera, Typhoid, Smallpox, Yellow Fever, Jaundice, and probably a few other appalling diseases. We had, as yet, no permission to climb in our largely untouched range up in the north of Chitral. The only definite information we possessed was the shape of the outline of our liaison officer's feet. He would be one Major Manowar Khan of the Pakistan Army. Our provisions included 24 bottles of whisky, 3 bottles of sherry, and about 200 cans of assorted beers. The third item was a last minute addition after Dick decided the van springs were not quite in contact with the shock absorbers.

The journey out was fairly uneventful and quite slow: down the Dalmatian coast, across to Istanbul and then through Turkey, Persia and Afghanistan to the Khyber Pass and so to Rawalpindi in Pakistan: about six thousand miles in all. By Istanbul I had developed a dreadful allergy to sun which, in those parts of the world, was unfortunate. This turned out to be Jaundice virus clashing with Cholera virus, and the trouble eventually cleared up. Just before Kabul, Dick mowed down a very tasty antelope which he and Rob cut up with the breadknife in a medieval scene (to quote our cook book). In Kabul Chris drove round in circles while Dick, the self-appointed whisky officer, haggled over the price for twenty of our bottles with two shady Indians concealed in the back of the van. Hashish may be legal and only fifteen shillings a kilo, but the Afghan Authorities frown on strong alcohol. Finally, coming down the Khyber in the twilight, Dick uprooted an army chain-barrier which forcibly reminded us that Pakistan enjoys martial rule.

---

44 Colin Taylor, *CCJ* 1969 pp 11-19
45 *Ed.* For some reason, this was never done but Dick's account appeared in *HJ* 1970 - See next article

In Rawalpindi there was a letter giving us permission to climb on Thui II, a peak of 21,401 feet in the Hindu Raj. We learnt later that this came as the result of a night's drinking by a friend of an American friend of ours with someone in authority. For the next week we were well looked after by Col. Buster Goodwin [See Footnote 12, p.17]. Day by day the temperature and humidity rose, until the former was over 100°F and I swore never to complain about a little heat wave in Manchester again.

Why were we not on our way into the Hindu Raj? Our liaison officer was creating problems. Major Manowar Khan is not very tall, running to fat a little, with a strong 5 o'clock shadow. He was, I think, hurt to be sent with so small and poor an expedition. He showed signs of wishing to lead the expedition. It was he who arranged schedules, ran press interviews, and issued instructions to all. At one point he even produced a sport-plan for our ascent of the peak. I began to see there was more in this Himalayan business than just climbing virgin summits. As Manowar saw it: "Time spent in Rawalpindi is never wasted". He was in no hurry to leave. We did not share this view and were. Eventually Manowar gave the word to leave after I had driven 100 miles down to Peshawar to get a chit from Pakistan Airways saying they could not fly in our gear. The van we left outside the police post at Dir; the road over the Loweri Pass into Chitral was too steep and twisting for anything but a jeep and 76 miles took ten hours. Chris and most of the gear followed with Tim Nulty, the American friend who had got us the permission, and his brother. They had hoped to come part of the way up Chitral with us but it was now too late.

In Chitral Manowar and his batman, who turned up as well, disappeared in to the Mess of the Chitral Scouts; at our expense as it turned out. Two days later a jeep arrived to take us twenty miles up the Chitral river to Maroi, leaving us ninety miles to walk up beside the river to Lasht, a small settlement north of the Shetor Glacier from which we hoped to climb Thui II. The plan was for Dick and Rob to go on ahead while Chris, Manowar, the batman, and I followed with ten donkeys in ten-mile stages. They would go up to the Thui An (pass) to see whether we should try our peak from the south instead and would meet us at Wassam twenty miles downstream from Lasht. They would also avoid seeing Manowar for eight days. To keep the number of donkeys down to ten, Chris and I added several items to bring the weight of our pack frames up to about 40 pounds – this effectively removed the pleasure from the walk to which I had really been looking forward.

On the first day as the sun rose higher in the sky, we nearly expired in the dust, and none of Manowar's advice prevented our feet developing really gruesome blisters. The schedule allowed no rest. When after seven more days, we hobbled into Wassam, I was unable to walk at all and rode a rather aged horse. Dick had turned up on the road the day before, also with blistered feet. Here Rob met us, down from the Thui An, fit and bronzed, with the news that there was nothing much to see of our peak from there. The schedule was scrapped and we decided to wait a day to recover in a rather fly-blown orchard full of goat-droppings. That evening Manowar announced that from now on he would need a daily food allowance to supplement the good things in our twenty-four food boxes in spite of his earlier brave declaration that: "Major Manowar will eat anything." Dick remarked sourly to one of us that he wished something would eat Manowar. Manowar also showed displeasure at Rob's excursion up to the Thui An which seemed now to be a breach of security despite earlier publication of the plan in the Pakistan Times. There followed a lengthy discussion between Manowar and Dick which seemed to be leading to an agreement. Then Manowar dropped his bombshell. The expedition would have to go back. He would give no reasons, and looking back, I wonder whether he had thought of any reasons at that stage. Dick and he sent off long telegrams via long distance runners and we sat in deep depression for the next seven days while our feet festered. On the eighth day Manowar announced that we would go on to Lasht to wait for the answers to the telegrams. So, two months after leaving Manchester, I arrived, still on a horse, at the bare settlement we had decided to call base. Only one man in the party was fit to climb our peak, now only 11,000 feet above us. We had, in theory, no longer permission to climb. All we knew of the peak was a comment in the 1968 AJ by Gerald Gruber that: "The ascent of Thui II will require a strong team and a massive outlay of equipment... it is the most beautiful and isolated summit in the Hindu Kush or the Hindu Raj."

Rather surprisingly, Manowar expected us to climb. A few lines will be enough to describe roughly the country about our peak. Lasht is some five miles south of the Pakistan-Afghan border which runs parallel to the Wakhan or Oxus river. The Shetor glacier runs north-west for about eight miles from a gentle col on the Kashmir border, down via a ferocious icefall, to run out into a couple of miles of moraine above Lasht. From the eastern bank of this glacier rise three peaks of over 20,000 feet. At the head of the glacier, to the west, stands Thui II, 21,401 feet high. There are six ridges, of which three, the NW, NE and SW are very long, they are all separated by steep ice faces to the north and rock faces to the south. The ridges are narrow and generally heavily corniced; they merge into a slender wedge with two summits at about 19,500 feet. The summit ridge is about 5,500 feet above the glacier. All in all Gruber's comments seemed apt. From Lasht our view was blocked by the 2,500 feet icefall but it was possible to obtain a glimpse of the summit of Thui II by walking a few miles up the main valley. No one, so far as Dick had been able to discover, had even been on to the glacier. We had a copy of the 1928, four-miles-to-the-inch map, which showed the main characteristics of the area, but the details we would have to find out for ourselves.

Rob was burning for action. On the first day at Lasht, he walked up to the icefall and found a precipitous goat track running up the steep moraine west of the glacier. We were fortunate that the moraine would lead right up to the level glacier, for the more I saw of that icefall, the less I liked what I saw. The immediate problem was to find someone to go up with Rob. As Dick put it: "Someone on this expedition has got to suffer." At the time this sounded as much a command as a statement, although Dick now denies the former. As I had cunningly ridden expensive horses for the last two stages, I was in better condition than he or Chris, so on 1st August Rob led nine porters up the hill while I tagged along far in the rear in a pair of plimsolls with the backs flattened down. We stopped halfway up the icefall at a tiny grass platform, just big enough for one tent, by a trickle of water. Next day Rob was suffering from a touch of the sun so I hobbled up another 2,500 feet onto the glacier to look around for a site for a proper base camp. If I were to fall out of my plimsolls down one of the hidden crevasses, they would probably become yet another example of unsuitable footwear in the hills. Within the next few days Rob and I made two sixty-pound carrys and I got one boot on. Then Dick and Chris appeared and started their share of the carry by cleverly getting porters to bring loads up to only 1,500 feet below the level glacier. On 8th August I got the other boot on, so Rob and I set off late in the morning to climb the 17,500 ft peak behind the tent to have a closer look at Thui II. What we saw of the NW and NE ridges appalled us. Either would be a worthy objective for a really competitive expedition. However, slightly further north, there was a worthy looking 19,500 ft peak with a tempting north-east snow ridge. We had grossly underestimated our training peak, for the east ridge we had climbed was about AD and the north ridge which we chose to descend was no easier. Naturally we carried neither torches nor duvets. Darkness found us front-pointing down a steep snow-ice gully with six or seven pitches to go. I only had dark glasses with me but Rob rose magnificently to the occasion and found the tent at 9.30 p.m. Since getting off earlier did not seem possible, we would carry torches in future.

Our next excursion, after a day of rest, was right up the Shetor glacier to the 17,500 ft col at the head. From here we could see not only the south-east ridge of Thui II but also Thui I and Thui Zom. The south-east ridge was very long with several minor summits, the upper part looked reasonable if only we could reach a col at about 19,000 feet below the final ridge. This ridge looked fairly gentle and not too severely corniced above a thousand-foot step of rock. To reach this col looked, from where we were, very difficult and stoneswept. After photographing every mountain in sight we returned to the tents feeling we were unlikely to get very far up the peak.

Figure 33 Chris Wood, Dick Isherwood and Colin Taylor heading upwards[46]
Photo: Rob Collister

46 *Ed.* Surprisingly there were no illustrations in the *CCJ* but this one has been provided by Rob Collister

Dick and Chris had now finished their stint of load-carrying so, being full of commendable enthusiasm to climb our main peak, they resolved to go up to the col at the head of the Shetor Glacier for a couple of bivouacs to have a close look around. Rob and I were now greatly taken with the desire to climb our 19,500 ft peak, ostensibly to look closely at the north-west ridge of Thui II. We set up a camp at 17,500 feet below the north-east ridge and climbed it the next day, on the 14th August. As our view of the peak had been a greatly foreshortened one, the ridge turned out to be quite straightforward. The north-west ridge of Thui II still looked a very considerable undertaking. Since my measurements showed our peak to be between 19,200 and 19,700 feet high we decided to name it Pachan Zom – the hidden hill – in the hopes that it would eventually prove to be just over the 'Munro' limit of 6000 metres.

Back down at base-camp the weather, which had hitherto been uniformly good, became stormy, and it was raining quite heavily when the others returned with great news. They had found an easy way up to the col on the south-east ridge. From the top of one of the lower summits on the ridge which they had climbed from the south, they had been able to see that, at the back of the cwm below the col, there was a concealed icefall. This in itself did not entirely solve the problem as the icefall was very steep indeed in its lower part. Being ingenious men, they climbed slopes to the south of the concealed icefall and then traversed into it above its steep lower section for 300 feet in complete safety along the lower lip of an enormous bergschrund. The icefall then led to a very convenient sheltered snow bowl about five hundred feet below the col. Although the weather remained stormy, as it was to do for the rest of our time on the mountain, on 17th August we all carried sixty-pound packs with food for six days up the Shetor Glacier to the col on the south-east ridge of Thui II at about 18,700 feet, via an intermediate camp. The ridge now above was rock up to about 20,000 feet where Dick and Chris had named two great pinnacles the 'Rabbits Ears'. For two days we lay in our tents as snow fell and plastered the ridge. The third day was fine so we all moved up to a bivouac at the 'Ears' hoping to attempt the summit next day. Much of the climbing was in fine position and, to the east I could see as far as Rakaposhi. One rock band which I had been thinking a lot about during the two bad days did turn out to be vertical but gave 200 feet of superb Grade III climbing on granite flakes. Properly photographed, this was the sort of climbing to make big mountain reputations – no one would believe it less than V+. After another five or six pitches Dick and I reached the 'Ears'. Meanwhile, an enormous storm was coming in from the south-west. We did another three pitches, just enough to see a clear way onto the broader and fairly reasonable looking upper part of the ridge and then descended to a convenient natural icehole – sixteen feet deep right on the crest of the ridge close to one of the Ears. Inside we passed the night in great comfort brewing up icicles while Rob and Chris chose to sit outside in the steadily falling snow below the Ear.

The one fine day we needed we were not to be given. Next day was cold and grey; great clouds were rolling in heavy with snow, dimly and occasionally visible through the whiteout. Snow continued to fall, but we were lucky that the wind, although cold, was not very strong. Dick and I went up for one pitch before agreeing that to continue further would be idiotic. The retreat through six inches and more of new snow was not so bad as I feared it would be. Six long abseils took us down the steep rock and on to an avalanchy (*sic*) snow-slope with a good run-out five hundred feet lower. I did not feel cold at any time, but as Dick and I reached the tents, I suddenly noticed I had lost any sensation in my toes. As feeling did not return in the big toes for several hours, I suppose I must have nearly got them frost-bitten without appreciating there was any chance of this happening. As Dick and I re-erected the tents which had collapsed under the weight of the snow, Chris made a direct and involuntary descent of the large bergschrund above the snow-bowl. By the time he and Rob had sorted themselves out, I was in my sleeping bag with a brew on. The following day we again continued to retreat through whiteout and falling snow back along the bergschrund lip, which had its moments of drama, down onto the Shetor glacier. Here the new snow concealed many of the crevasses and the weaker snow bridges. The visibility was often down to twenty feet and it was getting dark. Dick and I, in front in turns, were lucky not to do more than put a foot through half a dozen crevasses. Once I put my leg right through and found I could touch nothing in any direction.

At base-camp, there was a peremptory message from Manowar ordering us to return to Lasht with all our equipment as our permission to climb had now been definitely cancelled. We had, I suppose, been lucky to get 20 days at base-camp. We had climbed five new peaks in all, of which one was quite worthy, and we had come close to climbing our main peak. Failure to complete the climb of so fine a mountain rankled deeply. The immediate cause was the weather, but with less time wasted in the valley there would have been time for at least one more attempt and probably enough to have stocked a camp at the Rabbits Ears.

The rest of the saga is quickly told but took many days to unfold. In Lasht was the Colonel of the Chitral Scouts, the only officer in the valley outranking Manowar. He had just galloped 150 miles up the valley with orders to hold an enquiry into our disagreement. Unfortunately he was able to come to no useful conclusions so his journey was probably fruitless. The walk-out was notable for the enormous quantities of food stacked away by the expedition accompanied by the various inexplicable internal disorders, and the absence of Manowar. He had ridden off on a small pony followed by a small boy carrying his sack to the outside of were strapped a brand new axe and a pair of gleaming crampons, apparently on a secret mission – "Sometimes I shall be in front of you, and sometimes behind you." I think he wished to impress the locals in the villages we had not yet visited. At any rate, we had a message from one local official to say our leader had said we would sell him a tent cheaply. This made Dick apoplectic. Back in Rawalpindi the argument began; it all turned on whether Manowar could make us pay him £2 per day in addition to feeding him out of our food-boxes - this in a land where Chris had paid four shillings for three chickens. He accused us of everything from spying in Kashmir (Rob's trip up to the Thui An), to illegally importing equipment into Pakistan (to wit asking him to pay for the pack frame he took to carry away his purchases from Chitral). The situation was out of Kafka. We offered to pay anything to anybody with no effect, as no one could produce a bill even after seven days. After fifteen days a banker friend got Dick in to see the Secretary for Defence who settled the whole matter in three hours. We would have to pay Manowar £140 but would not have to pay his Life Insurance premiums for the year. Leaders of future impecunious expeditions may well consider the advantages of being an Official Expedition.

The return to England was swift, ten days to cover 5,500 miles not counting two days spent in a cholera quarantine camp on the Persian-Afghan border. In 14,000 miles we had no punctures. The alternator seized up near Kandahar but Chris had a new dynamo made in the bazaar from bits of old ones, and there were no other mechanical troubles. This was as well for none of us is much of a mechanic.

ATTEMPT ON THUI II
FROM SHETOR GLACIER[47]

(Members: R. J. Collister, R. J. Isherwood (leader), Colin H. Taylor, Chris Wood, Major Munawar Khan, Army Service Corps (liaison officer).

Our planning was greatly helped by Dr. Gruber's article and panorama in *AJ* 73 55 (subsequently corrected in *AJ* 74 216). Although the highest summit, Koyo Zom (6889m), was climbed in 1968 (*AJ* 74 217), the two other principal peaks, Thui I (6662m) and Thui II (6524m) were unclimbed. A third peak, Thui Zom (6158m) came to notice in the report of a small Japanese party as having a North face 'more impressive than the Grandes Jorasses'.

We drove to Rawalpindi and as a result of various difficulties over permission, etc., reached Lasht on 31 July, about two weeks later than expected. Only Rob was fit to climb immediately, as the rest of us, on account of very badly blistered feet, had completed the journey on horseback, a harrowing experience for the uninitiated on the steep zigzags above the Yarkhun river. At this stage, we still had not seen Thui II, but a three-mile detour up the main valley gave an excellent view. It seemed to live up to Gruber's description of it as the finest isolated peak in the area.

Rob began a reconnaissance and found an excellent route up the west flank of the Shetor glacier to bypass its big lower icefall. Porters were hired and in a few days we had established our Base Camp on a lateral moraine above the icefall at 15,000 feet – all, that is, apart from Munawar, who preferred to remain in Lasht. Load-carrying was completed by Chris and myself, while Rob and Colin explored the north side of the mountain and made a brief trip up the Shetor glacier to the col at the head. They climbed two peaks, one, which was tentatively named Pachan Zom (5,974m), was a striking snow-summit; but at the same time they established that there was no reasonable route for a small party on this the northern side of Thui II. Chris and I meanwhile, went up to the head of the Shetor glacier to look for an approach from the south or east. The south-east ridge seemed to provide a reasonable route, mostly on rock but not too steep, but the approaches to it were difficult to see. To get a better view we climbed two small peaks from a bivouac at 17,000 feet and, after struggling with waist-deep soft snow and crevasses situated surprisingly on the crests of corniced ridges, we were able to sort things out. There was clearly a route, threading through a system of bergschrunds to a snow-plateau below the south-east ridge.

Back at the Moraine Camp, we made plans. We hoped to put a camp on the snow plateau, at about 18,000 feet, and from there to climb the peak and return with one, or possibly two, bivouacs at a group of gendarmes just over half-way up the ridge. After a rest day we set out with enormous loads for a single carry, in two days, to the snow-plateau. On the second day the route was made through the bergschrunds; we were able to climb inside the lower lip of one schrund, and we surprised ourselves by reaching the plateau without using any fixed rope.

---

47 R.J. Isherwood, *HJ* Vol XXX (1970) pp. 278-281

We set up camp in a superb position with a view north toward the Pamirs, east to three fine unnamed summits on the Shetor-Ponarilio watershed, and further to the bulk of Thui I, and south to Thui Zom. This peak showed a very impressive North face – it too lived up to what we had read about it. We saw no obvious route from this side, Thui Zom would make a fine objective and there are many other fierce-looking unclimbed peaks between 18,000 and 21,000 feet in the area.

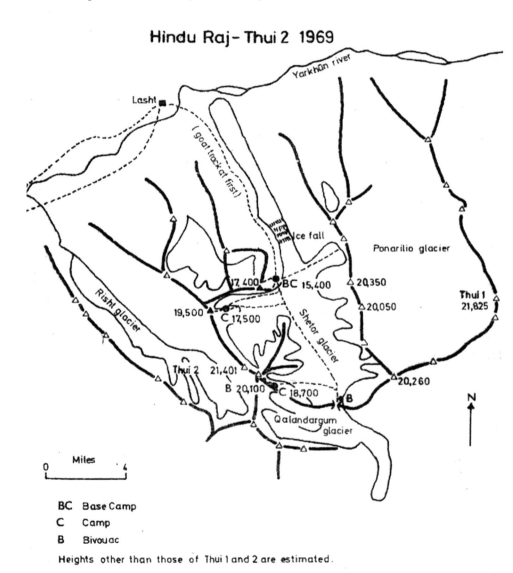

Hindu Raj – Thui 2 1969

BC Base Camp
C   Camp
B   Bivouac

Heights other than those of Thui 1 and 2 are estimated.

Figure 34 Thui II area, Hindu Raj showing the activities of the 1969 British party.
From material supplied by Colin Taylor

Heavy cloud built up that evening and we woke next day to several inches of fresh snow and a white-out. We had heard that the weather often deteriorated in mid-August, and it was now the 19th. The weather remained bad for two days and we were glad to have some reading-matter, but on the 21st we woke to a very fine, cold morning. For the first and only time we saw the Rakaposhi group far away to the east.

We set out with duvets, sleeping-bags, bivouac sacs and food to last two days. With limited climbing gear our sacs weighed around 30 pounds. A slope of snow-ice, fairly steep but made easy by the peculiar snow-fences of the Hindu Kush, led us to the rock ridge, which, from our camp, had looked very short and easy-angled. The rock was superb granite, though often covered in debris. We soon found that the scale was bigger than we had thought. Some sections were steep and single out-of-balance moves were very strenuous. One pitch in the lower section needed a peg; this and the following pitch were probably IV. Above here the ridge steepened, but Colin, in the lead, had seen a line to the left of the crest. He traversed out onto a nose, in a superb position, and the next pitch took me up a fine series of flakes to bypass the steep section.

The ridge eased off, and just after lunch time we reached the gendarmes, impressive 50-foot granite monoliths. We could now see to the south-west, where an ugly black cloud was approaching. Colin and I, ahead of the others, left our bivouac gear and went on. After an ice pitch leading up to the gap between two gendarmes and a short descent on the other side, two more pitches led to a point from which the way ahead was fairly clear; mostly snow and snow-ice to the summit ridge, which itself looked fairly straightforward. We were clearly above most of the difficulties, but, unfortunately, it was far too late to reach the summit that day. We descended to rejoin the others and choose a bivouac site.

Figure 35 Pachan Zom c. 19,588 ft to the north-west of Thui II.
The route of the first ascent was by the central snow ridge
Photo: This and all others: British Hindu Raj Expedition

At the foot of the two gendarmes was a flat area of ice, big enough for a tent if we had had one. This was an adequately sheltered site, but Colin and I were lucky. A little lower down a narrow snow passage between two blocks had collapsed and gave entry to a little cave. Fifteen feet down was a good niche for two, with stones to sit on. We were the first in; Rob and Chris decided there was not room for four and spent the night on the ice platform.

We all had a reasonably good night: I took a sleeping pill and had some weird dreams. Next morning we emerged to fresh snow, a dark grey sky and no option but to go down. We were aware that we were not likely to get another chance. The descent, ending in a series of abseils down the snow-covered rocks, took most of the day and the next day, still in bad weather and mindful of avalanches, we descended the bergschrunds. Chris fell into three of these in succession, happily without serious consequences.

The glacier was in heavy cloud and route-finding was difficult. Many times the leading man put a leg through, but we were lucky this glacier seemed to have very few big crevasses above its lower icefall. Just before we reached the Moraine Camp the cloud lifted to show Koh-e-Baba-Tangi and the other peaks above the Oxus transformed into a Christmas-card view. It seemed that winter had come.

Figure 36 View south from the Summit of Pachan Zom. The Photo shows Thui II, with the north-west ridge leading to the summit; the attempt was made from the other side, by the south-east ridge.

We had just time for another attempt provided the weather cleared, but after some false starts it settled into a monotony of dark clouds and snow showers. We packed up camp and descended to Lasht, where surprises awaited us. We discovered that our permission had been withdrawn two weeks previously and that at any moment an official investigation could be expected from the Pakistan Government. This was in fact carried out by a Colonel of the Chitral Scouts, a very friendly and impartial man; we heard no more of it subsequently. We returned to Rawalpindi on 12 September, and after a remarkable series of events, during which we were formally debriefed, given verbal clearance to leave Pakistan, stopped at the Khyber Pass frontier, and delayed a further nine days in Rawalpindi, we eventually left for home.

Figure 37 The ridge in the left foreground is the south-east ridge of Pachan Zom, while the Risht Gol is in the right foreground, with unnamed and unclimbed peaks behind.

Figure 38 Thui II from the east taken from the col between the Shetor and Qalandar glaciers.

THE DUGUNDUGOO[48]

Ihad only been in Hong Kong three days, and I had met all the active climbers. This was not so remarkable as it sounds – there were only four of them. On a Sunday afternoon, climbing on a small crag above the city and watching the traffic jams below us, we talked about expeditions. Three of us wanted to go somewhere in 1972. The Himalaya seemed a bit difficult to organise from Hong Kong, and in any case we wanted to go somewhere unusual. Someone suggested New Guinea; we all knew there were glaciated mountains there but we knew very little more. So an expedition was born, and surprisingly enough it survived from this abrupt beginning and took place with the original three members to the original objective at more or less the originally intended date.

Leo Murray had been in Hong Kong eight years and had learnt to climb there. Jack Baines had spent four years there altogether with the RAF, mainly in mountain rescue-collecting stranded picnic parties from steep hillsides. They knew one another, but neither knew me. Our first combined expedition was to the City Library to find out about New Guinea.

We soon put together most of the climbing history of the Carstensz range. First seen from the sea by Jan Carstensz in 1623, the mountains were approached unsuccessfully by two British expeditions in 1910 and 1912. They were visited by foreigners for the first time in 1936 when a Dutch party (*Ed*. It was then a Dutch colony), led by Dr A. H. Colijn, and assisted by an aerial reconnaissance, came in from the S coast and climbed Ngga Poloe (5029m) and the East Carstensz Top (c 5000m). Colijn's attempts to climb the Carstensz Pyramide were unsuccessful and only later did his observations show that this was marginally the highest peak[49].

After the war missionary groups began to open up the highland valleys N of the Carstensz and subsequent mountaineering parties have approached from this side, where the airstrips at Ilaga and Beoga allow one to fly over the worst of the West Irian jungle. The New Zealand expedition of 1961 and Heinrich Harrer's visit to the area in 1962 have been recorded by Philip Temple[50]. The New Zealand party suffered many misfortunes and were forced to retreat, half-starved, from the foot of the Carstensz Noordwand when an airdrop failed. Harrer, with Temple's experience, made a successful airdrop and in three weeks climbed all the major summits and a multitude of minor ones. The Carstensz Pyramide was climbed by a rather indirect route on its N face, giving pitches of IV and providing excitement for one member of the party, a Dutch district officer who had never climbed before.

In 1963 Dutch New Guinea became a part of the Republic of Indonesia. The Carstensz summits have been renamed once or twice since then, mainly in relation to the political fortunes of Sukarno. A Japanese-Indonesian mountaineering party in 1964 repeated the ascent of Ngga Poloe, then known as Puntjak[51] Sukarno, but the

---

48 Dick Isherwood, *AJ* 1973 pp 188-194
49 *Ed*. Paul Newby informed me "4884m is now generally accepted for Carstensz Pyramide and following an Australian visit in 1973, 4861m for Ngga Poloe"
50 *Nawok !* London, 1962 and *AJ* 68 78 (1963-1)
51 *Ed*. Paul Newby also elaborates: "At the time Dick was writing, the Indonesian language still retained Dutch spelling, hence Puntjak (now Puncak), Poloe (now Pulu), etc. The highest peak in Indonesia is now officially known as Puncak Jaya but mountaineers bent on the "seven summits" continue to refer to Carstensz Pyramide (or Pyramid)."

second ascent of the Pyramide was not made until late 1971 when Reinhold Messner visited the area with an Italian "client".

Permission was our first problem. Fortunately I was able to visit Djakarta, where the British Embassy put me in touch with an important gentleman in the Ministry of Home Affairs. He promised to do what was necessary and said it would take two weeks. Four months later we realised he was useless. Another trip to Djakarta enabled me to find the right people, the security police, and everything became simple.

We received a generous grant from the Mount Everest Foundation and support from a number of companies in Hong Kong, where begging mountaineers are still a novelty. Jack Tucker, our patron, wrote a splendid open letter in support of our cause, which made us feel like clean-living young men again, and the RAF were so impressed by our prospectus that they sent Jack Baines on a paid holiday to Kinabalu as training. The manager of a local supermarket told us, one Saturday afternoon, that we could take what we needed from his shelves, and fifteen memorable minutes later we had our food. The markets of Kowloon were scoured for beads, axe-heads and other barter goods and an emissary was despatched to Guam for twenty dollars worth of cowrie shells. Excess baggage was mounting fast when Cathay Pacific Airways gave us all free tickets for the greater part of our journey.

We left Hong Kong on 31 August 1972 and flew via Djakarta to Biak, a modest island off the N coast of New Guinea which achieved some importance in the Pacific war and boasts an 11,000 ft concrete runway, once the second longest in the world, and very little else. We had heard much about the operations of Merpati Nusantara Airways, the only commercial air-line serving the interior of West Irian, and thus it was a surprise to be taking off the next day in a chartered Twin Otter for the missionary airstrip at Ilaga.

The Ilaga is one of only three valleys in the highlands of West Irian which is sufficiently open to support a substantial population. Its inhabitants, the Western Dani and Uhunduni tribes, number around 6,000 people. They wear no clothes but are more "advanced" in some respects than their neighbours. Unlike the Danis of the Grand Baliem valley to the E, and the people livings S of the Carstensz range, the inhabitants of the Ilaga have no recent history of cannibalism. They cultivate sweet potatoes, their staple food, and smaller areas of corn, beans and taro, in a way which appals Western agricultural experts but which supports populations up to 500 to the square mile. Their first Western visitors were American missionaries in the 1950s, and the majority of the people are now practising Christians.

Ilaga is about 50 miles, in a straight line, from the Carstensz. The intervening country, though uninhabited, is fairly well frequented by the Danis who visit the Dugundugoo (high mountains) in search of birds and spiny ant-eaters.

With the help of the missionaries and the Indonesian Government representatives, and our own rudimentary knowledge of the Indonesian national language (now spoken fairly widely in the Ilaga), we were able to recruit porters without difficulty. Our cowrie shells were nearly all the wrong kind – the shell currency is remarkably complicated – but beads, shirts, and above all, bright-coloured nylon anoraks, were very satisfactory as payment. Only five days after leaving Hong Kong we were on our way to the mountains with thirty men and a vast quantity of sweet potatoes.

For a day and a half we climbed steeply up the valley side, through thick forest where tree trunks had been felled to make a footpath of sorts. The Danis ran along these with loads on their heads while we, the mountaineers, tiptoed unsteadily or gave up altogether and struggled through the undergrowth. On the second day we came out onto an uneven plateau of limestone karst, tussocky grassland and occasional thickets, which led us in another three days to the foot of the Carstensz Noordwand. Already our ultra-light Japanese tent was showing signs of strain and we were glad to use Harrer and Temple's advance base, a huge erratic block which provided ample shelter. Here the porters left us, promising to return two weeks later.

The following day Jack and I set out with loads to cross the New Zealand Pass to the foot of the Meren glacier, where we planned to put a second camp. The pass is conspicuous from the N side as a deep cleft in the Noordwand, but approaches to it are less obvious. I made an unpleasant direct approach up steep, decomposed limestone and knife-edge ridges of earth, while Jack explored a bit further and found the footpath, hidden behind a spur. From the top of the pass we caught our first glimpses of the Pyramide, but it was largely hidden in cloud, and we groped our way down into the Meren valley through mist and rain.

Figure 39 The face of Carstensz Pyramide from the Meren Glacier
Photo: R. Isherwood

The Carstensz glaciers are retreating rapidly and both the Meren and the Yellow valleys are desolate places, dominated by black, glaciated slabs and fresh moraines, with virtually no vegetation. Our tent seemed more inadequate than ever, but fortunately it was not put to the test as we found, close to the foot of the Meren glacier, the half-derelict base camp of an Australian scientific expedition. Their enormous tent must have weighed 100 lb, and even half collapsed it provided plenty of space and protection. The weather in the West Irian Highlands is very wet, all the year round. Ilaga has a rainfall of over 200 inches a year, and the mountains get even more.

We thought we were lucky as we had had rain every afternoon but none in the mornings, so to make the most of this "dry spell" we wasted no time in getting on to the N face of the Pyramide, which up to now we had scarcely seen.

Starting in the dark we crossed a low ridge into the Yellow valley and traversed the moraine to the foot of the face. We picked out a line leading fairly directly to the left hand of the two summits, and after a few scrambling pitches were soon moving singly. The limestone bedding on the Pyramide is steeply tilted and the N face is made up of large monolithic slabs, broken by rather discontinuous cracks and chimneys, and scored by shallow water-worn channels. The rock is generally excellent, though very rough and spiky in the chimneys, and disturbingly smooth on the open slabs.

None of us had been climbing regularly in the Hong Kong summer, and we were glad that the early pitches were easy. Several pitches of III and IV led to a big terrace from which we had a choice of routes. The continuation of our line led more steeply on to the upper tier of the face, while the terrace disappeared round a corner, suggesting an easy escape. As it was only lunch-time we chose the direct route and immediately wasted an hour exploring a cave and chimney which promised a route through the steep section. We were forced to do some real climbing, and I soon found myself at the top of a water-channel, facing a blank slab, with no rope left. Fortunately we had a continuous 300-foot rope, and by untying from the middle and pulling a lot more through, I was able to go on. Freak pockets provided two peg runners and after about 220 feet I found a belay ledge.

A big black hole in the face a little higher revealed itself as a natural arch, 200 feet across. We entered the bowels of the mountain just in time to dodge the first hail-storm, and Leo took the lead up some loose dark grooves. Back in the open some pleasant climbing up shallow chimneys took us quickly to the last steep section of the face. Here, with two hours of daylight left, the hail came again. I struggled with a small overhang, too tired to make a big move over it and too slow to spot the obvious place for a peg. Annoyed at wasting time, I rushed on up the pitch, wriggled into a narrow chimney and stuck tight. More time wasted. I finally crawled out, half undressed, on to a ledge and with cramped arms hauled up the sack, which stuck just as I had done. Leo climbed a gripping arête on a tight rope to avoid the narrows, and we had only one pitch to do. Again I became jammed in a hole, and when we were all up we had just ten minutes of daylight left.

We had brought little bivouac equipment, expecting to be down in one day, and we got into the bivouac sack, conscious of our duvets in the tent below. We shivered through the night and emerged to a fine morning and an easy climb up the ridge to the top. We found a tin left by Harrer's party and a new Stubai peg, which we took to be Messner's signature. Not having a pencil we scratched our names laboriously on the lid of Harrer's tin, took photos of various donated goodies and headed down.

We did not choose the best way down. The narrow E ridge took us down 500 feet or so, then continued on the level toward some unattractive gendarmes, while a scree gully led invitingly in the direction of the valley. We ran down the scree, by-passed a steep and very soggy snow-field, and got into a deep gully, invisible from above. One abseil led to another, culminating in three long and spectacular free descents through a series of caves. We reached the bottom shattered, slightly burnt, and short of pegs, trudged back to camp in the rain and slept for a day and a half.

The next part of our plan was to traverse the snow summits of East Carstensz Top, Sunday Peak[52] and Ngga Poloe, and to this end we rose very early and set out in crampons over the crisp snow of the Carstensz glacier. Trying to do a thorough job, we climbed a small rock peak on the way up to the main watershed, and by nine o'clock we were floundering in thigh-deep snow on top of an undistinguished hump, named by someone the Middenspitze. We gave up for the day and waded down. Next day we rose really early and reached the summit of Sunday Peak by starlight in very good conditions. A pleasant walk over the glacier took us to Ngga Poloe, where a narrow corniced ridge, with a creaking crust, led out to the summit, a snow-cone on the very edge of the Noordwand. From a rock ledge just below I collected another high-quality Austrian peg; from this we presumed that Messner had climbed the N face of Ngga Poloe, a conspicuous slabby ridge with steep steps. We continued, over several lower summits, to leave the glacier close to the New Zealand Pass.

Before returning to the N side of the mountains we made a detour down the Meren valley to visit the Freeport Indonesia mining camp, about four hours' walk below the foot of the glaciers. The "copper mountain" of the Ertsberg, a 1200 ft dome of unusually rich iron-copper ore, lies on the side of the valley at a height of about 3650 m, just above an enormous precipice. First described by the geologist J.J. Dozy who accompanied Colijn, its value was confirmed by a vice-president of the American Freeport Sulphur Company, an unusual executive who walked the 75 miles from the S coast. Now enormous men drive enormous bulldozers, gradually demolishing it, and a pipeline is under construction to carry pulverised ore to the coast. Investment, including the cost of a deep-water port, an airstrip, a small town and 80 miles of road, is approaching 200 million dollars. We traversed, unwittingly, across the line of fall of all the ore, waded through knee-deep mud to the foreman's hut and begged a night's lodging. Freeport could provide the easiest route to the Carstensz, but understandably are not too keen to have visitors. Our return up the valley the following day was notable mainly for my straying into an enormous bog in which I nearly drowned.

We had scarcely stopped moving since leaving Hong Kong, and once back at our base we spent two days sleeping and washing. Thoughts now turned to the Carstensz Noordwand, and in particular the faces of Ngga Poloe and Sunday Peak, close above our camp. It seemed very probable that Reinhold Messner had climbed Ngga Poloe from this side, but the face of Sunday Peak, so far as we knew, had not been climbed. A shallow groove in its centre made an attractive line between two very steep pillars. For me this had been the most interesting climbing prospect in the area from an early stage, but Jack and Leo were less enthusiastic. I began to work on them. Jack declared right away that he did not want anything to do with it, and Leo eventually decided he was not interested either, so I decided to try it alone, while they climbed a peak to the W of the camp.

I climbed up the central gully, full of old avalanche debris, and as soon as possible got out to the left, up a loose subsidiary gully, to the foot of the main face. Here a false start up steep vegetated rock wasted two hours, and ended in an abseil. I decided to explore further left, more to vary the descent than in a serious effort to find an

---

52 *Ed*. Paul Newby observes: "So named on Heinrich Harrer's map. Modern internet research and comparison with Dick's photographs reveal serious doubt about which peak is which, even among those who have visited in conditions of reasonable visibility! Sunday Peak may or may not be the one called Sumantri by some modern writers. See also *AJ* 85(329): 118–121 (1980)".

alternative, but once I was on the left-hand ridge the face took on a more reasonable appearance. I climbed a fairly easy gully, still grassy and full of burrows formed by some creature. Soon I was almost level with a conspicuous light pillar in the centre of the face, and traversing to it offered no great problems. The climb again seemed possible and I went on up slabs and grooves, occasionally using slings to protect myself on the short difficult sections.

In gathering cloud and spots of rain I reached a pair of parallel chimneys in the upper part of the face. Neither of these seemed difficult, but I had seen from below that the section above them was the steepest part of the route. The left-hand chimney led strenuously to a ledge, just below an overhanging rock band. The pillar separating the chimneys formed a pinnacle, linked to the overhanging face by a rather slender bridge. Peg climbing on my own was not at all what I had intended and I looked around for alternatives, but on either side I had to descend several hundred feet, and then the prospects were uncertain. I dithered up and down the chimney until a heavy hail-storm made the overhang the more attractive route. Sheltered completely from the weather, I uncoiled the rope on top of the rock bridge and tried to remember what I had read about solo artificial climbing. I tied on to both ends of the rope and made a big loop in the middle which I put over the high part of the bridge as a token belay.

Figure 40 The north face of Sunday Peak
Photo: R. Isherwood

Somehow I had only brought one étrier but I had a few slings to supplement it. I protected myself by tying loops into the two ropes alternately and remaining attached, as far as possible, to three pegs at once. The slanting fault in the overhang was loose and one peg popped out with me on it. Just below the chimney which led out of the overhanging band, I had difficulty placing a good peg, and I used a sling threaded round a flake as extra security. As I moved across I pulled on the sling and the flake fell off, hitting me in the face. Fortunately the peg was adequate and a few more feet of artificial climbing led to a big terrace. I climbed the final steep chimneys, hauling the sack behind me, and groped my way down the Meren glacier in thick cloud. Night fell as I returned over the New Zealand Pass and down to our boulder

Jack and Leo climbed a small peak on the following day. Then the weather deteriorated and we sat in our pits, waiting for the porters who were due two days later. When they did not come we gave them a day's grace and scoured the horizon with binoculars. We could wait no longer, as our plane was due in Ilaga five days later, so we abandoned everything non-essential and started walking. Definitions of essential varied among the three of us, but after a few miles and some heart-searching decisions we got our loads down to around 40 lb each, leaving gear all over the countryside. We hoped to get back to Ilaga in three days but we found it hard to keep to our schedule, especially as we took several wrong turnings in the maze of hunters' trails on the plateau. Fortunately, on the second day the porters met us. One man and three small boys made light of our loads, while the others went on for the remainder of our gear. We never saw them again – when the plane came for us, one day late, they were "still very close, coming tomorrow". As we had run out of food and were living on potatoes, we were content to leave our gear behind. We returned to Hong Kong just five weeks after our departure.

SUMMARY

- R. J. Isherwood; L. Murray; J. Baines – Carstensz Pyramide (New Guinea) by the N face, descending by the E ridge. N face of Sunday Peak – R. J. Isherwood (solo), August – September 1972

PARBATI 1973[53]

"It's all right, Sir," said the airline steward. "These overhead bins hold up to forty pounds." He helped me close the flimsy hanging door on my sack full of ropes and ironware and I passed the journey from Hong Kong to Delhi in fear of decapitation.

Rob Collister's four-man party had had some problems getting permission to do what we wanted in India and the last letter I had received said "I'm sure we'll find something to climb, but bring some extra pegs as it may be the Manikaren Spires." Vertical rock sounded better to me than vertical ice climbed in the 1973 style, so I took all my rock climbing equipment except for a brand new pair of Jumars that I didn't want to lose.

By the time Geoff Cohen, John Cardy and I had arrived in Delhi, our objective was decided. Point 20,101 feet in the South Parbati district of Kulu, was apparently unclimbed, just outside the Inner Line, high enough to be respectable, and impressive in photographs. In two days we had packed the food and were away by third class sleeper and a long bus ride to Kulu.

All we knew of Pt. 20,101 derived from an account by Charles Ainger [54] who had approached the mountain from the north by the Parbati valley. We decided to try a southern approach via the Sainj Nal (see map). Our map, based on a 1917 survey, showed footpaths in the upper and lower parts of the Sainj valley, but a disconcerting blank in the middle section. Majority opinion was that there must be a path all the way, but I had recently made that assumption about a similar valley in Nepal, and been proved wrong. The resulting four thousand foot climb through steep jungle was so fresh in my mind that I convinced the others we should go further south and take the footpath from Gosheni (Bandal) which looked very convincing on our map. It involved an ascent to 13,000 feet but this seemed like good acclimatization.

John and I went ahead to Gosheni and confirmed the existence of the footpath. While John returned to Kulu to bring the others I 'organised the porters'. This was done in ten minutes with the help of the local apple tycoon, and I spent an amiable day thinking how wise I was in the ways of the Himalayas. Next morning only nine of twenty porters showed up. The others had backed out 'because it was raining'. Eventually, the apple magnate, with the smile of a man who knows what he is doing, told us that the nine men would carry twenty men's loads – if they were paid twenty men's wages. The original deal of 15 kg per man was now seen in proper context. The rate of pay for carrying apples was good – and you only carry apples downhill.

It was August 30th, and it was raining in a way which suggested that the monsoon was not ending, despite what everyone told us to the contrary. On the 31st our nine porters actually did set out with all our gear, but sub-contracting in various villages soon increased their numbers to sixteen. We covered a remarkably small distance and stopped for the night in mist and rain, still in the forest.

---

53 Written by Dick Isherwood.
Ed. According to Rob Collister, who mailed me the original typescript, this article was intended for publication but it seems that this never happened in the end. I have shortened the original title so as not to confuse it with that written by Rob Collister in *AJ* 1974 pp 121-127 (which is not included in this book although I have used many of the photos). I have also undertaken some very minor editing changes which would surely have been done by Dick had this ever reached the publishing stage.
54 *HJ* Vol XXX (1970) pp 228-236

The next morning our porters appeared at 9:30 a.m. and immediately suggested a change of destination. Our "Sirdar" from Manali, who shall be nameless, agreed with them and even persuaded Rob to agree. The leader of the porters was so delighted that something was clearly wrong. We soon realised what was happening when we reached the crest of a subsidiary ridge and they headed down the other side on a route which would have taken us back to Gosheni. Here it became apparent that reasonable discussion was pointless: fortunately threats, expressed vigorously in English, were very effective. We had been told that we were the first climbing expedition to go through this area, and since we were twice asked if we were on "official business" we wondered if news of the political changes of 1947 had reached Gosheni.

After three days very enjoyable walking, during which the monsoon really did end, and one major strike, again broken by threats, we reached the village of Maraur in the Sainj Nal. Here the Gosheni porters quit: they were on foreign ground and a wide range of English obscenities had no effect on them. All the inhabitants of Maraur were diseased it seemed, and even acupuncture treatment was ineffective in persuading them to carry for us. In any case, a bridge had been washed away further up valley. Rob saw the Gosheni men telling the Maraur men in graphic detail of the hardships they had undergone at our hands.

We had considered ourselves a semi-lightweight expedition with a total of 700 lb of gear for four climbing members for four weeks. At this point we became lightweight. We abandoned the tomato ketchup, the orange squash, the rolling pin for the chapattis, the two girls and – the sirdar. The latter, at twenty rupees a day, was a burden we were happy to lose. He seemed keen to return in any case, vowing never to return to what I thought was one of the most beautiful valleys I had ever been in. He and the girls followed the well-marked footpath down the Sainj Nal.

The unbridged river was very nasty, and Rob came near enough to drowning, despite being roped, before we found a slender log bridge higher up the tributary valley. This was thrilling enough to justify a rope, and we hauled the gear over just before the shepherds arrived to reconstruct the old footbridge. We left them a huge tin of marmalade as we still had a fearsome weight of stuff. We thought two more days would see us to a base camp but in fact it took four, as we needed double carries to get all our gear up to the moraines beyond Rakti Tapta, and we moved awfully slowly.

The glaciers had retreated a long way since the 1917 survey. We could not see Pt. 20,101 from anywhere near our base, but the glacier which lead to it was directly above us, spilling over a cliff and disturbing our sleep. One side of it was a fearsome rock gully fringed with seracs, and the whole central part was clearly dangerous. This only left the right hand edge as an approach to what we hoped would be a snow basin below the peak.

This right hand edge was, in September conditions, a scoop of bare dirty ice rising for, as far as we could judge, five hundred feet, between the main glacier and the steep flank of Ainger's "Ridge Peak". The next morning we set out on the first of what we intended to be two carries up this scoop. The lower grass slopes seemed a long way and we realised that the ice section might be longer than we had expected. I also had a private realisation. As the others front-pointed upwards it dawned on me that my old semi-competence on snow and ice was rather badly out of date. I hand traversed up the edge of the ice and across a little crevasse till it fizzled out, and caught Geoff just in time to suggest roping up. A few minutes later a rock, the size of a small suitcase, bounced down and just missed me. Rob by now was seeking out boulder problems several hundred feet higher, apparently oblivious of his 50 lb pack. As Geoff was complaining about the size of his load, I saved face by offering to carry the bigger sack if he did all the leading.

We soon caught up as Rob and John reached a dead end in some séracs. By now it was after lunch time, the ice scoop was as active as a bowling alley and the route above still looked like 500 feet of ice to the top. Even the ice experts decided that it was not a suitable route for regular load carrying. I had long ago decided that I was not doing it again for anything. As we descended, Geoff commented that days like this put five years on your gear. Mine was already too old.

We concluded that we were on the wrong side of our invisible adversary. From our base we could see Ainger's "Snow Peak" and it seemed that we could reach the col to the west of it. This certainly seemed less hazardous than further efforts in the icefall so after a rest day we set out to cross the col and establish another camp on Ainger's "Glacier IV", on the Parbati side of the watershed. At this stage the food men decided that the rations could be halved. Since we hadn't started eating the real climbing rations, John and I had to agree without knowing what was involved. Anyway it was clearly a long way to the col, and anything that reduced the loads was welcome. We set off with around 65 lb each.

Figure 41 Ridge Peak from the SW ridge of Parbati South
Photo: Rob Collister

That afternoon we camped in a snowstorm a little way below the col. I was sharing a tent with Rob and witnessed a most impressive demonstration. Antarctic Man was in his pit, with a brew on, and without a single snowflake inside the tent, while I was still trying to unfasten my boots. I realised I was in the right tent; the others were still putting theirs up. He was the only one whose boots didn't freeze in the night too.

Next morning we had the first near view of the mountain – it convinced us it was really there, but it looked rather hard. By now we were seeing it as it looked in Ainger's photographs and the feeling remained that perhaps there was an easy route round the back. However, we had at least got to the side with the easy approaches – from our new base camp. This face presented a contrast to Ainger's post monsoon photos – it was virtually all rock. To my relief and to the disappointment of the Nordwanderers there was an easy glacier to the foot of the S.E. Face.

Ainger's party had left some food, and by now this had become a high priority; we found two tins of pork sausages which looked a bit green but tasted good as a change from Antarctic meat bars. The rest of his food was pretty badly decomposed, so we left it – though towards the end we were tempted by the candles.

We had had only a short second day on the route over the col, so the next morning we went to climb the "Ridge Peak", Rob surprisingly suggested an ascent over a pile of loose rocks in preference to the obvious ice ridge, and I was pleased to follow. We soloed all the way above the bergschrund. John was having acclimatisation problems – to the food, despite its limited quantity, and to the heights – so he retired while Geoff, rather late in the day, climbed most of the ice ridge to meet us.

Figure 42 Parbati South (6128m) from Ridge Peak. The SW Ridge attempt went up the central ridge. The SE Face finished along the E ridge on the right of the summit (see also Figure 41)

Photo: Rob Collister

From where we now found ourselves, the S.E. Face and then the E. Ridge of Pt. 20,101 was the obvious route to try. The face seemed to lie back at a reasonable angle with some steep steps, particularly at the bottom. The ice gully leading to the East Col was a rather nasty dark grey colour but was judged to be "OK in the dark". Above this, I at least thought, we should be out of stonefall danger and on reasonably climbable rock. The alternatives were the S.W. Ridge – a beautiful line and almost certainly the safest, but involving a vertical section of at least 200 feet, and a fair amount more of rather steep unbroken rock – and the N.W. ridge, a reasonable rock ridge but approached via a couloir several times longer and only a little less grey than the one leading to the S.E. ridge.

After some discussion, we agreed to try the S.E. couloir and face. John was still feeling bad, so he and I rested while Rob and Geoff climbed an ice face on a nearby peak. Rob and I started at midnight on September 16th with three night's food and reached the foot of the S.E. couloir and the climbing at 3 a.m. The next four pitches were for me the most thrilling part of the climb. The dark grey section of the couloir was ice with bits of rock stuck in it, and was not too well frozen. I persuaded Rob to put a rope on and followed him up a shallow waterfall running in the central groove. Fortunately the moon was full, so I could see the small bird-like marks left by his axe and hammer. I stuck my weapons into the same holes, but even my Chouinard ice hammer didn't seem to work properly, and I was thankful for the occasional rock big enough to pull on. I was very glad when even he decided that the gully was getting steep, and we traversed to the rock just before dawn.

The lower part of the face confirmed what we had seen – a steep lower section, which we had avoided, followed by some easier rock bands to a group of snow patches. The rock bands were, however, subject to some stonefall. We found a line up a rib which seemed relatively sheltered and soon reached the snow patches on a big terrace, from which most of the falling stones seemed to originate. We traversed left below a steep band of grey granite, looking for an easy way through it.

Rob climbed a nasty pitch, and I climbed another, with a couple of pegs, to a point below some rather steep walls. Belaying here, I realized we were not entirely above the stonefall. Most of the stones were small but the odd house brick came down too close for comfort. Rob traversed right to a rib which we hoped would give some protection. Following him, I took a lower line and found by accident a protected ramp leading to the south-east col. Three more pitches put us on the ridge above the col and our position was transformed. Above we could see the higher col on the south-east ridge, and the final ridge to the top which from here appeared to lie back at a reasonable angle. We had, however, seen a rope just below the S.E. col, and wondered whether the peak was in fact unclimbed[55].

After a brew we continued past the higher col, and up some difficult rock, the hardest of the route, to a group of ledges and a good bivouac site. We bivouacked at 19,800 feet in sleeping bags, without duvets, and had a good night; we appreciated being on a face which caught the sun at 6 a.m. and we had a magnificent view over Lahoul and Kulu. We also had a good view down Ainger's Glacier III which we thought might, in September conditions, give the easiest route to the S.E. col of Pt. 20,101.

---

55 The note in *HJ* 78 p 240 regarding the University of Aston Expedition which attempted Parbati South may explain the rope found at the S.E. Col.

In the morning we climbed to the summit ridge in three very enjoyable rock pitches on slabby compact granite. The summit proved to be a Y-shaped corniced ridge, disproving my theory that it was a football field. Ainger's Pyramid Peak to the S.E. appeared comparable in height while his Peak A to the North seemed a little higher. Other peaks in the immediate area were clearly lower – the Ridge Peak especially seemed less than Ainger's estimated 19,000 feet (assuming 20,101 feet to be accurate). We saw no traces of any previous ascent above the lower col on the S.E. Ridge.

We descended by the same route, mostly by abseil. In the lower part we abseiled down the steep face to the west of the S.E. couloir, ending in a fairly exciting 160 feet descent to the ice on a 150-foot rope. We reached our camp as night fell.

Geoff and John had ambitions to climb the peak too but John's intestines were still rebelling. He and I carried more food over from our base while Geoff and Rob prepared for an attempt on the S.W. ridge. They spent the day of September 20th on the lower parts of the ridge, making slow progress up the rather compact rock. In the late afternoon they abseiled off after a thunderstorm from a point below the big ledge; they would clearly have taken several days to complete the route.

We were now limited in time, in that Geoff and I had to be home to earn our livings. There was time left for John to climb the Ridge Peak, for Rob and Geoff to climb two peaks in the "Snow Bowl" to the S.E. of our camp, and for me to wander up the Parbati Glacier in search of the Pin Parbati Pass, which I couldn't find. Therefore we put our remaining equipment and food on our backs and walked out, in four days, down the Parbati valley to Manikaren, hot baths and, eventually, civilisation.

Figure 43 John Cardy, Dick Isherwood and Geoff Cohen ready for the walk out from Base Camp
Photo: Rob Collister

HIMALAYAN GRANDE-COURSE[56]

Rob Collister

Moonlight upon a glacier; two figures picking their separate ways over the ice. Two minds conscious of frozen beauty in the silent black and silver mountain-scape, but dwelling more perhaps on cold oats settling heavily in their stomachs. Overhead, rock looms higher, casting a cold forbidding shadow far across the glacier. Into its chilly embrace, reluctantly, with a sense of the irrevocable; up an avalanche-cone encrusted with fallen stones as thickly as the sky above with stars; by devious bridges over a bergschrund, to stand at last peering up the streak of grey ice which is the slip-road to the face above: a typical alpine situation.

Not the Alps, however, but the Himalaya. The lesser Himalaya, certainly – the mountain is only just over 20,000 feet high and, from a distance, its broad, wedge-shaped south face – 3,000 feet of striated, almost snow-free rock – reminds one of the Dolomites. No icy giant, but the Himalaya nevertheless; the South Parbati region of Kulu in Northern India, to be precise.

Twenty five years ago, Tom Longstaff, possibly the most widely travelled of all Himalayan climbers, wrote apropos Everest: "I hope and believe that one day it will be climbed. Then, when no higher 'altitude record' is possible, mountaineers can turn to the true enjoyment of the Himalayas, most likely to be found at about 20,000 feet or less." For most climbers it is not the height that makes the Himalaya so attractive; not once they have experienced altitude. Leaving aside the special fascination of the valleys with their ancient trade-routes, simple, contented people and exotic flora and fauna, it is the fact that climbers can be, must be, self-sufficient. By inclination, I am an alpinist – Harrison's Rocks appal me, the South-East Ridge of Everest attracts me, if anything, even less. Yet, except in winter, the Alps are being reduced to the status of outcrops, albeit serious ones. The alpinist must look elsewhere for a wholly satisfying test of his skill and judgment. And, while the great peaks of the Himalaya still tend to demand not so much skill as endurance and tenacity, the more so the harder the route, the lower peaks do provide such a test.

John Cardy, Geoff Cohen and Dick Isherwood must have thought something similar, for I had little difficulty in persuading them to come. Already Geoff and I had climbed a fine ice-face, resembling the right-hand pillar of Piz Palu in length and difficulty. And now Dick and I were attempting the big rock peak, the nameless Point 20,101 ft, which dominated our particular glacier.

Dick, who does not like ice, has described the initial couloir thus:

"The next four pitches were for me the most thrilling part of the climb. The dark grey section of the couloir was ice with bits of rock stuck into it and was not too well frozen. I persuaded Rob to put a rope on and followed him up a shallow waterfall running in the central groove. Fortunately the moon was full, so I could see the small bird-like marks left by his axe and hammer. I stuck my weapons into the same holes, but even my Chouinard hammer did not seem to work properly, and I was thankful for the

---

56 Rob Collister, *Mountain* 39 (October 1974) pp 14-17 The photographs from *Mountain* however have not been reproduced. *Ed.* This presents an interesting comparative description of the same climb described by Dick Isherwood above although a third article about the same trip has not been reproduced in this book (Collister, *AJ* 1974 pp 121-127). Some photographs from the *AJ* and fresh ones from Collister have however been added to both of these articles.

occasional rock big enough to pull on. I was very glad when even Rob decided that the gully was getting steep, and we traversed to the rock just before dawn."

We had timed it perfectly. As we traversed ice-coated slabs to a terrace running the breadth of the face, the sun began to caress the skyline above, and minutes later the first stones were clattering down the couloir. Below us lay a blanket of cloud, smothering the glacier and the camp on its edge; above the cloud stood the mountains we had climbed and were to climb, the 17.000 ft col we had crossed to get there and the summits of a myriad other peaks stretching away into the crystal distance of China and Garwhal. It was another perfect day.

Figure 44 Parbati South from Advanced Base Camp.
The SW Ridge attempt (left) and the SW Face Route (right)
Photo: Rob Collister

Figure 45 Dick on the SW face of Parbati South
Photo: Rob Collister

Our satisfaction was short-lived, however. As Dick started up steep rock from the terrace, weaving an improbable but, in the event, fairly straightforward way through a maze of little roofs, stones in ones and twos came bounding down the face itself. The climbing above was not sustained, in fact there were several sections of scrambling, but in places the rock was loose, with the looseness of tottering blocks stacked on top of each other, and increasingly frequent whines, thuds and crashes kept our nerves on edge. The stones flurried me more than Dick. "They're only small and small ones can't do much damage," he commented, imperturbably. I was impressed by his calm, but unconvinced by his reasoning. However, retreat would be no safer, so I pinned my hopes on the theory that most of the stones were coming from Snow-patch Terrace – another broad terrace about halfway up the face where a solitary patch of snow had lingered providing a conspicuous landmark.

Hurrying from relatively sheltered rib to rib, belaying where possible under overhangs, we made good time and by mid-morning were sitting at the top of the terrace, watching little stones, freed from their casing of ice, topple over, roll slowly to the edge and disappear on their long journey to the glacier. With our backs to a plumb-vertical smooth grey wall, we felt safe from above. But where now? The only two visible lines would clearly need much pegging, not at all to our taste though we had the gear for it. The wall stretched across the face, a good 300 feet high, unrelenting in its steepness. The only hope lay in a recess some way to our left, into which we could not see. Suddenly a pebble arrived beside us with a smack. Dick didn't turn a hair but the place had lost its charm for me and I could not start climbing again too quickly.

Figure 46 Dick on Grade IV rock at 6000m on the summit slabs
Photo: Rob Collister

Traversing left along a sharp rim of ice, where the snow patch lapped against the rock, using it now for hands, now for feet, delicate without axe or crampons, I found the recess to contain a long scoop slanting back rightwards. The angle, compared with the sheer walls on either side, looked easy. "It's a piece of duff," I yelled back jubilantly, promptly to discover that the difference was only relative. Breathless and out of balance, I found myself lunging for resting places which vanished as I reached them. Moreover, the holds were covered with a fine rubble which, it occurred to me briefly, could only have come from above. Predictably, the rope came tight in the midst of my struggles. Luckily, a sense of urgency must have been communicated down the rope, for although he could not hear me. Dick loosed his belay, enabling me to climb a few feet higher to a good foothold which would serve as a stance. Dick had climbed over me and, with the aid of a couple of pegs, had emerged on to an easier slab when, with a whistle, a salvo of rocks came down right on top of us. There was a rattling on my helmet and something large gave me a nudge as it passed between me and the rock. I gripped the rope tighter, waiting for a weight to come on it. Nothing happened; Dick, to my surprise, was unhurt. Nevertheless, even he must have been shaken, for he shot up the rest of that pitch to a friendly overhang, and when I next saw him his sharp features seemed to have become slightly sharper, though he said nothing. For my part, I peered upwards with great care, like a cautious tortoise, before scurrying over the exposed slab. Fortunately, I could see an apparently sheltered line slanting rightwards for at least the next run-out. I say fortunately, because otherwise I would not have continued and, as it turned out, that was the last time stonefall was to bother us until the descent.

At the end of my pitch the rock was once more vertical and I was wondering if it could possibly go free, when I noticed that Dick had disappeared. Investigating a lower line, he had come to a hole beneath some blocks; ever curious, he took off his sack and crawled through it to discover an overhung but easy-angled ramp cutting through the verticality. This proved the key to the wall and in effect to the whole climb. The only bulge was well-endowed with jugs and at its top, we were on easy broken ground. The chimney-line which formed the continuation of our original couloir was only a rope-length to our right, and not far above was the crest of the east ridge, where presumably nothing solid could fall on us. We were at about 19,000 feet and for the first time could allow ourselves to feel confident of success. Suddenly, to our amazement we spotted a white rope hanging down the chimney. Later we learnt that it had been left the previous year by an unsuccessful party from the University of Aston; but at the time it took the wind out of our sails to discover climbing litter on 'our' virgin mountainside.

Following the line of least resistance leftwards, it was several more rope-lengths before we reached a snow shoulder on the ridge and could look down upon a new glacier and across at new peaks. Disappointment seemed to have reduced our impetus though we had, we were surprised to find, been on the go for fourteen hours. Either way, a brew was called for. The usual afternoon cloud was swirling up and sweaters and windproofs were pulled on hurriedly in a sharp flurry of snow. It did not last however, and through windows in the mist we could see the ridge rising up above in a monolith of orange granite, its east side sheer and almost featureless, the south face equally compact but set back in a sweep of comfortably angled slabs.

Morale improved by the cup of tea, we descended a little snow slope to a notch in the ridge and set off up the slabs. The climbing was glorious in golden evening sunlight, the cloud still boiling about the smaller peaks but dropping just enough to leave us unmolested. Big holds were few and far between but the rock was so rough that it sliced open finger tips, and was covered with tiny knobs and pockets on which bendy boots felt like PA's. Only once, when, leaning sideways from a peg, I swung across in a committing mantelshelf over a short wall on to a slab steeper and smoother than usual, demanding the utmost concentration for a few moves, was the climbing hard enough to preclude conscious enjoyment of every moment. One stance, squatting beneath a long square-cut roof, reminded me of Rebuffat's route on the Midi, and the climbing was not dissimilar to that of the famous "red slab".

Two pitches higher we came to the ideal bivouac site, complete with icicles for water. There wasn't room for two side by side, so we took separate apartments Dick excavating himself a coffin-like trench, while I built up a platform of flat blocks taking care to add a parapet. The Hilton had nothing on that bivouac. Not that it mattered, we were tired enough to sleep anywhere. It had been a long day, and though the climbing had been easier than expected it had had its moments all the same altitude tending to make difficulties feel perhaps a grade harder than they would in the Alps. We were carrying sleeping bags rather than duvets and slept the clear windless night through, not bothering with the bivi sack.

After luxuriating in our bags until the sun came up next morning, three rope lengths of the same superb slab-climbing brought us to the summit ridge. This was snow, rimming the rocky face like froth on top of a pint. Almost horizontal, rising very gently to its highest point about 200 yards away, it was also sharply corniced, so that far from being the football pitch we had half expected, it was more like a screwdriver. A few minutes later, one at a time because of the cornice, we were on top, letting our eyes sweep slowly round through 360 degrees of mountains. On every side lay a parched brown landscape splashed with grey, turbulent and empty. Neither welcoming nor hostile, it was unmindful of us, waiting thirstily for the winter snows.

POSTSCRIPT

The south-west ridge of Pointe 20,101 ft offers another fine climb (see Figure 39 and Figure 41). Geoff and I attempted it a few days after the South Face ascent, but after a day's climbing we had made depressingly little impression on it. It is a superb natural line, likely to be on good rock all the way and apparently free from stonefall. The ridge appears easy-angled at first but this proved deceptive for the crest is too sharp and jagged to be followed for long, and we were soon forced on to the steeper south facing side-wall. The climbing was more sustained than the South Face, and as we were making slow progress we decided to retreat. A route of calibre deserves to be climbed well, and a competent, well-acclimatized party should be able to climb the ridge with just one bivouac. An alpine type route, it would he a pity to climb it with fixed-ropes and a multi-day epic. If it is climbed in good style, it will give a climb comparable in quality to anything in the Alps. Even if this fine project fails to provide sufficient challenge for the ambitious alpinist there is always the adjoining West Face...

SUMMARY

Kulu Himalaya: Point 20,101 ft. An account of the first ascent of the South Face by Rob Collistcr and Dick Isherwood. The article suggests further possibilities on the mountain. Other members of the expedition were Geoff Cohen and John Cardy.

LAMJUNG HIMAL[57]

Permits for virgin peaks in Nepal have become rather scarce in recent years, as most of the peaks on the Nepalese Government's permitted list have been climbed. Mike Burgess, fortunate in being on the spot in Kathmandu, got one for Lamjung Himal, at the E end of the Annapurna range, for the 1974 premonsoon season, and thus another expedition started. This one, like many others, nearly died several times – lack of a leader, lack of climbers, and lack of money all presented problems at different times. Eventually, Mike was elected leader (at a meeting held in his absence), people were recruited from England to swell the inadequate ranks of Hong Kong climbers, and fund raising in Hong Kong enabled us to stay solvent.

Figure 47 The route of ascent.
Photo: Joint Services Expedition to Lamjung Himal

We were, nominally, an Army expedition mounted from Hong Kong. We even had a military code name. However, as the number of experienced Army climbers in Hong Kong in 1974 was scarcely sufficient to mount an expedition to Llanberis, the original plan had to be modified along the way. The team finally included three Army climbers based in England (Mike, John Scott and Derrick Chamberlain), Frank Fonfe from Brunei, Phil Neame from the RAF, and even a civilian (me). The original Hong Kong Army criteria were filled only by Jeff Barker (just about to be posted away) and our two Gurkhas, Angphurba Sherpa and Sange Tamang. Angphurba's father had been on Everest in 1921, which seemed a good start. When we assembled in Pokhara in March 1974 only Mike knew everyone else in the party.

We were a large expedition for the size of our mountain, but an underestimate of its difficulty made us a fairly lightweight one, and force of circumstances made us a low-budget one. We took no Sherpas, thus saving much money and probably some trouble, and confounding the newspaper correspondents in Kathmandu, who told us improbably, that we were the first expedition ever to leave without them. I convinced myself, from one or two distant photographs, that 1,500 feet of fixed rope would be the most we would need, and in fact it was just enough, though I suspect we would have used twice as much if we had had it. Frank, temporarily in Nepal paying Gurkha pensions, struck a very good deal with the 1973 Dhaulagiri IV expedition for their surplus food, which saved us time and customs duty. Mike and Jeff obtained most of our tents and climbing gear on loan from various Army units. My simple belief that Army climbing expeditions were all paid for by the British tax-payer was shattered at an early stage, but we received a grant from the Mount Everest Foundation, and we managed to raise some cash in Hong Kong which kept our personal contributions down to £100 each plus personal gear. Our total expenditure was £4,000.

Figure 48 Dick emerging up the E col
Photo: Phil Neame (*Ed*. This photo was not in the *AJ* article)

Jimmy Roberts had suggested the E ridge of Lamjung, approached from its S side, as the best route. This was the route taken by the only previous party (*AJ* 73 249). An exciting aerial reconnaissance confirmed this as our choice.

After Mike and I had been up on foot to choose the base camp site, we set out from Pokhara on 23 March with 60 porters and just under 2 tons of baggage, including 7 weeks food for 10 people. Our approach was short, not more than 30 miles, and we thought we were safe in allowing 4 days to base. A heavy snowstorm on the third day out confounded us by causing two-thirds of our porters to quit, half way there, and the 2 feet of new snow on the rest of the route slowed us down very much. We even had to fix a rope in one place.

Before our base was set up on the snow at around 4100 m, we were out of porters altogether, and I for one had done as much load carrying as I had expected to do on the whole trip. However, we had stuck to our resolve not to touch the climbing food before we reached base, and the tubes of cheese and other tit-bits in the climbing rations provided a welcome boost. We also managed to get the beer all the way. Soon after our base was set up, a diversion occurred. Our head porter-cum-cook was sent back from base to bring up a load and never returned. There were several avalanches across the trail that day. Much discussion ensued as to whether he had run away or been killed. The climbing was almost postponed in favour of a search but reason finally prevailed, and Jeff went down to Pokhara to find him sunbathing. He was not much loss as he had been unable either to control the porters or to light a primus effectively. In contrast, our mail runner, one Baktabahadur, was a small human dynamo with unlimited energy, a permanent grin from ear to ear, and a great ability to produce mugs of tea at crucial moments.

The route to the E col (5404m) between Lamjung and the "Lamjungspitzen" lay up the flank of a rather nasty glacier, into a snow bowl, then up a 1500-foot ramp on the flank of the W Lamjungspitze to a point just above the col. A large transverse serac wall, colourfully banded like Neapolitan ice-cream, threatened the lower part of the route but in fact caused no mishaps. The snow bowl, which could have been full of appalling crevasses was in fact very easy, and the ramp was straight forward steep snow, albeit sometimes in foul condition, and with the odd ice patch near the top. When Phil and I abseiled down to the col with the first batch of loads on 11 April, we felt we had been fairly lucky so far[58]. The next day, we took a rest – fortunately again, as 3 substantial avalanches cleared the soft snow off the ramp exactly 24 hours after our descent.

The campsite on the col was a windy spot with gales blowing from N and S variously. Two Arctic Guinea tents pitched face to face made life reasonably comfortable, and we had fine views, in the mornings, of the mountains N of the Marsyandi Khola toward the Tibetan border. The high winds generally prevented the regular afternoon snow building up here, as we waited in vain hope for the two-week spell of clear weather which we had been told to expect sometime in April. It turned out that this was just one

---

58 Phil Neame recalled in 2013 "Regarding the picture of Dick and axe, it was taken after the pair of us had opened the route up to the E Col. This involved a 1500 ft 45 degree slope from a cwm at the bottom on the flanks of Lamjung Spitze, before a short abseil down to the Col. It was like climbing a slope of ball-bearings, and took us 7 hours. The next day we planned a carry up the slope, but when those below at BC said they were taking a day off, we – a little self righteously – decided to do likewise. Half an hour later, brew in hand, sitting in the sun outside the tent, we watched as the whole slope avalanched top to bottom, with the cone coming to rest just 10 yards from the tent. We congratulated ourselves on sound mountaineering judgement and a good decision!

of those bad seasons – but it was at least always clear in the mornings, and higher up the mountain we did not get much heavy snow. From the col our foreshortened view of the E ridge gave rise to some optimism. A series of snow couloirs led to the ridge which, it seemed, gave access via a short serac wall to the upper, glacier-capped ridge. This, as we knew, or thought we knew, from the plane trip, led in easy snow slopes to the top. Phil stirred up the rearguard by asking on the radio for the summit flags, and we set out for a look the next day, full of hope that the job would soon be done.

Figure 49 Carrying loads to the E col
Photo: Joint Services Expedition to Lamjung Himal

We found we had been somewhat premature. Six hours up the couloirs and along a narrow and not too stable snow crest took us to a junction of ridges, and a superb view to Manaslu and Himalchuli away to the E. From here a kink in the ridge line, hidden from below, revealed a thousand feet of particularly nasty narrow, rotten, steep-sided, cornice-topped snow ridge leading to a suddenly impressive wall of seracs. We clearly needed fixed ropes, not summit flags, for the time being. We also needed a campsite, for which there was no obvious location. After some thought, we scratched out the beginnings of an ice cave in a very exposed position and retired to bring up the gear and let our minds digest the thought of the forthcoming bivouac.

At this point, the Expedition's secret weapons came into play. These were monumental stakes, made by the Royal Engineers to my somewhat extravagant design out of one of the world's more expensive alloys. They weighed about 3 pounds each and were strong enough to hold a falling tank. They had been conceived, over a few beers in Hong Kong, as ice stakes, but when someone pointed out that you would need a piledriver to get them into ice we started calling them snow stakes. It turned out that in steep soggy snow they were ideal. This meant, incidentally, that my equally extravagant home-made dead-men could continue to support the kitchen floor in base camp. We gathered the snow stakes from their positions on the main guys of the base camp tents and humped them up the hill with all the rope we had.

Figure 50 Lamjung (6983m)
Photo: John Cleare

Phil and I were relieved of our soul-searching about the ice cave when Mike decided we had been in the lead long enough, and went up himself with John to fix the ropes. John had been looking forward to this and they turned our scratchy hollow in the ice into a presentable bed-sitter – just as well, as they spent 3 nights in it, rather than the one which had been anticipated. Even in soggy snow the big stakes needed a lot of driving. After 2 days and 1,200 feet of rope-fixing, John and Mike reached the serac wall. It was around 200 feet high, not 30 feet as I had thought from below, but they found an almost miraculous route through it by a big crevasse, big enough to locate a temporary camp. Derrick, Phil and I joined them – 3 in a two-man tent to save weight – and at 6030 m on the altimeter we began to feel we were getting close.

We still had some food in a dump at the ice cave, so on the next day John and I carried this up, while Phil and Derrick set off, self-contained, for the top, hoping to make it with just one more camp. The serac wall was followed by an exciting snow-bridge and another 200 feet of fairly steep ice, after which they were on the broad glacier-capped ridge leading toward the summit. This had one catch in it, a small overhanging ice wall which made them get out the ice pegs and étriers, and caused some hard breathing. They pitched their top camp, on 24 April, at around 6520 m on the saddle above the conspicuous snow dome.

Above this camp, the broad ridge continued easily at first – then it steepened into a turret-like summit crest, rather more distinct than it appeared from below, and a good deal steeper. An easy snow ramp ran to the E around the base of this, and may have led to a relatively easy route to the top, but this could not be seen, so Derrick and Phil took a direct route. Three hundred feet of steepish ice took them to a sharp crest, which ended in a short vertical snow-wall below the summit. They needed pegs again, for what proved to be the last pitch. The summit plateau was long and narrow, but otherwise remarkably like the top of the Cairngorms in winter. Despite a late finish they got a view of Annapurna II rising 3 miles away beyond a very large snow saddle. They just got back to their camp in daylight.

John and I repeated the climb 2 days later, following the original route exactly despite my preference for exploring round the corners and avoiding the ice climbing. We had electricity buzzing around our heads on the summit and saw about as much as one usually sees from the Cairngorms. We had a thrill on the descent when we abseiled down the top wall from an ice channel in the snow; the peg held me adequately but pulled out just as John finished his abseil. It meant we saved a peg. Mike, who had earlier descended to the col with a heavy cold, now persuaded Phil to repeat the climb with him, again following the same route.

By this time, several people had been continually above the snowline for a month or more, and we had had enough, so after some heart-searching we left the fixed ropes and headed for home. The main party returned by the approach route, marvelling at the difference in speed of the same porters going up and coming down. Frank, John and I for a change went down the N side of the col, sliding for miles on our trousers seats in the snow, and incidentally discovering that access to the col was much easier from this side. After a few passages of grade 6 pine forest, we reached the beautiful and impressive Marsyandi Khola at Chame, and followed it down in 5 days to Khudi, Dumre and the road to Pokhara.

Figure 51 Load carrying on the E ridge, Lamjungspitze behind
Photo: Joint Services Expedition to Lamjung Himal

Figure 52 John Scott on the final section
Photo: Joint Services Expedition to Lamjung Himal Himal

BIRDS OF SWAT AND GILGIT[59]

In June and July 1975, Rob Collister and I trekked from Matiltan, in Northern Swat, via the Kachikani An to Sor Laspur, thence via the Shandur Pass to Gilgit, and subsequently to Chalt and the Bola Das valley. For various reasons we achieved no climbing whatever [see p.123], but we did record around seventy bird species, and an account of these may be of interest to others following the fairly popular Swat-to-Gilgit trekking route.

Around Kalam and Matiltan, the Swat river and its tributaries gave us the usual range of riverside birds, including pied and grey wagtails (with young at this time of year), plumbeous and white-capped redstarts, and the violet whistling thrush. Rather more notable was a small forktail, seen in a torrent at Bahrain.

From Matiltan onwards, the wooded hillsides provided continuous interest. Russet sparrows, meadow buntings, crowned willow warblers, rufous turtle doves and the occasional common rosefinch appeared on our first day out. There were woodpeckers around, but we never stopped long enough to allow a search for them.

Higher up the valley, as the trees began to thin out, a new range of birds appeared. Yellow-headed wagtails became progressively more common, on the riverside grassland and in the low scrub, until at around 12,000 feet they became the most abundant species in the valley. The Kashmir race of the black redstart became common in the more stony areas, and red-fronted serins frequently appeared in small groups. Indian black tits were seen in one of the last pine woods. In the river we saw both the brown and European (white-breasted) dippers, the latter being more common near the snow line; we saw a pair swimming in a pool in the ice below Kachikani. A number of common sandpipers were chasing one another up and down the river; they may well have been breeding, but we saw no definite evidence of this. Both the common and the alpine chough appeared in some numbers. We saw one European cuckoo and heard several more. A flock of five snow pigeons was an attractive sighting.

Before crossing the Kachikani pass, we spent a night in a group of shepherds' huts at around 13,000 feet. Here, the river meandered through beds of dwarf willows, on the tops of which sat male yellow-headed wagtails, evenly spaced, around twenty yards apart and presumably laying claim to breeding territories.

On the stony hillsides around the snow line, we saw brown accentors, a horned lark and a dead coot, while I pleased myself by spotting the vinaceous-breasted pipit (Anthus roseatus). One of our best sightings was of a wall-creeper on one of the highest patches of exposed hillside.

In the Kachikani Gol on the north side of the pass, we saw a number of great rosefinches and, in the river bed, one out of place green sandpiper. Lower down, European swifts, crag martins, and house martins appeared in succession. A wren appeared briefly out of a hole in a rocky hillside.

Near Sor Laspur, where small willows grow in the river bed, we saw and heard chiffchaffs, lesser whitethroats and a number of common rosefinches. Wheatears (black and pied) appeared in the drier areas, and we saw flocks of the plain mountain finch. Six Turkestan rock pigeons flew up from the first cultivated land areas outside Sor Laspur.

59 R.J. Isherwood, HJ Vol XXXIV (1974-5) p 130

On the grassland on the top of the Shandur pass (13,000 feet) were many horned larks, all of the Pamir race with the black facial ring, and generally very tame Skylarks (probably the Eastern skylark) were also abundant. A flock of small finches must have been either linnets or twites, but we saw no adult males, and were left in doubt.

The path from Shandur top descends into the Ghizar valley at a point where this is probably a mile wide, and filled with small willows. A detailed search of this area would probably be very rewarding. We merely followed the trail, but were rewarded with a bluethroat (white-spotted), Himalayan gold-finches, and many more chiff chaffs

From Teru, we travelled by jeep to Gilgit, and subsequently on to Chalt, on what must be one of the more exciting public transport routes of the world. Bird watching was limited to frequent sightings of golden orioles and hoopoes in the cultivated areas

Above Chalt, I recorded a white-capped bunting in the open fields, and a scaly bellied green woodpecker on a rocky hillside. Higher up the valley, the "enormous vultures" recorded over the Baltar glacier by one previous climbing expedition were definitely not in evidence; however, we added Tickell's leaf warbler to our list, seeing a number of them among the chiff-chaffs in the willows, I saw a number of other *Phylloscopus* warblers which fitted neither of these species but never in enough detail to permit identification.

One of the disappointing features of our trip was the scarcity of birds of prey; occasional kestrels were the only common raptors seen. In Gilgit, just before my departure we saw a European hobby on the air-field and also a light-phase booted eagle. Three vultures, seen high over Chalt, could have been white backed or Himalayan griffons.

My final, and perhaps one of our more unusual sightings, was of a gull-billed tern hawking insects over Gilgit airport.

In terms of the variety of species seen, the upper Swat valley seemed markedly richer in bird life than the Laspur area, Ghizar II valley or the lower Hunza valley. However the drier, less vegetated Ghizar and Hunza valleys yielded several birds which we did not see at all in Swat, notably the wheatears and willow-warblers.

A SUMMER IN GILGIT (1975) PT I[60]

Rob Collister

Ed. Sometimes you climb something – sometimes you don't...

Ever since we had shared a tent in Kulu in 1973, Dick Isherwood and I had been plotting a 2-man expedition to the Karakoram. I use the word 'plotting' advisedly, for we would be in no way official and of planning there was little, and that hindered by the peripatetic nature of Dick's job in the Far East. One of the last communications I received was a card scribbled in an aeroplane and posted in Japan. It read:

'*How about Distaghil Sar? Buy a goat in Hispar and drive it up the glacier. Dick.*'

Distaghil Sar is 7885m high. Investigation revealed that despite several attempts it had only been climbed once, and then after a struggle involving ice-cliffs, avalanches and violent storms. However, the Hispar Glacier is 40 miles long and surrounded by peaks only slightly lower and considerably less dangerous, so I was quite content to head in that general direction.

With 7 pounds of potato powder and some meat bar to supplement the goat, I flew to Pakistan on 21 June. I was met by Dick with the news that Hunza, the northernmost province of Pakistan and the only feasible approach to the Hispar Glacier, had been closed to foreigners. After being a prohibited area for over 10 years, it had been re-opened in 1973. Now, suddenly, it had been closed again, ostensibly because of work on the so-called Karakoram Highway. Following an old Himalayan trade-route but built for political and military rather than commercial reasons, the 'K-K Highway' runs from Islamabad to Kashgar, in Chinese Turkestan, over the Kunjerab Pass (where according to Dick who had reached it clandestinely the previous year, there is nothing save a sign reading: "CHINA, DRIVE ON THE RIGHT").

Work still goes on, however, widening, metalling, and endlessly repairing the road. The ban on foreign (though not on Pakistani) tourists seems to have been prompted mainly by the objection of several thousand Chinese engineers and labourers to being so much camera fodder. Another possible reason, strenuously denied by officialdom, was the disturbance caused the previous winter by the government's arbitrary assumption of power in Hunza, depriving the Mir of all authority. This move cannot have been entirely unexpected as the semi-autonomous kingdoms of Negar and Chitral had already suffered the same fate. Nevertheless, some, at least, of the Hunzakuts resented the imposition of policemen, magistrates and a Hilton Hotel, all of which they had managed without quite successfully for some centuries. Be that as it may, our plans to climb around the Hispar Glacier had to be shelved.

We had other strings to our bow, but the immediate problem was to reach Gilgit. This scruffy but strategically-placed little town, once the corner-stone of Imperial defence policy in the Great Game with Russia, is the unavoidable gateway to the W Karakoram. Unfortunately the road up from the plains was also infested with Chinese and out of bounds to foreigners. With the road closed, air flights were even more heavily subscribed than usual, with a booking list stretching into August. That in itself meant

60 Rob Collister, *AJ* 1977 pp 158-164

little, but Rawalpindi was suffering from the vagaries of its erratic monsoon and many
of the daily flights had been cancelled. Rawalpindi was full of long-faced expeditioners
of many nationalities, some of whom had been waiting a fortnight already. Neither
Dick nor I are good waiters and, besides, Dick only had 4 weeks' holiday. So, after one
abortive visit to the airport, we decided to take the long way round through Swat and
Chitral, small states to the S and W of Gilgit. The plan was to walk up the Ushu Valley
and over the Kachikani An (4766m) to Sor Laspur in Chitral. From there, we would
have to cross the Shandhur Pass (3700m) and travel down the long length of the Gilgit
Valley, much of which can be done in a jeep. The journey would take at least a week
compared with an air flight of one hour, but the time would be infinitely better spent
than stewing in Rawalpindi.

Two days' travel, mostly by minibus, saw us at Matiltan in Swat State, the end of
the road. The village boasts an unusual flyover irrigation system of hollowed-out tree
trunks on stilts. Set amid fields of maize, wheat and potatoes, its solid stone-built
houses are shaded by huge walnut trees and enjoy a view of the twin Bateen peaks.
But, to our surprise, its people were grasping and unfriendly. We had both been to
Swat before and had the fondest recollections of the place. Dick, in 1964, had climbed
Mankial *Ed. See p.13*, a fine peak conspicuous from the road as one drives N through Swat
while in 1968 I had been with a party which travelled up the neighbouring Gabral Gol
and climbed peaks on the Swat-Chitral watershed. Things had changed considerably
since then. We found that organized trekking, both by foreigners and Pakistanis, had
become extremely popular and the route we had chosen threatens to rival the Pennine
Way in the traffic it receives. Partly because of this trekking boom and partly because
Pakistan, like everywhere else, is in the throes of inflation, wages had increased by a
factor of 4 or 5 and porters were not inclined to haggle. In Matiltan, those who were
found themselves set up by a vigorous Trade Union movement, the militancy of whose
members seemed to be directly related to their affluence. It was only with difficulty
that we found 2 (*sic*) men, or rather a man and a boy, sufficiently impecunious to defy
the militants and accept our terms.

The Ushu Valley, though not without its arid sections, is a lovely place. Its stands of
pine and deodar, its water meadows dotted with ponies and cattle, and the snowy peaks
visible at either end, make it as picturesque as anything in the Alps. Springs of fresh water
bubble up among banks of orchids. Beside the path bloom familiar flowers – cinquefoil,
forget-me-not, comfrey, celandine, gentian, even the ubiquitous dandelion. And there are
birds everywhere – beside the turbulent white glacier stream, dippers and white-capped
and plumbeous redstarts; where the river has flooded, sandpipers and a striking black
and yellow wagtail; on open rocky hillsides, kestrels and black redstarts; and among the
trees, rose finches, and cuckoos calling insistently. Dick, ever on the watch with his Leitz
glasses, was compiling a checklist which had soon exceeded 50 species.

The only discordant notes in this idyll were struck by our predecessors. Earlier the
same month a party led by one Mr Langlands had travelled up the valley. We knew
this because either Mr Langlands or one of his acolytes appears to suffer acutely from
the 'Kilroy was here' syndrome. At least once in every day's march the legend 'Mr
Langlands' and the date, artistically enclosed in Urdu script, would appear painted on
a prominent rock. We were compelled to follow the progress of Mr Langlands all the
way up the Ushu Gol, into Chitral and even some of the way down the Gilgit Valley.

We wished that, like Kilroy, he could have confined his activities to lavatory walls.

Two days ahead of us from Matiltan was a commercially-organized trekking party of 15 Americans led by a Pakistani, with a huge number of coolies. Of their passage, too, we were left in no doubt, following a trail of Kodachrome boxes, sweet papers and fruit drink packets until, near the end of the second day's walk, we caught up with them, camped in a birchwood not far from the snow-line. They were so affable and welcoming, however, that I did not have the heart to give vent to my feelings.

Figure 53 The N face of Rakaposhi from near Chalt
Photo: Rob Collister

The Kachikani An proved straightforward enough, though without a guide the correct route might not have been obvious and from the opposite direction would I suspect, be even less so. We spent most of the day in the snow. The coolies were not strong and in their plastic shoes made heavy weather of the steep sections. I was no faster. A 'touch of the sun' the previous day had made me feel so poorly that I had eaten and, more important, drunk virtually nothing. As a result, I became badly dehydrated and found every upward step of the pass an effort.

Another day's walk through a very different, near-desert landscape brightened only by dog roses and purple vetch, brought us to Sor Laspur – a prosperous village sited like most in these parts, on an alluvial fan and totally dependent on irrigation from the glacier river. Here we had to change porters, the villagers being jealous of their territorial rights.

Finally, in a 25-mile day, we crossed the long plateau of the Shandhur Pass to reach Teru. In December 1895, the Pass was the scene of an epic crossing by Colonel Kelly, on his way to the relief of a beleaguered garrison in Chitral, when unfortunate sepoys from the plains of the Punjab had to drag their cannon through 5 feet of snow In summer, though, cattle graze upon it and there is even a polo ground laid out. In days gone by, the annual polo match between Chitral and Gilgit, held on top of the pass in August, was the social event of the year. Alas, the advent of the jeep has made the ownership of a horse a luxury rather than a necessity, and the match has not been played since 1968.

The sight of a blue-throat, so rare in England, only a few feet away and quite undisturbed, enlivened a dull walk on the far side. But almost as memorable for their homely associations in that foreign setting, were house martins swooping over the broad white river and, in Teru, skylarks singing above the fields. Over the last few miles, however, I noticed little. In the glare of mid-afternoon, my feet swelled and swelled until, like the princess in the fairy tale, I seemed to feel even the tiniest pebble through the thick soles of my shoes. The two coolies from Laspur must have found it a long day also, for they arrived late in the evening driving their loads before them on a donkey.

A rough road runs right to the top of the Shandhur Pass but only occasionally do jeeps go even as far as Teru. We were in luck, for one arrived that night which took us 60-odd miles down the hospitable Gilgit valley the following day, more than once being flagged down to sample the first fruits of the apricot harvest. Rather than continue to Gilgit itself we had decided to branch off up the Ishkoman Valley to the Karumbar Glacier, from which we could attempt Kampire Dior (7143m). After various vicissitudes involving jeep-drivers and bouts of a mysterious fever, we eventually reached the roadhead at Imit, renowned locally for its opium poppies. On the way we had been given every assistance by the police but here we met a self-important gentleman from Military Intelligence who was quite emphatic that a permit was needed and that 'law is law'. Despondently, we walked 12 miles back to the next village where we found a jeep going to Gilgit.

Gilgit is an unprepossessing place full of jeeps and flies. Expedition accounts tend to confine themselves to the comforts of the Residency and the hospitality of the DC. However, appearances are everything in Pakistan and we did not receive the usual invitation to take afternoon tea. In fact, I seemed to have offended the orderly bureaucratic mind, for I was asked by more than one puzzled official 'Are you Tourist or are you Hippy'. At all events we lost no time finding another jeep and next day drove, on the opposite side of the river to the K-K Highway, along the spectacular mountain road to Chalt, 30 miles N of Gilgit in the Hunza gorge. In addition to the usual oft-described horrors of such rides we found ourselves perched high up on top of sacks of flour and lumps of rock salt, in imminent danger of decapitation by branches, telegraph wires and overhanging rock, though in good position to help ourselves to apricots.

Foiled twice now, we were making for 2 unclimbed peaks of 6872m and 6885m respectively, at the head of the Kukuay Glacier. Again, the local police were friendly and helpful – 'You are our Guests' – and as there is no frontier in the vicinity, this time there was no sign of the army. Putting our belongings on a horse and marvelling, on the way, at the stupendous N Face of Rakaposhi, we reached Bar, the last village in the valley and started the lengthy process of finding porters.

In Gilgit we had pared our baggage down and, with only a fortnight of Dick's holiday left, we needed less food. The 2 loads weighed less than 70lb each and normally we would have had no hesitation in shouldering them ourselves. In fact, the following morning when negotiations broke down, we did so and were not bluffing. Nevertheless I, at least, was relieved when, after half a mile, the porters and their representatives caught us up and agreed to our price. More than Dick, I was finding the searing heat and the dryness of the atmosphere very trying. (A German expedition to this region, in 1954, estimated the relative humidity to be often less than 10 %).

The coolies agreed to our rate of payment but insisted on lighter loads, and by the time we had taken our own climbing sacks they were left with very little more than 40 lb apiece. With loads so light they might have been expected to travel relatively fast. Instead, the distance we covered that first day from Bar was so paltry that we would have paid them off there and then had I not been feeling, again, the effects of dehydration.

We spent that night outside a goatherds' shelter which had clearly been occupied by the goats as well as the herds, and I put in some determined drinking. As a result I went much better the next day. Initially, we tried to stay with the coolies, but they were impervious to hints and the combination of a rest every quarter hour and a pace that would not have been out of keeping in a dead march, was too much for our patience. Anxious not to walk through the heat of the day unnecessarily, we went on ahead, vowing to pay the coolies off that night.

Having crossed the moraine-covered snout of the Baltar Glacier in a long detour enforced by an unfordable river, and returned to the stony wastes of the main valley we reached, about midday, the place called Toltar – or what we took to be Toltar. There was nothing there but a few charred sticks and some dry stone walling beneath a boulder. But the coolies had made it clear that Toltar was the day's objective, so we sat down to wait for them.

They never came. Every hour or so we carefully scanned the valley with binoculars but there was never a sign of them. Dick read Richard Burton on Sindh. Having rashly left my book behind in the interests of weight, I contemplated alternatively the sky and my navel. The hours passed and we began to feel hungry. Finally, as evening drew in,

we unrolled our sleeping bags and tried unsuccessfully to stave off the pangs in sleep
Just before dark, Dick had a final look round but still there was nothing to be seen, not
even the smoke of a fire.

Figure 54 Gilgit, Chalt and lots of other places
Ed. Surprisingly, there was no caption in the *AJ* – so I added something

Next morning our hunger was no less, but convinced that the porters must
be nearby, we left our sacks and back-tracked a mile or so, searching and shouting.
We were certain that they could not have passed us. Not only were we keeping a look-
out, but at that point there is so little room between the mountainside and the river

that they could hardly help but see us. But there was neither sight nor sound of the 2 men. With nothing to eat, there was no alternative but to beat a retreat to Bar, by now a highly desirable land flowing with chapattis and salt tea.

At the insistence of the villagers who professed themselves certain that the porters would return any moment, we spent 2 days in Bar, lying in the shade of a walnut tree. An almost morbid fear of the police stemmed, we learned later, from a successful raid in search of stolen property only a fortnight before. So strong was this fear that it induced the local prophet to go into a convulsive trance, wherein he was bold enough to foretell the very hour of their arrival. Unfortunately, he was wrong. In the meantime, we lived on what the villagers chose to provide, mostly mulberries and chapattis of mature vintage, sometimes eggs and, on one memorable occasion, a packet of vermicelli, a tin of cheese and a large quantity of sugar boiled up together into an edible glue.

However, 2 days seems a very long time when one is a public spectacle throughout the hours of daylight and has nothing to do but debate the likelihood of villainy or disaster. Eventually, when requests that we should stay showed signs of hardening into a refusal to let us leave, we flitted on a dark moonless night to Chalt – our noiseless departure marred only by Dick describing a somersault from one terraced field to the next, wrenching a knee in the process. In Chalt we made a statement to the Inspector of Police and, after a day of over-indulging in apricots and sweet biscuits, returned to Gilgit full of gloom.

With a damaged knee and his holiday almost over, Dick cut short the fiasco of our 'expedition' by taking the first available flight back to Rawalpindi. Within minutes of his departure I met a policeman from Chalt in the bazaar and learned that our baggage had been recovered. Back in Chalt, I was told that the coolies had brought it in themselves, claiming to have carried it all the way to the Kukuay glacier and back and demanding 9 days' wages for their pains. Unfortunately the Inspector believed them. Apparently one of them had made the pilgrimage back to Mecca and 'They are very gentle men'. Secretly, I wondered if a man who had been to Mecca might not be all the more anxious to con an infidel. Aloud, I voiced the suspicion that they might have spent most of those days reclining in the shade of a birch grove beside the Baltar Glacier with some goatherds. But there was no convincing the Inspector and it is no easier to argue with the Law in Pakistan than anywhere else. Reluctantly I handed over the money.

Before I could depart with the baggage, however, there was a formality to be observed. 'Please check that everything is here', said the Inspector. He had already done so himself, using the list attached to our statement, but now it had to be done again. I was rather embarrassed as 2 fascinated constables, like children with a Christmas stocking, drew forth ropes, ice-axes, hammers, pitons, karabiners, crampons and high altitude boots in quick succession. But the Inspector seemed unperturbed. Despite our insistence that we only wanted to 'visit the glaciers', he was no fool and must have known better. The important thing, as far as he was concerned, was that we were not an Expedition.

The ruling of the Pakistan government is that Expeditions to climb mountains must apply to Islamabad for permission, whereupon (maybe a year later) they are charged a royalty of $1000 US, given a liaison officer whom they must fully equip and, more often than not, informed that they may climb a totally different peak to the one requested. But, as the Inspector knew from personal experience, Expeditions have at least 8 members and require an army of porters. As patently we were not an Expedition, he could see no reason why we should not climb mountains if we wanted to: though *why* we should want to was beyond his comprehension.

Dick had gone home without setting foot on a mountain. I was more fortunate, having plenty of time and having already arranged to meet 2 other friends, Rob Ferguson and Dave Wilkinson, to climb in the same area. There was hope yet. I returned to Gilgit to spend 10 hot, sticky, interminable days waiting for them.

(To be continued) [61]

KANJIROBA 1976[62]

The arrangement of the big mountains in Nepal is so compact that after flying from India to Kathmandu a few times you can feel that you know them, even when you have not actually been near them on the ground. Kangchenjunga, Makalu, Everest, Manaslu, Annapurna, Dhaulagiri – they all line up for their photographs as the tourists climb over you with their big cameras. I think it was partly this experience which made the Kanjiroba Himal – which you do not see in this way – seem more attractive to me than the other areas of Nepal available for climbing. Ron Giddy felt the same way, and after reading John Tyson's various articles we soon had a plan for a small expedition in the autumn of 1976. Dave Holdroyd joined us a little later; we reckoned 3 people plus a climbing Sherpa would be just enough, and so in fact it was.

Our initial plan was to approach Kanjiroba Main Peak (6883m) from the W over the Patrasi Himal – almost the only route which Tyson, in his 3 exploratory expeditions, did not try. We changed our minds, however, when we saw an account of the first ascent of the peak by an Osaka City University party in 1970. They had taken this approach, crossed the Patrasi ridge at 5500m and spent a fortnight descending a steep loose face to the base camp, using a good deal more hardware than we intended to take in total. This did not sound like fun, so we looked at the maps again. By piecing things together we calculated that John Tyson's original attempts up the Jagdula Khola had reached a point only 2 or 3 miles short of the lowest point to which the Japanese party had descended. "What's 2 or 3 miles?", we asked ourselves, and opened some more beer to mark our finding a workable plan which still had some exploration in it.

Organization in Hong Kong was simple, though fund raising was hindered by the presence of a "rival" – the Army expedition to Annapurna South Peak[63]. We did, however, receive substantial and very welcome support from the Mount Everest Foundation, the British Mountaineering Council and a number of individuals and companies in Hong Kong.

"You'll be lucky to fly into Jumla before October 1st", said the pundits in Kathmandu. This was over 2 weeks away and the alternative – to fly to Surkhet in the lowlands of far W Nepal – involved an extra 9 days walking. We had a total time or just over 7 weeks, and Mike Cheney's comment that people with limited holidays and rigid deadlines should perhaps avoid remote areas began to seem relevant.

Fortunately Royal Nepal Airlines had a more flexible view of things. One day they were sure they could fly us in, and our spirits rose. Next day there was water on the runway at Jumla. Then the story came that they had no contact with Jumla at all, but thought there might be water on the runway. Finally we took off on 18 September to give it a try – 3 expedition members, 2 Sherpas, liaison officer and gear just fitting into the Twin Otter. Cloud obscured all the mountain views but cleared as we reached the Kamali river system, and we landed in beautiful weather. Need less to say, there was no water on the runway.

---

62 Dick Isherwood, *AJ* 1978 pp 37-42
63 In the autumn 1976 season one third of all foreign expeditions in Nepal were from Hong Kong. We even outnumbered the Japanese.

The people of Jumla seem to be notoriously bad porters even when there is no festival in the offing, which is very seldom. With the Desira celebration approaching we had difficulty finding 25 people, and our first group lived up to the local reputation covering a very short distance in 2 days and then staging a sit-down strike. Fortunately replacements were close by at the Tibetan refugee village of Chotia, and they served us very well.

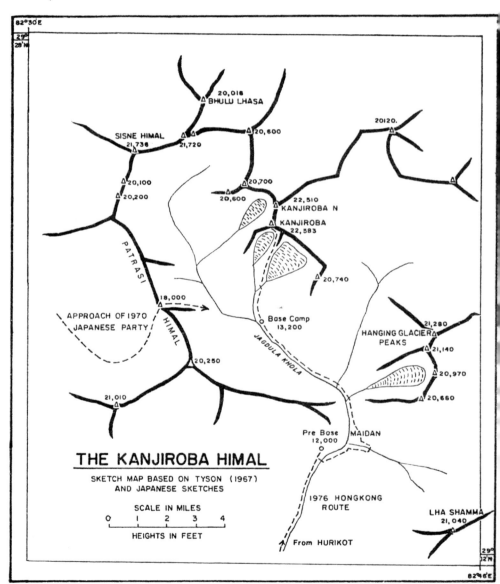

Figure 55 The Kanjiroba Himal

We reached the village of Hurikot, at the foot of the Jagdula Khola, in 5 days from Jumla, and found to our surprise an excellent new footpath leading up the valley. The Government, we were told, was building a road to Kanjiroba. Our porters, furthermore, knew the route all the way to the Base Camp, and it would take us only 3 days from here. We were still wondering whether to be pleased or disappointed by all this when, after 2 more days, we came to Tyson's 1961 Base Camp site and were shown a mountain, in totally the wrong place, supposedly called Kanjiroba. Further questions revealed that all the mountains for miles around were called Kanjiroba. We began to appreciate John Tyson's achievement in finding and mapping the highest peak of this complex group despite the total inaccuracy of the old Survey of India map. Armed with his map and some other recent material, we were able to point ourselves in the right direction with reasonable certainty, and to persuade our porter to leave the "government road" and follow the trackless flank of the main Jagdula.

It was here that we really appreciated our Tibetan porters. The route lay across some very steep grass, at first high above the river but later descending to the bed to avoid a series of rock buttresses. We passed the remains of one shikari (hunter) whose quest for musk deer had come to a nasty end, and heard of another who had disappeared in the gorge.

In the river we ran into problem. The cliffs descended to water level and the obvious route involved 2 crossings of the worst deep water. Dave and I tried to set an example, taking a load across safeguarded by a rope, but the porters were totally unimpressed. "OK for tall Europeans, but we will be up to our necks in that", they said. Fortunately Pemba, our sirdar, found a route through the cliffs above, ending in a 150-foot abseil down vertical grass to rejoin the river. We began lowering loads down this section, but the novelty of swinging on ropes soon infected the whole party, and several porters went down hand over hand with 70 lb loads. Rates of pay by now had doubled to Rs 40 per day but at least we were still progressing.

Figure 56 Looking north up the Jagdula Khola towards the main peaks of the Kanjiroba Himal.
Photo: D. Isherwood

Four days beyond Tyson's camp we reached a meadow overlooking a major junction in the valley. Here, it seemed, the route really became difficult, and none of the various alternatives was likely to be suitable for porters. We paid them off and established our pre-base camp, an estimated 8 miles from the mountain, which none of us had yet seen. Directly opposite our meadow was the "maidan" reached by Tyson's 1964 party who had used a much longer route over the flanks of Lha Shamma (6413m) to the E of the river.

We soon saw that a continuation on the W bank of the Jagdula was not feasible. The river here ran in a most impressive crevasse-like gorge, above which was a monstrous fissured rock wall, reminiscent of those parts of the Dolomites which you only see when you get lost on a descent. Dave and I climbed some very steep grass to explore the high ridges above, but the prospect here was just as bad – days of climbing across steep loose rock with no water whatsoever. Ron and Pemba found the depths of the gorge equally daunting, but they did spot a possible roundabout route to the opposite bank and the maidan.

The following day the 4 of us set out for a longer exploration. The river crossing again needed a rope, but a tenuous route through the cliff on the E side proved easier than expected thanks to well rooted juniper bushes. Five hours strenuous work, across steep rock and grass, took us to the maidan. Earth cliffs loomed through the birch forest ahead but were fortunately avoidable, and after some scrabbling and steep loose slope, too near the brink of the gorge for comfort, we reached the river bed above the crevassed section.

Figure 57 Crossing the Jagdula Khola
Photo: D. Isherwood

We were still well short of a base camp but we thought we were over the worst, so I took a chance and sent Pemba back to begin ferrying loads with Pasang Gyan, our cook. Dave and I went on for another long day, up and down the valley sides, in and out of the river, and reached a camp-site below a mountain which we thought was probably Kanjiroba. The upper valley was much more open than the gorge below, and we had some excellent close-up views of "bharal" (blue sheep) on the juniper covered hill sides.

A search of the slopes around the camp revealed a small pile of Japanese refuse, so, reassured that we were in the right place, we looked for a route up the mountain. A rock band separating 2 icefalls seemed to offer the only safe approach to the S face, but did not look too easy. We left the tent and returned to pre-base. On the way down Dave thought he saw a kangaroo, but this major zoological discovery proved on second sighting to be a large deer of some kind.

This expedition was my first experience of Sherpas. I had been convinced by Ron that a sirdar was a good idea, and by Mike Cheney that one Sherpa on his own would be lonely, so we decided to take a cook as well. I had, however, heard so many unfavourable reports in recent years that my expectations were not very high. Pemba's early performance as an organizer of porters had not altered my views, but now he and Pasang really showed their value. They had been left with a request to do a carry through the difficult section of the gorge – a long strenuous day as a round trip – and with the suggestion that they might do a second carry if they felt like it. Two carries were done in 2 days, and they were ready without complaint to do a third with us the day after our return. This was sufficient, with a certain amount of overloading all-round, to get all our essential gear to a half-way camp in the gorge.

Figure 58 Crossing the Jagdula Khola again
Photo: D. Isherwood (*Ed.* according to the *AJ*, although this one is OF Dick!)

Dave's rock climbing enthusiasm was stimulated by the rock band, so he and Pemba went ahead with rope and iron-ware, while Pasang, Ron and I completed the carrying to base. Three days later we were established there, all agreeably surprised by the discovery that the rock band was very easy. One more carry was enough to put 3 of us in a camp at 5200m with, we hoped, enough food and gear to finish the job. At this stage, unfortunately, Dave was suffering badly from altitude sickness, which left Pemba and myself as the climbing party.

We had hoped to find a new route to the summit of Kanjiroba, but from the S glaciers, whose edge we were now on, the original Japanese route was by far the most obvious and safest way. This climbs a subsidiary spur running S off the long SE ridge of the mountain. Access to the spur looked difficult as it ended in a line of ice cliffs, but we found a ramp of steep snow/ice leading easily through these. After avoiding some large crevasses we reached the crest at lunchtime, and camped just below the first steep section of the spur, at 19,500 feet (5950m) by the altimeter.

Next morning we continued up the spur – all snow, but steep and narrow enough to need belays in some places. Higher up it merged into the S face of the mountain. I had been expecting ice here but the good snow continued all the way. We were both feeling the height now, having come up 7,000 feet in just over 2 days. My competitive mind had considered the possibility of "burning off" a Sherpa, but dismissed it as too likely to rebound on me – so it was with some warped satisfaction that I felt the rope go tight and looked down to see Pemba leaning over his axe, breathing very hard. He really did smoke too much.

We reached the SE ridge and had our first good views of the E basin of the Kanjiroba group – Serkhu Dolma, Tshokarpo Kang, the "hanging glacier peaks" below which we had come, and others further away towards Ringmo lake. In the far distance we could see the Dhaulagiri range, the Annapurnas and the Manaslu group, all looking very close together by comparison with the vast expanse of lower mountains stretching into Tibet.

From here Pemba took the lead for a while. In most respects he was very safe, but his attitude to the large cornice was a little too casual for me. At one stage he stood astride a junction between old and new sections of the cornice pointing to a small crack between his feet – "Look, sahib, crevasse". It was difficult to decide whether to break all the trail myself or stay behind to watch him. Really I wanted to unrope but this hardly seemed fair.

We followed the ridge to an almost level spot at 6500m which was probably the bivouac site of the 1970 Japanese party. As it was only 11.30 we planned to go on to the summit after pitching the tent, but as usual the camp-site was not as level as it looked, and after 1½ hour's digging we had had enough work for the day. We spent a long afternoon brewing-up and periodically worrying about the wisps of high cloud moving over from the W – the first hints of bad weather for 2 weeks or so.

Fortunately we woke to another clear morning on 16 October, and an hour's climbing took us, surprisingly, to the top, where we were relieved to see that we were higher than anything else for a long way around. The view again was magnificent, and we could see the Patrasi and Sisne Himal to good effect. We picked out the Japanese approach route; it seemed unlikely that they had hit on the easiest crossing of the Patrasi.

Figure 59 Camp 1 on Kanjiroba.
The route follows the spur in the foreground till it joins the main (SE) ridge (right skyline)
Photo: *Ed*. This appeared in the HJ, not the *AJ* but the photo is not accredited

The N summit of Kanjiroba, which I had imagined to be a ½ hour walk from the main top, now looked a long way off – probably a 2-day round trip for us in our half-emaciated state. Lack of food was an adequate reason for not attempting it, and Pemba's fascination with the summit cornice was a further incentive for going down, so we were soon back at our camp for a second breakfast. The descent was straightforward all the way and we rejoined Dave the same afternoon.

Dave by now had recovered and was keen to climb. Ron, however, had decided that 45 was an appropriate retiring age for mountaineers and was busy burying his ice axe. Neither Pemba nor I could face a repeat performance, so reluctantly we prepared to go down. I spent a pleasant day in the sun, drinking gallons of tea and observing the remarkable spectacle of Ron hiding expensive equipment under the boulders to lighten his load, while the 2 Sherpas were simultaneously sorting the Japanese refuse for anything saleable. A good aluminium ice stake fetches Rs 50 as raw material for cooking pots. Pasang found a very heavy white rock and was persuaded only with difficulty that it was quartz and not valuable Tibetan salt.

The return was straight forward; at pre-base we found 2 of our former porters and 3 local shikaris, surrounded by large quantities of meat, and anxious to do 10 men's portering for 10 men's wages. The lower gorge was studded with small traps set for maize-hares, weasels and the like, but we never discovered how they trapped the bharal whose carcases appeared here and there on the return route. At Hurikot we switched to dzos (yak-cattle hybrids) and reached Jumla, with a week in hand, on 31 October.

BOOK KEEPING[64]

John Ashburner

I was delighted when Paul Fox, Senior Treasurer of CUMC reported that he had managed to track down the CUMC Minutes book in the University Library. He carefully photographed all the pages covering the two years '63 to '65 and these also included records of the Committee meetings. I noticed that at the committee deliberations on June 4th 1963

"The Librarian's Allowance of £10 was agreed upon. This is the normal sum allocated".

I thought that was a bit paltry as the Wherry Library[65] in those days had a splendid collection of books which were constantly in demand. There was also a "Comments" book in the little room in St John's[66] which attracted a regular stream of messages, a sort of Blog I suppose you might call it these days *(maybe someone should track that one down too and record snippets for posterity?).*

So I also looked at some of the Club accounts pasted onto to the pages of the Minutes. In 1961 for instance the current account had a total expenditure of £168 including the cost to provide journals for the 158 members at that time, charged at five shillings a throw. The printing costs were £160 but £115 was collected from advertisers – I sense some strong arm twisting took place!

The records however, were not always too clear and at the Annual General Meeting of the Club on May 26 1964 the then Treasurer (Bob Courtier)

"...took the meeting on a rapid and somewhat baffling tour of the accounts, which were complicated this year by the presence of two journals instead of one. He was clearly proud of having to report a loss on the year of £128-19-8 but assured us that the finances were alright since the two figures at the bottom of the page were equal."

It can get a bit boring to hear about how little everything seemed to cost "in those days". I was always very patient when listening to such stories as a youngster but the problem was that rarely was any yardstick offered by which to gauge the scenarios described. So let me try to add a sense of perspective...

Let's try scaling up from 1969 when I landed my first (and only ever) "proper job" in the UK. I was offered a post as a Scientist with a government research institute and the salary was around £1300. Instead, however, I managed to latch onto a Lecturer's post at a quasi-university with an annual salary of about £2000. So these sorts of figures may offer an idea of scale. In contrast in 2013, I believe similar posts might attract salaries of between twenty and thirty thousand so perhaps 15 times these rates.

---

64 Contributed by John Ashburner
65 The Wherry Library is sadly perhaps better described today as a pile books and papers in locked cupboards in corners of the Supervision Room, O Basement in Pembroke College.
66 The "Room" was loaned to the Club for many years. The Minute book refers to the Committee Meeting held on June 2nd, 1964: *"It was decided to approach Mr. J.A. Crook, owner of the room housing the Wherry Library, and to offer him Honorary Membership* (he gratefully *"accepted but asked not to be dragged up any mountains"* – Minutes of the Committee Meeting of January 21st 1965).

So now let's look at some trips:

1964: Cambridge Chitral Expedition (*well we all know they actually went to Swat!*)*See p.42*
Total cost: £659 (for the team of 4, travelling overland)

1965: Cambridge Ala Dag Expedition (*Dick was not on the team but I was and still have the report*)
Total cost: £791 (for the team of 7, also travelling overland but only "halfway" – to Turkey)

1966: Cambridge Hindu Kush Expedition
(*again Dick was not on the team but I do have this data too!*)
Total cost: £885 (for the team of 3 as usual travelling overland)

1969: British Hindu Raj Expedition
Total cost: £1,253 (for the team of 4 plus a Liaison Officer, overland again. The L.O. was a pain in the neck and quite costly)

1974: The Hong Kong Mountaineering Expedition to Lamjung
Total cost: 45,741 HK$ (roughly £4,500) (for the team of 9 flying in from Hong Kong)

1976: The Hong Kong Mountaineering Expedition to Kanjiroba
Total cost: 36,264 HK$ (also roughly, £3,500) (for the team of 3 flying in from Hong Kong) *This to me looks a bit expensive. Perhaps there was not much sponsorship.*

So casually glancing over the above covering a 10 year period, it seems that it was costing from £150 to £300 per head although in all cases there was sponsorship to a widely varying degree. Apply the magic multiplication factor of "fifteen" I suggested earlier and then maybe we are in the range of £2,000 to £4,500 at today's prices.

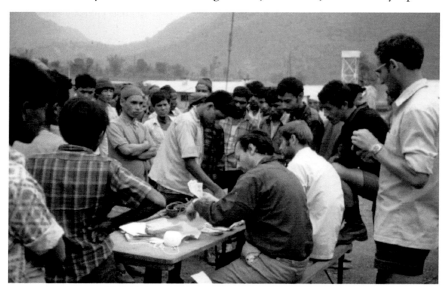

Figure 60 Dick Isherwood observing pay-day for the porters, Lamjung 1974
Photo: Phil Neame

Now pull out the colour supplement from your favourite Sunday newspaper – I think you may find that the higher figure of £4,500 might get someone about as far as the Indian sub-continent for a couple of weeks exotic holiday but not much longer. The trips illustrated above were at least twice as long.

Browsing through the costs for a trekking holiday seems to indicate perhaps £2,000 for three weeks excluding international flights. Going for an 8000m peak would take just over a month and cost perhaps £8,000.

There was a very persuasive article written back in the 1970s supporting the idea of small-scale expeditions[67], particularly in the light of the frequent problems and costs of employing the famous "Liaison Officer". He was required both in India and in Pakistan in those days. In conclusion the author suggested selecting peaks in the lesser ranges and turning a blind eye to officialdom. This meant that the cost for a 3-man trip could be kept to within £1,000 including air travel. Of course, this is very much in the spirit of the philosophy of Shipton and Tilman, Dick Isherwood having followed in the footsteps of the latter on many occasions as described in various other articles in this present collection.

So let's apply the fiddle factor of fifteen again, making the cost for a 3-man trip add up to £15,000. There are a few friends I know who nip off to the Himalaya every now and then on an entirely private basis. Dick indeed did just that only last autumn (2012). So I enquired as to whether some of them thought this sort of figure was about right for a sortie these days.

The first to reply was leaving the following week for the Himalaya (August 2013) and confirmed it wasn't far off. Another actually replied from the Kulu valley and also confirmed the figure was about right for a climbing party but if trekking, £10,000 would be a closer figure.

So it looks as if the true costs haven't changed much over all these years despite some folk complaining that it has become so much more expensive nowadays.

---

67 Rob Collister. Small expeditions in the Himalaya. *AJ* 1979 pp 166-172

ANNAPURNA II
Rob Collister

**Ed. There is a brief entry in the Nepal section of the
AJ Regional Notes of 1979 which reads as follows[68]:**

Annapurna II (7937m) Dick Isherwood writes that he and Rob Collister attempted a 2-man ascent post-monsoon in September 1978. They reached 7000m on the W ridge of Annapurna IV following the original route climbed by Jimmy Robert's team in 1960; they had previously hoped to find a direct N face route but abandoned the idea because of the heavy covering of fresh snow. Deteriorating weather forced a retreat – however they felt another 3 days of fine weather would have given them the chance of reaching the summit.

Figure 61 Dick Isherwood on a recce for Annapurna I and II, Dec 1977
Photo: Arlene Blum[69]

Rob Collister was asked to add further details:

In 1978 Dick was living in Kathmandu, working for ODA ^{See p.219}. On a trek in the Manaslu region he had spotted a possible line on the north face of Annapurna II which fired his imagination. It was not long since Messner and Habeler had climbed

---

68 *AJ* 1979 p 231
69 *Ed.* This photo arrived unexpectedly and when the script was already with the Graphic Designer. The trip is not recorded at all in Appendix 2. Arlene told me that it was *"on route to Annapurna North base camp in the Kali Gandaki with Dhaulagiri in the background"*

Hidden Peak (Gasherbrum I) in impeccable alpine style, so two-man expeditions were very much in vogue, and as Annapurna II is just under 8000m it seemed highly unlikely anyone else would be on it. When Dick asked me to join him I jumped at the chance before stopping to consider how I was going to pay for it. As I was earning a pittance at the time as an outdoor pursuits instructor and had a family to support, I pinned my hopes on winning a Churchill Fellowship in the Adventure category. Thanks to references from Noel Odell and Peter Boardman I was short listed, but the makeup of the interviewing panel was distinctly old school and they were not at all impressed by the concept of two men alone on a big peak. I think Rum Doodle was their preferred style. I was sent away with a flea in my ear, regretting the cost of the train fare to London. At this point Dick offered to pay for the whole trip if I could get myself to Kathmandu, an act of generosity I reluctantly but gratefully accepted.

Figure 62 Machapuchare from high on Annapurna IV
Photo: Rob Collister

Dick was always highly organized in a quietly efficient way. Years later I discovered he had detailed check-lists for everything but rarely referred to them in public. In Kathmandu the shopping had been done and the formalities largely completed by the time I arrived. All I had to do was attend a final briefing, the main purpose of which was to stress the importance of displaying the Nepalese flag alongside the Union Jack on the summit. Somehow, Dick managed to sidestep that one.

The walk in up the Marsyandi valley was a delight with such an informed companion. Dick had learnt Nepali which enabled him to haggle with villagers and banter with the porters as well as being a mine of information on flora and fauna. We persuaded our liaison officer that Base Camp should be in the village of Pisang where he could comfortably stay for the duration. Reaching Advanced Base Camp, where we would stay, was more problematic. We knew from the report of a German expedition that there was an ideal plateau at about 5000m, but we were not much over 4000m when we came across a small cairn which the porters declared was our destination. Fortunately for us, the cloud came down reducing visibility to a few metres. This allowed Dick to disappear up an ever steepening hillside building cairns as he went, while I stayed with the porters who clearly believed we were following a route put in by the Germans.

Figure 63 Dick rehydrating on chang after descending, October 1978
Photo: Rob Collister

We had been at this camp only a couple of days, acclimatizing, when our plans changed radically. The sight of a huge avalanche sweeping down the north face over the line of our proposed route caused a rapid re-think. The only viable alternative was to reach Annapurna II by traversing over Annapurna IV, which looked straightforward enough though not a first ascent. In the event, when we finally set out we were pinned down by bad weather for three days at 7000m. It was a struggle to get that far. I was suffering from a mysterious malady which had no obvious symptoms apart from lethargy and a total lack of energy. Although I could put one foot in front of the other, to my chagrin Dick had to do all the trail-breaking, a task even he found exhausting. When the weather improved, giving us dramatic views of Machapuchare, it was clearly no more than a lull, and with little food and fuel left we beat a retreat.

Predictably enough, the steep snow slopes we had toiled up were now smothered in soft but wind-blown snow, creating an unavoidable avalanche trap. Very soon I released a slab several inches thick. I found myself self-arresting on a small section of it which stopped moving while the rest of the slope accelerated silently downwards. The next few hundred feet were safe, the snow scoured crampon-hard by the avalanche. Then we arrived at some little ice bulges running across the face, possibly the line of a bergschrund, beneath which the debris had accumulated. Being of a suspicious nature when it comes to snow, I insisted on roping up. Dick passed the rope around his ice axe by way of belay but I made him adjust it so that his leg was braced against the shaft of the axe and the rope ran over his boot as well as round the axe, a New Zealand foot belay. I took one step downwards and the entire slope to a depth of nearly a metre broke away taking me with it. My full weight came abruptly on to the rope and Dick held me, but only just. We looked at each other, shaken, but said nothing – there seemed nothing to say – and continued on down without further incident, the avalanche having cleared the slope almost to the bottom.

As I wearily removed crampons, neoprene overboots, and massively heavy double-boots, it was in the certain knowledge that I would not be rushing to put them on again. We could have sat at ABC for another three weeks until an unseasonably late monsoon eventually ended when we could have tried again with every chance of success. Others would have done so. But I was the father of two small children and my interest in the mountain had evaporated. Dick was equally unenthusiastic about the prospect of hanging around for another attempt and we headed for the valley more relieved than disappointed.

Figure 64 Dick at almost 7000m on Annapurna IV just before their descent
Photo: Rob Collister

BUNI ZOM[70]

O ne of the advantages of living in the Himalaya is that you can organize your
climbing trips fairly casually. The expense is relatively small, and you have the
feeling that if you fail this year you can always come back next year if you so
desire. It encourages a more light-hearted approach to things than most people can
afford to take when they plan a trip from England.

Joe Reinhard and I went to Buni Zom (6551m) in the summer of 1979 in this way.
I had a long-standing interest in the area since I had walked by both sides of it at
different times and had never even seen the highest peak. The height seemed right for
a light 2-man party and, we thought, it was far enough W to have reasonable weather
even in August.

We had access to a few journals in Kathmandu, and we read what we could about
the climbing history of Buni Zom, which was not much. Dr Gruber's article in the
1970 *Himalayan Journal* lists all the peaks meticulously, but does not tell you who
climbed the highest one, or how. His sketch map however was very useful, as our
photostat copies of the 1: 250,000 maps were almost illegible.

Figure 65 En route to the Kachikani Pass
Photo: Johan Reinhard

70 Dick Isherwood, *AJ* 1980 pp 147-150. However the published photographs have been replaced by others kindly
supplied by Joe Reinhard

We had planned to go through Chitral, but stories in Islamabad of 100,000 refugees there, and probable restrictions on the movements of foreigners, made us opt for the longer walk from Kalam in the Swat valley, via the Kachikani[71] Pass and Laspur In fact, as I subsequently discovered, there were no problems in travelling through Chitral to Mastuj and Laspur, and not many refugees either.

My casual approach to the trip extended to leaving half my clothing in a Rawalpindi taxi by mistake. Fortunately the only critical thing I lost was my breeches. Pakistani pantaloons seemed less than adequate, but I was lucky to be able to borrow a pair of woollen trousers from an American friend. They were somewhat old, and I did all my climbing with a gaping fly. Joe, who had been much more careful in his planning found himself limited to a one-month stay in Pakistan, in total contradiction of what their Embassy in Kathmandu had told him. Thus our projected 3 weeks' climbing dwindled to a rather meagre 12 days. We left Rawalpindi, inauspiciously enough, at dawn on the first day of the holy fasting month of Ramazan, with very empty bellies.

In Kalam in 1964 we had recruited porters for 4 rupees a day, and they had provided their own food. Now you pay 50 if you are lucky, and feed them as well. Ramazan was, of course, advanced as a reason for not working, or working reluctantly for very high wages. After allowing for return pay, we finally paid out over 80 rupees per man per day of actual carrying. Anyway we were able, on 27 July, to move out of Kalam with six Pathans, who put aside their religious convictions as soon as they had passed the last villages, and wasted long hours each day in leisurely chupatti-making.

After 5 long but pleasant days in excellent weather we reached Phargam, close under the E side of the Buni Zom group. Our Kalam porters were keen to go all the way with us, but the Phargam people tried to insist that we pay them off and take locals for what was described as 1½ days of very, very rough walking on a trail which strangers could not possibly follow. We compromised by taking one "guide", and next day we reached Kulakmali, our base camp site, in 5 hours easy walking up an excellent and unmissable grazing path, with the "guide" lagging far behind. My impression of the Phargam people as porters remained very low throughout our trip.

We intended to go to the W side of Buni Zom, *via* the Khorabort glacier, as we had been told that this was the easy way. This information came from a hospitable shopkeeper on the Laspur-Mastuj road who described himself as a guide but, I suspect, had not been far up Buni Zom. His story, anyway, was contradicted by another guide who assured us that the Gordoghan glacier on the E side was the usual way, and only one party of Japanese had ever been up the Khorabort. Since we had had enough of porters for a while, we decided to pay them off at Kulakmali as planned, and stick to the W route.

From Kulakmali, at around 4000m, the route to the Khorabort glacier lay through a steep and rather continuous rock barrier. We spent a half day soloing on some very loose grey granite before I stumbled on a reasonable route – 3 pitches of about Alpine Grade IV up a small gully line leading to long moraine slopes and the upper glacier. In contrast to the other lines we had tried, the rock in this gully was excellent. The reason was brought home to us that afternoon, when rain forced an early abandonment of our carry and we had to descend through waterfalls.

---

71 *Ed.* The original article spelt this as *Katchakam* Pass but it seems the correct name is Kachikani Pass or Kachikani
An

Two more strenuous days saw us camped at 5025m by the glacier, with a week's food, minimal climbing gear and not quite enough fuel. Fortunately we found the remains of a Japanese camp littered with, of all things, firewood. It had been there for years and burned reluctantly, even with kerosene to encourage it, but it helped us to make our 5 Gaz cans last for the climbing.

At this point the bad weather which had been just a nuisance so far really hindered us. Day after day storm clouds came in from the W, visibility was poor, and there was a thunderstorm almost every afternoon. Not at all what I had expected, and led Joe to expect (sic). The Hindu Kush is supposed to have good weather.

Figure 66 Dick approaching the West face of Buni Zom (right)
Photo: Johan Reinhard

The weather did, however, give us time to evaluate Joe's new and very expensive tent. It was a tunnel type, with a silver-plated double skin, long tapering ends and a very sleek, streamlined appearance. It looked rather like one of those exotic 4-seater Italian sports cars, but without windows. It even had air intakes below the doors at each end, as if it were meant to travel very fast. Its maker had some unconventional ideas – it was the only tent I have ever seen with an impervious upper part and a permeable groundsheet. I sat in it watching the drips gather on the ceiling and wishing I had known more before leaving my old Vango down below. The theory was that you closed the doors and put your faith in a "chimney effect" from the air intakes at the bottom and little ventilators at the top. Unfortunately it did not work. It was days before I could persuade Joe to let me open the doors; it was nice to see the view too. In fairness, it was an excellent tent in other ways, and the hoop design was very roomy and very stable. The same manufacturer, believe it or not, also makes an impermeable, non-breathing, silver-plated sleeping bag, presumably for people born without sweat glands.

On a half-fine day we climbed Khorabort Zom (5850m), an easy snow-walk, and had our first good view of the W side of Buni Zom. The long, narrow and rocky W ridge descended straight towards us, ending in a steep buttress; it looked as though it would give a fine 2- or 3-day climb in settled weather, but at present it was plastered. To its N an easy slope led up to the col between the main peak and Buni Zom North, but the continuation to the main summit up a steep gendarmed ridge was uncertain. The alternative, on the S flank of the W ridge, was a steep couloir of snow, or possibly ice, which joined the ridge at about 6350m. We decided to try the route first, and the next day we carried our camp to 5480m in the northernmost branch or the Khorabort glacier.

After another day of poor weather but, fortunately, little new snow, we set out at 5am for the col. Dawn was fine, but as we ploughed up the deep snow it clouded in, and on the col we were in thick mist. The upper ridge was very narrow and corniced, the face on the far side very steep, and the snow like custard. After a few rope-lengths of waist-deep wallowing in visibility so poor that it was hard even to see which side of the ridge was corniced, we decided to give up, and floundered down. By good fortune the lower slope did not avalanche until the next day.

So, what to do? We had time for one more attempt. We really had no basis for giving up the N col route, and it was tempting to try again if the weather improved. On the other hand the upper section did not look easy. We eventually decided to give the S face route a try, even though we had not looked closely at it. We should have moved our camp round to the S side, but inertia prevailed until the snow was too soft, and I argued persuasively that we should save our energy and merely start an hour earlier in the morning. There would be a long return round the end of the W ridge – but then we might be able to traverse the mountain and come down by way of the N col.

That afternoon the weather cleared. At least the high cloud stopped moving over from the W, and we thought a real change had come. We set out at 3am under a starry sky, and hoped it would at least last through the day.

At dawn we were on a snow-ramp leading to the S face couloir, and finding reasonably good snow conditions. The sunrise was magnificent, but far too colourful for comfort. As we moved higher we could see a big mass of multi-coloured cloud to the SW with ominous dark streamers coming our way. We were making quite good progress, we thought, and hoped to be off the hill before anything too dramatic happened.

The couloir contained more snow and less ice than we had expected, but some of the snow was unstable and the angle was sufficient to encourage us to take rock belays when possible. Ten rope-lengths up the couloir seemed to go fairly quickly, ending in some very soft steep snow, and we reached the ridge at 11 o'clock.

Here we had expected to find a pleasant picnic spot, but the col, like the ridge above and below it, was rather narrow and exposed. The weather was still clear to the NW and we had a splendid view of the main Hindu Kush from Tirich Mir to Lunkho. One hour to the top, we thought, but somehow it took three. The snow-covered rock, and the final none-too-stable snow-ridge were both quite easy, but the altitude must have been affecting us and we were both very slow.

The summit was an airy spot – the junction of three corniced ridges. We could see our footsteps on the N ridge, but no easy way up past the rock gendarmes. We still suspected that there was an easy way somewhere on the E side, but we could not see it. Awi Zom, the second peak in the group, appeared fleetingly through the cloud, a fine steep rock pyramid.

A thunderstorm gathering on the Sohnyoan glacier peaks immediately to our S put paid to any ideas of traversing the mountain and we hurried down the way we knew. Before we reached the col it was snowing and the air was buzzing and crackling. I sat on a horribly exposed belay as Joe climbed the last pitch to the col, listening to my karabiner sing a song, and wishing I could hide under one of the very small rock outcrops.

Figure 67 Buni Zom
Photo: Dick Isherwood

It was 5.30pm and we were fairly tired. There was a doubtful bivouac site under a rock and I was in favour of stopping, but Joe persuaded me that we could get down – rightly, as it turned out. We kicked steps rapidly down the couloir, hammering ice axes in for a notional security, and trying to dodge the spindrift avalanches. The snow was softer but actually seemed more stable than on the ascent. We found our way off the snow-ramp in gathering darkness and wallowed down to the glacier through piles of new powdered snow. Here exhaustion hit us, and it was midnight before we made our way back, in mist and wet snow, to the other glacier and the tent. Two days later we were back in Phargam and on our way to the apricots of the lower valley and the Jeep road to Gilgit.

APPENDIX

I have subsequently traced 2 previous ascents of Buni Zom. The first, by Berry and Tyndale-Biscoe in 1957, climbed the N ridge, scene of our first attempt, from the Gordoghan glacier by traversing Buni Zom North *(NZAJ* 1959 283). The second, by a Japanese party, reached the S face from the Gordoghan side and took a line to the right of ours *(Iwa-To-Yuhi* No 48 1976). There have probably been other ascents.

A YEAR OFF WORK[72]

I hope and believe that one day it (Everest) will be climbed. Then when no higher 'altitude record' is possible, mountaineers can turn to the true enjoyment of the Himalaya, most likely to be found at about 20,000 feet or less.

Tom Longstaff, This My Voyage

Figure 68 Dick scrutinising Dorje Lakpa, Jugal Himal, showing the two camps on the West ridge
Photo: John Cleare (*Ed.* This was not included in the original *AJ* article)

---

72 Dick Isherwood, *AJ* 2010/11 pp 168-177

In mid 1979, after 10 years of varied work in several countries of the Far East I found myself at age 35, still single, unburdened by employment or other responsibilities, with a bit of money in the bank, and a desire to climb a few more Himalayan peaks before I got too old. Geoff Cohen had a sabbatical year coming up at Edinburgh University. Sabbaticals are meant for mind-enlarging study at other academic institutions but Geoff had just discovered that there was in fact no rule to that effect, and reckoned he could expand his mind in the mountains as well as anywhere.

When we met in Manchester I had a brand new copy of John Cleare's *Collins Guide to Mountains*, autographed by the man himself, with whom I had just led a Baltoro glacier trek. The cover had a photo which had got my attention. Dorje Lakpa is in the Jugal Himal, almost directly north of Kathmandu, and is one of the most striking mountains you see from the plane window as you fly in. It was reportedly unclimbed, apparently not too hard, and at 6966m about the right height for a small light party[73]. Tilman had been almost all the way around it in 1950, but he was there in the monsoon and never even saw it. The approach from the south went via Panch Pokhari, a pilgrimage site and occasional trekking destination, so we had a cover story in case anyone wanted to see our permit. With good luck we could cross the col Tilman had used and come home down the Langtang valley. It seemed the perfect objective for a discreet trip. Dave Broadhead and Anne Macintyre were taking a year off from teaching in Scotland so we had a team.

We met in the Kathmandu Guest House in early October, bought our food locally, including an enormous round cheese, arranged 15 porters through Mike Cheney, and caught the bus to Chautara, east of the Kathmandu valley and at the end of the road. The monsoon ended obligingly a day after we set out. The porters took us, over several days, to a group of summer grazing shelters at around 4500m, close to the moraines of the glacier descending from Dorje Lakpa, and right below where John had taken his cover photo [74]. Anne guarded the camp while Dave, Geoff and I looked for a way up the mountain.

We first explored up the main glacier but it was a mess of moraines and melting ice. The ablation valley on the left was much better, but we had to leave it where a side glacier came in, and descend some steep moraine. On the other side we re-ascended to a hollow with a pair of tridents by a pool – the holy men even got up here. We now had access to the branch glacier leading to the west ridge of Dorje Lakpa.

---

73 *Ed.* You will notice that on the caption to Figure 65 "the man himself" quotes a height of 6989m rather than 6966m. I raised this matter with John Cleare and he described his thinking.

"As you know lots of Himalayan heights, at least those of the smaller, un-famous peaks, are vague. I notice that several different heights are given for Dorje Lakpa by different sources on Google. I personally use the Japanese master Mountain Maps of the World, Himalaya volume, which gives a height of 6990m (I may have used other sources in the past to compose my captions – before I obtained this hugely useful tome).

The first party to attempt Dorje, back in the 1960s, was Japanese and doubtless they obtained a height for it – which was probably 6990m? Nevertheless, I'm always a trifle suspicious about 'rounded' heights – are they exact or are they 'to the nearest' ??? My rather old Indian mountaineering reference book gives 22,927 ft = 6988.15m however. This would have been, I think, the 'official' Survey of India height, while, dare I say it, Feet are more precise than Metres.

We should also bear in mind that after a heavy monsoon a height can likely change by a foot or two on certain configurations of summit... Since I was last there, a new map (Schneider-type 1:50,000) has been produced of the Langtang National Park area which MAY extend to Dorje Lakpa. There may even be a GPS height - ? I did once examine this expensive map in Stanfords and found major discrepancies depicting places I knew well. So the height label I have placed may not be as precise as it appears."

74 *Ed.* A different photo of the mountain by John Cleare is shown above on the previous page

We found a way through an area of crevasses and made a camp right below the ridge at around 6000m. After a bit of acclimatisation time we started up the ridge that was initially easy snow. We found an ancient fixed rope on terrain we were wandering up solo. It steepened and narrowed, and we made a dump on a high point, beyond which things got a bit more serious. A couple of days later we came back with all the gear and camped in a spectacular spot. There was barely enough room for the tent, and only then because we had piled rocks under one corner. We were sleeping three in a two-man tent – it was a bit cramped, but very cosy if you got the middle berth.

Figure 69 Dorje Lakpa (6966m) from the south
Photo: Dick Isherwood

The ridge now became corniced and rather steep on its flanks. We roped up for a while, then went back to soloing on the southern side, on excellent névé. There was an area of bare green ice which came rather close to the cornice at one point, but the corridor between was wide enough, and we found ourselves on a flat snow platform, below a large bergschrund, at just the right time to stop for the night. It was a perfect campsite as it got all the evening sun. Next morning we were off in the dark, leaving the tent, and Geoff led a steepish ice pitch above the 'schrund. I led us into some rather rickety snow – three dimensional lattices of icicles, very close to the cornice at times – and we reached a basin of deep soft snow, up which we ploughed slowly to the summit.

A layer of cloud had come in during the day, and we were at the very top of it. The sun was on us and we could look over the cloud layer, but it didn't clear enough for a view. As it was after 4pm we couldn't wait longer. We got back to the tent in the very last light. An extremely slow descent over the next two days took us back to the base camp.

Geoff and I climbed Bauddha (6151m) with some exciting soloing near the top. We got separated on a fluted snow face and chose separate flutes. As mine steepened

I wished I had a rope, but too late. Each little flute was hard ice on one side and loose powder on the other, and the layer of hard stuff was disturbingly thin. We reunited for one steep pitch to the summit and came down more conventionally.

We had done what we'd come for and the food was running out – even the cheese. We packed everything up and set out, with loads of 30kg or so, for the obvious col west of Bauddha. Just below the col we had to cross a gully in the snow down which some stones were falling. The plan was to choose a quiet moment, drop into the bed of the gully, and run across and up the other side. It wasn't very far but at 5800m with big packs it was easier to plan than to execute. Three of us made it safely but Anne got a blow on her upper arm from a brick-sized rock. We thought she might have broken a bone, but it was just badly bruised. The rest of us took her load and we continued over the col and down into the upper Langtang above Langsisa. We waded the Langtang Khola and finished our last scraps of food before descending to Kyangjin Gompa the next morning. The route we had taken has become widely known as Tilman's Col, but if you look at the original edition of *Nepal Himalaya* it's clear that Tilman crossed a different col, further east and right at the foot of the west ridge of Dorje Lakpa. He even has a photo of the tridents by the pool. The way we went was probably easier.

Figure 70 Dave Broadhead at the first ridge camp on Dorje Lakpa
Photo: Dick Isherwood

It was mid November and the weather was fine. Geoff and I thought we just had time to get another trip in before the winter snow came. We bought three weeks' food and set out with three of Mike Cheney's finest to carry it all, bound for the Rolwaling valley. We had some wonderful views of Gauri Shankar from the approach, and some exciting moments on the trail – in those days the main footpath to Beding used three bendy tree branches to negotiate a rock wall above the river. The boys got us up to a base camp above Nar and overlooking the Rolwaling lake, took their pay and scampered off. There were a few thin high clouds around.

We'd decided to try a peak called Tsoboje (6689m) which is right above the north side of the lake, by now very frozen. We had no idea whether it had been climbed but it had an attractive ridge dropping down from its eastern end toward the lake. We were camped in a tiny hollow right below this ridge and thought we were well set. Unfortunately it then snowed.

It snowed for two days and we dug the tent out more than once. Then it cleared, the sun came out, and – guess what next – it all started to thaw. I emerged in the morning sun, looked up and saw a huge icicle, dripping water, right over the tent. Time to move, fast. We dragged everything down the slope and found a safer place.

Off up the hill, through various rock bands, to another campsite on an area of scree before the real ridge. This was very steep on our side but we found a neat way out to the sharp ridge crest and round on the other side things looked a bit better. Geoff led one of the more impressive pitches in my memory, up a steep rock groove with very little protection, in double boots and with a 15kg sack. We ended the day in a reasonably good position, in a little saddle on the ridge with maybe 500m to go to the top.

We'd brought the inner tent as a bivi bag, and work was needed to make a ledge big enough for it. Unfortunately the snow we stood on rapidly gave way to ice as we dug. The ice was mixed with rock and I broke the pick of my axe. We dug on, but by the time we had a platform big enough to use there was light in the eastern sky. We got in anyway, and slept, after a fashion, still roped up.

It may have been the short night, but in the morning I was not feeling at all brave. There were lenticular clouds coming from the north-west, which is where the snow comes from in Nepal in the winter. Geoff wanted to finish the job but I am ashamed to say that I chickened out. He was very good about it but we missed a great opportunity, as we were almost certainly above all the difficulties and the weather in fact did nothing much for days.

We descended and camped above the lake. It was a calm night but suddenly the tent was rocked by a series of wind gusts. Then it all calmed down again and we slept well. When we got out in the morning we saw that a huge icefall had come down, within a hundred metres of the tent, and made a mighty hole in the ice on the lake, which was a couple of feet thick. There but for fortune... We attempted to cross the Tesi Lapcha, with rather large loads, but it snowed some more. Winter had come. We gave up and went to India, where we bought traditional single speed bicycles and toured Rajasthan – but that is another story.

Eventually, after a short trip to the Valley of Flowers See p.165, it was time to do some real climbing in the Karakoram. In early July we travelled by train from Delhi to Lahore, enduring a wait of four hours at the Wagha border while the Indian customs checked the baggage of travellers *leaving* India. In Rawalpindi we met Des Rubens who had just flown from the UK.

As usual the flights to Skardu, on little propeller planes which had to fly around Nanga Parbat, were chaotic. We kept showing up at the airport very early and got on a plane on only our third day. We had managed to hit the start of Ramadan, but it proved to be a bonus – double breakfasts for us on the plane as the Moslems weren't eating. Having no permits of any sort, we kept a low profile and got out of town as fast as possible in a rented jeep to Khapalu, and the roadhead below Hushe.

We had various loose ideas for climbing. One was an attempt on Masherbrum by the original southern route, but when we saw it from the Hushe valley we thought it was a bit big for us.

It seemed a better idea to go up the Charakusa Glacier, to the east. With five porters we headed up the valley, past flowering roses and small cypress trees – this bit of the Karakoram is quite well vegetated. The trail led to summer grazing settlements to which people were just beginning to bring their cattle. Beyond, big lateral moraines flanked the glacier and granite walls appeared out of the mist – the weather was not great. We paid off the porters, with the usual difficulties, and were glad to be alone in great scenery. The whole valley was one of the most beautiful I have ever seen. We camped among yellow poppies and looked at the enormous and very steep north face of K6. This was obviously too much for us, though it was fun sketching theoretical lines up it. More realistic was a peak on the north side, 21,700 feet on our map, and apparently close to K7, which we had difficulty identifying.

A side glacier led up to a face on Pt 21,700 which didn't look too steep, at least from well below, so we decided to give it a try. We put a camp in a snow basin at around 5000m and plotted a route up a series of snowfields and rock bands. It didn't look hard at all, but we got a series of shocks. The granite here is very monolithic, with few cracks, and the rock steps were deceptively steep and uncompromising. We found ourselves repeatedly climbing runnels of ice between big bald chunks of rock. Geoff did some impressive leads on the first day that took us to a tiny snow ledge, just big enough for the Vango tent.

We had gained about 700m and decided to leave the tent here, as there was unlikely to be a place for it any higher up. Des was feeling the altitude, having just come out from the UK, and this may be why he left his sleeping bag in the tent the next morning. Not a great idea.

Figure 71 K7 West, showing the high point reached
Photo: Dick Isherwood

On the second day we took ages to climb the next (fourth) rock band, first up a very steep chimney full of ice, then a traverse across some steep ice with bits of rock sticking out of it – almost a hand traverse. We got out onto a steep snowfield which led to a notch in the west ridge of the mountain, but by now Des was very slow – falling asleep on the stances – and the weather was not looking good at all. Geoff found a ledge on the rocky ridge crest just big enough for three to sit on. The view down to the Kaberi glacier on the other side was enough to give me nightmares.

Figure 72 Des Rubens on Drifika, Karakoram
Photo: Dick Isherwood

We organised ourselves in the twilight and were lucky to drop no more than Des's mug. We put him in the middle, since he had no sleeping bag, and huddled together. The boots got passed to me at one end and I hung them all by their laces from a big chock placed in a crack – at least I thought I did. We had a surprisingly warm night though it was all a bit cramped. In the morning I carefully passed the boots back and discovered that I'd failed to clip in one of Des's – it had spent the night merely wedged between two others. I didn't dare confess to this and sat in silence as Geoff said speculatively:

'I wonder what would happen if you dropped your boots from here?'

Des replied:

'I doubt if you'd get down.'

I spent the rest of the climb wondering just what we would have done.

Above here it was steep – like overhanging – for the next 20m or so. Geoff tried manfully to climb it directly, then we decided to traverse around the steep bit. We went down and across for a couple of rope lengths, then back up left in some icy cracks and onto a rock ramp. Seven hours of effort saw us 30m directly above our bivouac. It might have been quicker just to peg up the overhang, even at this height.

At this point Des very nobly decided to opt out. He was still going very slowly, so he abseiled down directly back to the bivvi ledge. We let him take one of the two sleeping bags and the stove and pot. Geoff and I continued, initially up straightforward snow, but then onto rather hard green ice with a cover of loose powder. By the time it eased off again, below a sérac wall, it was sunset – the clearest evening we'd had so far – and I had trouble dividing my attention between the climbing and the tremendous views – north to K2 and the other Baltoro peaks, east to the Golden and Silver Thrones, and west to the huge mass of Masherbrum.

We found a snow hollow under the séracs and shared the one sleeping bag and one Karrimat. Supper without a stove didn't take long. Above us was a huge hanging disc of ice which might have wiped us out if it had decided to fall, but we were too tired to care. Amazingly I slept fairly well. We knew we were close to the top, but in the morning it was snowing and we could see very little. I led a pitch up the ridge above and was surprised when the mountain hit me in the face – the visibility was so poor I couldn't see that it had suddenly steepened. Time to reconsider. It was extremely frustrating, as through gaps in the cloud I glimpsed the edge of a big snowfield, crevassed but basically easy, that seemed to lead to the summit. However with no stove or food, and only one sleeping bag we couldn't wait it out, so we went down.

We picked up Des and descended very slowly to the tent, doing some impressive abseils over the rock bands. Our uneaten shrimp curry from three days ago tasted great, even with bits of ice in it. The descent the next day should have been efficient but somehow wasn't. The rope got stuck after one big steep abseil and Geoff did some desperate rock climbing back up a very steep groove to free it. On the next abseil it happened again and Geoff was again the hero – both Des and I were far too shattered for this. Somehow I had lost both front points off one of my crampons by now. We shambled down across the bergschrund and into the lower gully, which we got out of just ahead of a large avalanche.

We had been five days on this climb and we were all very tired. I had slightly numb and tingling fingers and toes, and lay in the grass feeling as if I was in a shell. My body didn't want to do anything but my mind was very active, thinking of all the things I could do in the future provided I continued to survive experiences like this.

Figure 73 Geoff Cohen on K7 West
Photo: Dick Isherwood

We went down to our dump for more food, taking two days over what should have been a four-hour round-trip, and then considered our options. We really had to get to the top of something. The only peak of respectable height in this valley system which looked any easier than the one we had just failed on was marked on our map as 21,150 feet. It was a sharp pyramid, looking a bit like the Obergabelhorn, and was up the southern branch of the glacier, to the south-west of K6. After a couple more days' rest we set out, working through a messy icefall, and taking two days to a camp at around 5700m below the north-west ridge of the peak. We found we were following a trail of Japanese debris – someone had been here before. They had left the label from a quart of Suntory whisky, but no sign of the contents. From this camp we could look back at Pt 21,700 and realise just how close we had been to the top.

Figure 74 Geoff Cohen on the south-east ridge of Tsoboje, Rolwaling, Nepal
Photo: Dick Isherwood

Next morning was fine and clear, and we soon reached a col on the west ridge, from which we had a magnificent view of a large part of the Karakoram. Good snow continued to within 300m of the top, then it got steep. We climbed a rock chimney, initially trying to ignore bits of Japanese fixed rope but eventually using them. Des led a very scary pitch across steep rock slabs with a thin and fragile ice cover, and we reached a narrow and very corniced summit ridge. It was almost horizontal but of course the real summit was at the far end. Sections of fixed rope peeked out of the snow and we clipped our rope into them, having no idea what they were attached to.

Somehow it was 5pm when we got to the top. We had probably the best long distance mountain view I have ever had – most of the Pakistan Karakoram, dominated by K2, Chogolisa and Masherbrum, a huge extent of the Indian Karakoram, and some very steep granite pillars closer to hand, south of K6. We could see Nanga Parbat to the west and distant peaks in Sinkiang beyond K2. We took a few photos and wondered what to do as we were clearly not going to get down to our camp. I must have been very tired as I wanted to dig a deep snow hole right there on the summit ridge, but I was rightly overruled. We began abseiling down, rather diagonally. I was last off the ridge and I eyeballed the piece of line looped around a granite spike sticking out of the snow, willing both of them not to fail. Crossing the rock slabs was very skittery, especially with front points on only one crampon.

Then it got dark. We had very limited head-torch batteries and Geoff proposed that only the first man down should use his – the other two could just follow the rope down in the dark. This worked for a bit, then all the torches failed when we were still on steep ground. We cut three modest thrones in the ice, belayed to bits of rock and an ice peg, and made the best of it. We had very little bivouac gear and it was too exposed to take off your boots or anything, so we all had a miserable night. We had only one more serious diagonal abseil to do in the morning, for which Geoff again pulled out amazing reserves of energy. By 11am we were asleep in the tent.

This peak now goes by the name of Drifika (6447m). We probably did the second ascent and by now it has had several more. Pt 21,700, now known as K7 West (6858m), had its first ascent by Steve House and party, taking a different route, only in 2007.

It was a very memorable year. I can hardly believe it was 30 years ago. We may have gone a bit over 20,000 feet, but I think we were doing very much what Tom Longstaff had in mind.

A FORTNIGHT IN GARHWAL[75]

Geoff Cohen

Not long ago my good friend Dick Isherwood described in the *Alpine Journal*[76] some climbs we did together in the Himalaya in 1980. However he omitted to mention what I thought had been possibly the most successful of our campaigns. When I asked him why, he said that as they were not new routes he didn't think they were worth describing. Now very sadly, at too young an age, Dick has gone off to climb in another world. I cannot write as engagingly and wittily as he always did, but in remembrance of a good friend here is a short account of a memorable two weeks.

We met up in Joshimath on 21 June. Dick immediately constructed a shopping list and in the evening we went to the bazaar and purchased a generous quantity of fresh vegetables – cabbages, peppers, aubergines, tomatoes, cucumbers, onions, and of course garlic which Dick loved inordinately (he once used a surplus of several pounds of garlic to make a garlic soup!). This was supplemented by rice plus tins of butter, cheese, tuna, bacon rashers, chicken curry and a 'mystery' tin. Next morning Dick persuaded two Nepali porters to come with us to the Valley of Flowers at the princely rate of Rs 20/- per day. At that time, and possibly still, there was such poverty in western Nepal that there were always Nepalis available for work on the Indian side of the border. Our lads were sent off to get themselves shoes and blankets while we bought bus tickets for the hour's ride down to Govind Ghat, where the trek to the Sikh holy temple at Hem Kund starts. After a wet night at Ghangria we walked through the Valley of Flowers, where Dick the naturalist identified for me the beautiful yellow lilies and violets, blue cranesbill, purple pea, dwarf orchids, primulas, red, orange and yellow potentillas and many others. Base camp (one two-man Vango tent) was set up at about 13,000 feet at the far end of the Valley and our two brave lads sent back to warmer nights below.

After a day's reconnaissance we set off to attempt the north-west face of Rataban, the most accessible and reasonable objective given our limited time. Our spare food was stashed in a small cave. We took with us two ropes, three ice screws and a few small wires. As afternoon wore on we found ourselves floundering in thick mist on a glacier shelf at about 16,000 feet listening to the sounds of avalanches coming off the crags above us. We reckoned we could camp far enough from the cliffs to be fairly safe and hope for better visibility in the morning. As it turned out the weather remained poor but we managed next day to weave around a variety of crevasses and ice cliffs to reach the col below Rataban, where in cold, wet and windy weather we got the tent up and crawled inside. Later in the afternoon Dick went outside and watched avalanches coming off the slopes of Rataban, one of which crossed our tracks and would have obliterated us. The following day was foul too and my memory is of snuggling down all day with our books – Dick read the recently published 'Snow Leopard' by Peter Mathiessen and I had a Hindi grammar book; luckily he was very tolerant of me muttering my exercises.

On the 28th June the sun began to emerge, so we climbed a short way to a snowy bump north-west of the col, enjoying tremendous views of Chaukhamba, Nilkantha, Mana, Kamet and nearby Nilgiri Parbat; we allowed this day for some of the fresh

75 By Geoff Cohen - submitted for inclusion in *HJ* 2014
76 *AJ* 2010/11 A Year of Work pp 168-177 (see p. 155 above)

Figure 75 Dick resting below the NW face of Rataban
Photo: Geoff Cohen

snow to clear. Though it snowed again in the night and was cloudy at 5 am next morning, after discussion we decided to attempt the peak in spite of the ominous weather. We were away by 7 am, crossing avalanche debris to reach a spur on the right of the north-west face. A little way up this we found a fixed rope; although apparently in quite good condition much of it was buried in snow and thus not very useful. We climbed eight pitches of mixed ground at about Scottish grade III, during which the cloud thinned and some patches of blue sky appeared. Either side of our spur the ground plunged down in steep mixed faces of impressive depth. At noon we reached a place a few hundred feet above the last rocks, where it seemed safe to unrope. Above us was a snow ridge at an angle that did not seem too challenging, so we left our sacks and just took one rope and a bite to eat. Dick stormed off up the snow at a terrific pace and I panted along in his steps. An hour and a half later, after passing a few icy steepenings, we rested in the cloud on top with nothing to view. Dick announced with satisfaction that it was his tenth 20,000 foot peak, but after waiting in vain for a clearing we started down. For a couple of hours on the descent the weather deteriorated to a cold, wet afternoon, but the evening brought another clearing. Abseils were slow – we had only one sticht plate between us, as Dick had not yet acquired such up-to-date technology, so he hauled mine up for each abseil! But by dint of down-climbing where we could, we got back to camp by 7.30 pm.

Figure 76 Dick on the NW face of Rataban
Photo: Geoff Cohen

Figure 77 Dick below the NW face of Nilgiri Parbat
Photo: Geoff Cohen

We were lucky and got a reasonably fine day with only thin cloud around the tops. As usual, Dick led nearly the whole way making steps in the snow with inexhaustible energy. Here and there we tried to move fast where there was some risk of serac fall, and we needed a little bit of traversing to get around some ice cliffs; otherwise there were no serious obstacles and we only needed to rope up for about three pitches. On the way up we had excellent views north towards Mana and Kamet and, much nearer, the elegant Mandir Parbat, but from the summit views were limited by cloud.

We were back in our tent after only ten hours, a fairly short summit day by Himalayan standards, feeling mighty pleased to have got this peak in only four days after Rataban

On 4th July we descended the Khulagarvia glacier, climbed back up to the col and back down to the Valley of Flowers. On this last descent my legs began to feel so weak that I couldn't trust them to support me, doubtless the consequence of the last few strenuous days, and when I tried to run down the last few hundred feet above base camp they crumpled completely. Dick however remained strong enough to climb back up to our stash and retrieve pack frames, walking shoes, and cooking pots. We descended next morning with 60 pound packs as far as Ghangria, where we managed to negotiate a horse and man to take our loads back down to the road. We just made the last bus and reached Joshimath in a torrential downpour, where we gorged on coffees, samosas, and burfi.

Figure 78 Dick moving round some ice cliffs on Nilgiri Parbat
Photo: Geoff Cohen

There are many styles of Himalayan climbing. Nowadays, with the growth of commercial agencies that do the local organisation, many expeditions have extensive support even for quite straightforward peaks around the 6000m mark. Looking back at this short trip, it was satisfying to have climbed two quite easy but respectable 6000m peaks from different valleys in a fortnight, with little bandobast or expense and only a day and a half of support from two porters. Success was only feasible because our peaks were fairly accessible and thanks to Dick's huge energies. The Himalaya being so vast one hopes there will always be opportunities for small parties to be nimble and climb 'under the radar'.

OF JIMMY AND THE TCHADOR[77]

At Christmas 1998 I got an e-mail from Leo Murray in Hong Kong – "Hey, come on this unique trip – the Zanskar ice trek – walking on the frozen river."
He added a few more details – the plan was to walk up the Zanskar river gorge from a roadhead near Leh to Padam and back, taking around a week each way. It did sound very good, and Zanskar and Ladakh were both high on my list of places still to see. Unfortunately I had a job, and my 1999 holiday allowance was already spoken for. I held off replying and, by great good luck, within a month an early retirement offer had landed in my lap. I grabbed it with both hands and got on the e-mail. Don't, as they say, leave it too late.

Leo had done lots of homework on Zanskar, including telephoning several people who had travelled the Zanskar gorge in winter before. Excerpts from his transcriptions flew over the Internet:

'It was very cold.'

'Sorel boots are the thing – good and warm.'

'Jimmy is the key guy in Zanskar. He is basically a good man but a bit sharp.'

'Jimmy says no one has ever fallen in the river and drowned.'

'Jimmy is the Congress Party representative in Zanskar.'

'We only had to wade in the river once. The porters carried the ladies.'

(This from a Royal Marine officer.)

'Sleeping in tents cuts you off from the porters and their culture. It's better to sleep in the caves.'

'I got pneumonia twice in the same cave.'

We had engaged Jimmy and brought lots of antibiotics, so we figured we were well prepared. We had also bought Sorel boots which are made in Canada in various models. The pair I bought were extremely warm and seemed designed for the great Canadian male-bonding ritual of ice fishing rather than for climbing or even trekking. I brought along a half-gallon of very cheap whisky to make them feel at home.

Five of us gathered in Delhi early in February. Leo and I had been to West Irian together in 1972 and realised to our joint surprise that this was our first trip together, apart from occasional day hikes, since then. Terence Lam I knew from rock climbing in Hong Kong long ago – he had since become a solo round-the-world sailor. Mike Whelan and Steve Hale were friends of Leo and helicopter pilots in Hong Kong; it was their first time in the Himalaya. After a fairly disorganised scene at Delhi airport in the early morning darkness, we got ourselves onto a flight to Leh and were treated to fine distant views of Nanda Devi on the way.

Leh is very quiet in February, with few tourists and many of the lodges and restaurants closed. Military helicopters buzzed overhead, to and from the Nubra Valley and the areas of confrontation with Pakistan. The irrigation ditches on the edges of the fields contained old hard ice. We stayed in a fine small guest house at the upper end of town, recommended for its homemade central heating system. Hot water was piped to radiators made of two steel sheets half an inch apart, welded together around the rims. The noises were a bit disconcerting but it worked, if anything, too well. The owner claimed to have the only e-mail connection in Ladakh – we went to his house and stepped carefully around his small son, sleeping on the floor, to type our messages home. It worked too. From the windows we had a fine view across the Indus valley to the peak of Stok Kangri and I recalled Ashley Greenwood telling me that he and his wife had climbed it at the age of eighty – now there's a long-term objective for the ageing mountaineer to shoot for.

After a day of monastery tours – not to be missed in Ladakh – we were ready. Jimmy and his men had walked in from Padam along the river so we knew the ice must be OK. A three-hour bumpy bus ride took us to the roadhead, passing the confluence of the Indus and the Zanskar rivers *en route*. To my surprise the Zanskar was twice the size of the Indus, and both were clear blue-green. The Zanskar river was conspicuously not frozen here, but became intermittently so as we went up the lower part of the gorge to the roadhead.

First stop was lunch. I sat by a dirty road construction camp and watched a very small boy fetch water from the stream. He had shoes at least five sizes too big and a water-can almost as large as he was. He was further handicapped by having to use one hand to hold his pants up all the time. He hadn't washed for a while but he had a hell of a smile. It took me back a number of years, and I realised how much of life I was missing by no longer living in the Indian subcontinent.

We set out onto the Tchador – a Zanskari word, I believe, meaning sheet, or veil. It is still an important part of the scheme of things in Zanskar, as the road into Padam from Kargil is only open for about four months of the year, and the Tchador is half the length of the other walking routes over the passes. The ice in the gorge is sufficiently solid for travel for two to three months, typically January to March, and it is well used.

We had with us a young lady with a very engaging smile who didn't seem to be carrying a load. I asked Jimmy who she was.

"She is Oracle. Coming to Leh for three months' training under a high lama. Now returning to Zanskar."

Starting out onto the rather glassy smooth ice, I thought she was probably a good person to follow. Unfortunately, within fifty yards, Little Miss Oracle was sprawled on her bottom, giggling uncontrollably as the shutters clicked. Clearly she needed further training. I resolved to stay very close to Jimmy and tread only where he trod until I had got the measure of this place.

We all found the ice a bit skittery at first. Terence started out in alpine boots and set the record with 35 falls on day one. The softer Sorel boots were much better as they seemed to mould to the contours of the ice. The porters, of course, did fine in either traditional felt-soled Zanskari boots or Indian Army plastic wellies.

The ice soon turned into shelves on either side of the river. Slushy bits floated down the fast-flowing water in the middle, to disappear under the next closed section. It didn't require much imagination to realise what would happen if you fell in.

The shelves got narrower, till it was not obvious how to progress, especially if you were carrying someone's kitbag mounted sideways on your pack frame. Jimmy now came to the fore, clad in a long woollen coat and carrying a large white stick which made me think of him as a Tolkien wizard. He did various manoeuvres using a half stable ice flow, before deciding that the time had come for a bit of rock scrambling – the first of several. The rock proved to be quite good where it wasn't covered in scree.

At times we were a couple of hundred feet above the river, but the only hazard was kicking rocks onto one another.

Figure 79 A promising icefall in the Zanskar Gorge.
Photo: Richard Isherwood

I should say, for the record, that Jimmy lived up to every reasonable expectation we had of him. He is a very sophisticated and capable person, excellent company, and definitely a good guy to go with, on this trip at least, and probably to most places in Zanskar.

Next landmark was the junction of the Zanskar and Chang Chu rivers where we were to experience our first cave. Unfortunately a German trekking group was in occupation. Eyes turned to Jimmy whom we assumed, in addition to his other offices, to be lord of the caves in these parts. For once he had no quick fix for the situation, and we headed on into the gathering darkness, on and off the ice and up and down the moraines and small cliffs. Two hours upstream we did find another cave, but a very small one, good for the kitchen but not much else. We bivvied on a sandbank; it did get very cold when you stopped, and we learned to put duvets on quickly.

For the next two days the gorge scenery was superb – huge walls of rock folded to an amazing degree. The ice varied from full cover to narrow shelves, up to three or four feet thick in places, not always flat, and from rough to very smooth indeed. We all learned to adopt the Zanskari shuffle, scarcely lifting our feet on the smooth bits. At one rest stop we watched a big male ibex pick his way along the opposite wall of the gorge, 200 feet above us. Dippers swam in the water – one wondered what they found to eat. Jimmy had us looking through the ice for fish, without success.

Temperatures went down to around minus 18°C, not as low as we had been told to expect. Out of the sun, though, it rarely rose above freezing.

At the end of our second day the ice became very narrow, to the point where we had to crawl under a rock bulge, pushing packs ahead of us. We could see the night's designated cave a quarter mile ahead, but the next stretch of river ice was covered by two feet of water – totally unexpected as it had been dry when the porters came from Padam a week earlier. We stayed off it, by climbing over a rock buttress, and again had to make do with a very tiny cave.

We met traders carrying grain into Zanskar from Leh, and another group dragging timbers along the ice for a new school in Lingshed. There was an interesting two-way traffic in lumber, with the trimmed wood, presumably supplied by a government agency, coming downstream from the summer roadhead in Zanskar, while untrimmed poplar trunks from the side valleys were being carried the other way by private enterprise. I saw a pair of golden eagles in a side gorge while Steve, with the sharp eyes of a former military pilot, established himself as chief ibex spotter – he would see them with the naked eye on slopes I had scanned unsuccessfully through binoculars.

There was great excitement on the fourth morning as the porters found a recently dead ibex. The word was that it had just been killed by a snow leopard which had run away at our approach – of course no one saw it. The meat seemed fresh enough, at least when curried, and the head was a great trophy for the first man at the scene. He carried it by one horn, even in spots where I preferred to have two hands on the rock.

By the end of day four we were in the open Zanskar valley, its northfacing slopes under a few inches of snow. In the village of Zangla we stayed in the King's house – by far the biggest in town. His Majesty was not around but we made ourselves at home. I was watching the dinner preparation when an old lady came in to pick up some firewood. She was introduced by the cook as 'King's wife'.

'So is she the Queen of Zanskar?' This seemed unlikely. 'No, she is King's wife.'

'How many wives does the King have?'

'Only one.'

'Where does the King live?'

'King lives in Padam when he is not in Delhi.'

We left the mystery at this point.

It was a sunny afternoon and we attracted a crowd on the King's flat roof. Leo had photos from his last visit in 1981, and someone in the crowd recognised his father in one of them. We taught the kids three-legged races until the royal ceilings began to show strain.

Jimmy pointed out an alternative route home, via the Chang Chu and the Markha valley, over two 5000m passes – another route which is only followed in winter and late autumn when the rivers are frozen, as otherwise it involves something over a hundred river crossings. I was strongly in favour of this, to add variety and get us out of the valley bottom, but time did not permit.

From here it was a very gentle walk up the valley to Padam. We visited the striking monastery of Tongde, perched on the mountainside above its village, and had magnificent views of the back, as it were, of the Kishtwar peaks over the watershed to the south. I saw a fox running across the main trail.

Figure 80 The gompa at Tongde, Zanskar
Photo: Richard Isherwood

Padam at this time of year was very quiet and half closed down – the trekking and rafting operators had gone down to Srinagar or somewhere. The few motor vehicles we saw were all winterised and under tarpaulins, though there was (*sic*) only a couple of inches of snow on the ground.

We returned down the north side of the valley, via the large village of Karsha and another superbly situated monastery. Small boys skied in the street on lengths of split plastic water pipe with wire bindings. There was even a game of cricket going on, with a rag ball.

The return was uneventful, though it was warming up and the ice was getting a bit soft in places. I went through it once, fortunately onto rocks and not into deep water, so Jimmy's record remains intact. It was 20 February when we returned to Leh, and the consensus was that the Tchador had another two weeks at most to go.

I recommend the trip. Mandip Singh Soin, an AC member, runs Ibex Expeditions in Delhi, and made all our arrangements. He can be found at *www.ibexExpeditions.com* Alternatively, you could do it on your own with a good sleeping bag and a few Mars bars. Be quick, though, as the forces of progress are planning to extend the road through the whole gorge.

Figure 81 A monk at Tongde with a heavily decorated conch shell
Photo: Richard Isherwood

POKHARKAN SOUTH FACE, NEPAL[78]

Dave Wynne-Jones

*H*ey, *bhaje!'*
Kaji, our sirdar and the fastest man up Everest, was waving to us from up ahead. We'd arrived at base camp, and by now we were all hailed as *bhajes* or grandads. I knew I'd just turned 50 but what was I getting myself into? I suppose Dick Isherwood was responsible for starting it. With a full white beard, he bears more than a passing resemblance to Father Christmas, especially with his red woolly hat on. Speaking Nepali, he quickly recognized the joke and was quite able to hold his own in repartee with the Sherpas, but that just gave the whole thing currency. In fairness, his wasn't the only white or grey head amongst the team; at least two admitted they actually were granddads. It was just that some of the team were of an age where grandfatherhood hadn't occurred to them, never mind the female contingent who also seemed to have become honorary *bhajes*. In a funny way it was a term of respect, perhaps affection, and reflected the care the support team took of us. Of such things are relationships made.

We were in the Damodar Himal, just north of Phugaon, moving up to find a base camp. What had begun with Steve Town suggesting to a bunch of AC veterans that they might like to do a trekking peak or two had developed into a fully-fledged expedition after the Nepalese authorities released 103 new peaks from the restricted list. The complication was the Maoist insurrection, which deterred at least two potential members of the team. David Baldock had kept a record of reported 'incidents', mapping them to ascertain 'safe' areas. Ultimately he gave the thumbs up after NMA advice recommended Pokharkan (6350m), lying north of the Annapurnas and west of Manaslu.

Numerous teams had explored the Peri Himal, which lies to the east and includes Himlung, Gjanj Kang and Kang Guru. Similarly the Chulu trekking peaks to the south are frequently climbed, but research showed that very little had been climbed in the Damodar. Apart from Pokharkan there were at least five other unclimbed peaks including Amotsang, Jomsang, Chhib and Saribung, all around 6300m. Of course, Tilman had done some exploration hereabouts in 1950, attempting to circumnavigate the Damodar. He was forced to retreat and eventually made his way west via the Pukhung to the Kali Gandaki. Our best efforts turned up neither photographs nor anyone who had visited the area since. Still, with a couple of centuries climbing experience between us why should we worry?

The approach to the Damodar follows the Annapurna circuit from the Besisahar roadhead as far as Koto. There we had some bad news. A descending Sherpa told us that he had climbed Pokharkan from the north two weeks earlier with a lone Japanese client even older than most of us. Subsequently some doubt has been expressed as to whether the highest of the three summits was climbed, but in any case the report of waist-deep snow-plodding decided us to attempt the peak from the south.

---

78 Dave Wynne-Jones, *AJ* 2004 pp 24-28
Ed. Although this article describes the same mountain as that in the following account, it deals in greater detail with the mountaineering aspects.

The Naur gorge, north of Koto, turned out to be less formidable than a French expedition report had suggested, with new bridges erected and gallery paths quarried into the sheer sides of the gorge. Once off the tea house trail, villages were deserted. Thus far, John Fairley had been a focus of attention whenever he sat down to sketch with his watercolours. Children jostled to look over his shoulder as he worked and he would delight them by going through sketchbooks in a very grandfatherly manner. Now he mostly sketched alone.

After three days we reached the village of Phugaon, passing through a landscape of soaring rock walls, ruined forts and gompas, stupas, chortens and mani walls, whilst high above shone the cold peaks. Phugaon itself was busy enough, but there were abandoned buildings and fields on the periphery. At a temple complex on the ridge of a moraine hill opposite, the gompa was locked and empty. From camp in Phugaon's dusty fields we spent a day reconnoitring Pokharkan which proved to be a much more complex mountain than maps had suggested.

Figure 82 Dick with the friendly old Nepali yak herder
Photo: Dave Wynne Jones[79]

My first foray to 5200m took me to a pass west of Phugaon crossed by Tilman. But although there was a little lake just below the crest which could provide a good campsite, the ridge to the north, falling from Pokharkan, was barred by cliffs. The vast screes beneath them did nothing to inspire confidence in their solidity. Those who had gone east returned with better news, and the evidence of John's sketches and David's digital camera screen. There seemed to be a moraine ridge that would give access to a deep col on the south ridge, enabling a traverse onto the east face.

---

79 *Ed*. This photo was not in the original article but according to DWJ, for Dick the old man "was the real thing"

This looked to have a feasible snow and ice route winding up around sérac barriers towards a summit – perhaps *the* summit.

On the way to establish base camp at 4800m below this face, we set up an overnight camp below an apparently deserted village. Dick and I were walking up to enjoy the last of the sunshine when we encountered a lone yak herder, muffled against the cold (*see Figure 79*). With a face the colour and texture of old leather, he seemed tough as old boots and of equally indeterminate age. Dick chatted away to him in Nepali, but we declined an offer to share potatoes at his home since there was a meal waiting for us at camp. Sadly, at base camp, illness and the bitter cold meant that we lost Steve and David who decided to head for lower, warmer trekking. And then there were eight.

The rock and moraine ridge to the south did indeed prove to be the key to gaining the deep col, where advanced base camp was established. On that first trip to ABC, Toto Gronlund and I climbed the easy north ridge of the peak to the south of the col. It began as an attempt to confirm the feasibility of traversing from the colon to the east face, but by the time we had a clear view, the subsidiary summit was barely half-an-hour away.

On top, cloud lowered and obscured the view, but not before we had realized that Pokharkan had not one south ridge but two. A south-west ridge, long with rocky steps in it, led down to Tilman's pass, but a huge glacier bay separated that from a south-east ridge, terminating in the summit we had climbed. We promptly christened it Pokharkan South-East (5700m). The east face route would go, but the weather was worrying. Snowflakes drifted past throughout our descent and by morning base camp lay under six inches of snow, putting paid to any further load-carrying to ABC for a day. After much dossing around, we turned out for tea to find the cook team had built a snow stupa just outside the mess tent.

Next morning most of us helped break trail up to the ridge so that another carry could be made to ABC, but cloud and cold deterred us from any further efforts. The following day's fine weather was encouragement enough to pack up for a summit push from ABC before the winter snows arrived in earnest.

While the team settled into ABC, our sirdar, Kaji, and two other Sherpas went on to scout the huge glacier bay between the south-west and south-east ridges. They returned bubbling with enthusiasm for an attempt on the south face. There was some very grandfatherly humming and chewing of beards before we decided to go for it. Keeping the east face in reserve, we decided to place another camp at 5600m in the glacier bay and try the south face first.

Cold and illness was taking its toll. Pete and Sara Spillet had been forced to descend to base camp feeling distinctly unwell, leaving only six of the original 10 members of the expedition dug in at high camp for the summit attempt. Next morning, as I left high camp in the biting before-dawn air, I called 'See you' to John and Dick, but when John caught up at the crampons stop he was alone. Dick had succumbed to a chest infection that had long troubled him and wisely decided to descend.

The route first climbed a glacier ramp rightwards from the lower left edge of the face, where it abutted the buttresses of the south-west ridge. The ramp steepened to reach a shelf with serac barriers above. Climbing up through the seracs at about 5900m, I found Kaji backing off an ice cliff that barred the way. I borrowed his ice hammer and Kaji belayed while I led a 10m pitch of steep ice that proved to be the crux of the route. Ngima Sherpa took the route on into a huge crevasse, bridged with debris, up a second easier-angled ice cliff, breached by a crack just wide enough for some nice crampon bridging moves and out on to another glacier ramp. This led rightwards again in a long rising traverse, steep in places, to reach the south-east ridge at about its mid point.

The only drama was when Bill Thurston went through into a crevasse, managing with *bhaje* tenacity to hold himself on the brink while Kaji got a rope to him. Buffeted by strong winds on the narrow south-east ridge the situation suddenly seemed more serious. Ngima's glove was snatched away and he headed down for shelter until the ever-resourceful John dug a spare out of his rucksack. The nearer summit was just a totter away, but I had a nasty suspicion it was lower than another about a kilometre further across a windswept saddle. There was only one way to be sure. I climbed the ridge. The summit of what we christened Pokharkan 2 was definitely lower at 6250m. There was nothing for it but to go on.

Figure 83 Kaji and Martin Scott on the summit of Pokharkan (6350m), Nepal.
Photo: Dave Wynne-Jones

I broke trail across the saddle while the rest of the team ascended Pokharkan 2. From a scrape of shelter at the base of the summit ridge I could see the others descending. It suddenly seemed a very lonely place until Kaji and Martin Scott began following my trail across the saddle. 'They've had enough,' Martin said when he arrived. The three of us swung out into the wind, bending to the slope of the final summit ridge. Even Kaji was gasping at times and there was no way he was a *bhaje*. Heads down against the wind, with crampons biting into ice or crunching snow, it was almost a surprise when the angle eased. Looking up I found myself surrounded by a fantastic panorama of snowy peaks. There was another, slightly lower, snow peak just to the north, but we were there, on the summit. To the south-west the view was dominated by the Annapurna range, dazzling in the sun, while to the north shining peaks stretched way into Tibet.

After some unreserved handshaking, backslapping and photography, we turned to the descent. By ploughing straight across the saddle we could traverse beneath

Pokharkan 2 and meet the line of ascent lower down the ridge. Retracing our steps all the way back to high camp took just two hours now we were no longer fighting altitude, but this was 17 November and the light was fading. Another night at our high camp was inevitable. Next day we descended to ABC for a large late breakfast, before continuing to base camp where consensus graded the route at AD+, reflecting the ice pitch and objective dangers.

Figure 84 Descending through ice cliffs following the first ascent of Pokharkan's south face.
Photo: Dave Wynne-Jones

We had intended to carry out a reconnaissance of other peaks in the area, but our disabilities had mounted with Martin's frostbitten toe, and the cold was getting into our old bones. We retreated to Phugaon where John could sketch the children and sing folksongs to them while their faces registered complete incomprehension. Finally came news that our planned exit via the Kang La, a high pass leading to Manang, was impassable owing to snowfall. Concerned that there might be further heavy snow, we retraced our steps to Koto where the tea house did us proud with a bonfire and pitchers of chang. Climbers, Sherpas, cook team and porters danced in a very *un-bhaje* way, in the moonlight under fluttering prayer flags.

Next day, John and I defected with Ngima for a rapid completion of the Annapurna circuit while the others returned to Besisahar to find a heavy army presence. The Maoists had given notice of their intention to attack the town so our party left quickly next morning, returning to Kathmandu via some recovery time in Pokhara.

SUMMARY

An account of the first ascent of the South Face of Pokharkan, Nepal, by a group of mature AC members, November 2002.

BHAJE EXPEDITION[80]

"However well a man in his 50's may go up to 20,000 feet, I have come regrettably to the conclusion that above that height, so far as climbing goes, he is declining into decrepitude"

(H. W. Tilman, Nepal Himalaya)

I had not been to Nepal for five years, and was feeling I should go there again when I got an email from Steve Town about a proposed *Alpine Club* trip in the post monsoon season of 2002. I proved to be the 13th potential member of the team, but any superstition over numbers was allayed by various people dropping out, leaving a final party of ten.

There was a time when expeditions were organized, if not literally on the back of an envelope, at least largely on one individual's desk. Email has changed all that. Everything relating to this trip was expounded multilaterally over several months. We speculated at length about Nepal's volatile political situation, the long list of obscure 'discount' peaks (those not needing a liaison officer), the weather, the rival trekking agencies, the gear list, etc, etc. It was not all enlightening but at least it didn't cost postage. Other resources of the internet age were also mobilized, including a source of satellite images which, if you studied them very carefully, confirmed that the Kali Gandaki river really did flow between Annapurna and Dhaulagiri.

After a flirtation with the Rolwaling valley we agreed on the Damodar Himal, north of the Annapurnas and Manang, as an area of relatively unvisited moderate sized mountains suitable for a group of climbers largely well past their prime. I found a 25 year-old slide taken from Annapurna 2 pointing in this general direction, and it did all look attractive and not desperate. Pokharkan, 6346 m, seemed accessible from the Phu Khola, the scene of some of Tilman's explorations, and it wasn't too steep, at least from the north, if you believed our trekking maps. We couldn't find any record of an ascent but that didn't mean too much. Bikrum Pandey's "Himalayan Expeditions" gave us a reasonable quote for a month long trip with all supporting services, including a sirdar with five Everest ascents under his belt. We decided to stop worrying about Maoists, and we were set to go.

We met in Kathmandu at the beginning of November – a bit late in the season but this had been forced on us by the business commitments of a prospective member who decided at the last minute not to come at all. This was remembered later in the month when it became very cold. Not everyone knew everyone else and I, having been out of the UK for longer than I care to remember, knew only three others. I had kept in regular touch with Steve, the trip leader, but hadn't seen David Baldock since North Wales in the 60s. Bill Thurston reminded me that he and I had climbed The Ramp on Gogarth together back then. The four of us, with John Fairley and Martin Scott, comprised what Tilman might have called the decrepitude platoon, though some of us proved markedly less so than others. Dave Wynne Jones was a significantly younger early retiree, while Toto Gronlund and Pete and Sara Spillett were the young end of the team.

---

80 Dick Isherwood, *CCJ* 2002-03 pp 15-20
Ed. This account contrasts with the previous article and is particularly colourful in its description of life in the approach valleys.

First things first. We had declined to pay in advance due to all the political uncertainty, so Bikrum's men hustled us from the airport to his office, without even time for a shower, to get that taken care of before we met any cut-price operators in the street. Good business practice.

We were all looking forward to meeting Kaji, the five-time Everest summiteer. He did not disappoint us. Barrel-chested and beaming, he greeted us all warmly. He discovered I spoke some Nepali, tugged my white beard and named me 'Bhaje'. I had to go to my dictionary to find that this meant grandfather. Others were better qualified for this rank, but 'Bhaje' I was for the duration of the trip.

I was impressed again by the traffic congestion in Kathmandu, so different even from the 80s when I last lived there. Someone told me there is a UN-sponsored vehicle emission control program, but you'd never guess. Walking in the back lanes of Thamel is not much fun anymore with taxis and motorbikes swerving around the potholes everywhere. There were conspicuously few tourists – a fair number of individual budget travellers but not many trekking groups and none of the upmarket air-conditioned bus Agra-Nepal-Varanasi tour groups which used to keep the souvenir stalls going. Times were clearly hard for the tourist industry, but the rest of the domestic economy seemed to be thriving. Certainly, lots of people were buying motorbikes.

I hadn't been in the Marsyangdi valley since the 80s and was interested to see what had changed. The road went further, the bazaar towns were bigger, and the trekking accommodation had multiplied. Further up the valley the dry lake-bed settlement of Tal, which I remembered as two cowsheds and a minimal teashop, is now a small town with close to 20 trekking lodges. The steel-cable suspension bridges, which by the 70s had largely replaced the hairy old indigenous structures, had themselves been superseded by bigger better versions provided in part by German aid. Electric power had spread way up the valley and IDD phone service was offered, though not always actually available. I spotted a microwave tower on a ridge several thousand feet above us and way off any main trail. Corrugated iron roofs, traditionally a sign of relative wealth in rural Nepal, were everywhere, even in the smaller villages way up the hillsides and far from the tourist route. There was a lot more fruit and vegetable production – oranges were in abundance at this time of year. There were no obvious changes in the extent of the forest cover, but less bird life along the trail, perhaps reflecting the increased traffic. Most positive of all. a huge landslip on the west side of the valley near Bahundanda, which I remembered as it encompassed a whole village, and which Tilman had noted as long ago as 1950, had stabilized – the previously raw and active earth slips were now covered in alders and other secondary forest growth. Like Mike Thompson, I have long been sceptical of the many expert predictions of imminent ecological collapse in Nepal, and these observations did seem to suggest that someone is doing something right.

The trekking lodges, though, were clearly not prospering. A few years ago, we were told, the Annapurna circuit saw 75,000 trekkers a year. In early November, perhaps a little after the peak of the season but not by much, occupancy was below ten per cent. There must have been some good deals available as Kaji kepi offering us lodge accommodation to save his men the trouble of putting up tents.

We tried to do our bit for the local economy by buying beer at every opportunity. The price increased by ten rupees a bottle with every day's walk up the valley, leading to speculation that you could calibrate your altimeter by it. Rakshi, of which I once thought myself something of a connoisseur, is now hard to find, as Kathmandu whisky of various interesting flavours seems to offer more profit.

In a friendly hostelry below Chame we met a friend of Kaji's who had just – guess what – climbed Pokharkan with a Japanese client[81]. This was a bit of a blow, but at least it told us the mountain was climbable. They had gone way round to the north and up a lot of deep snow. The Sherpas were on their way home while the Japanese guy was crossing over to Muktinath with a single kitchen boy for company. Each to his own.

At this point we left the beer and fried noodles scene and turned north up the narrow Nar Khola. the entrance to which is marked by a cliff very like a small El Capitan. I had wanted to go up this valley for a very long time. The trail was formerly tenuous, so much so that the standard approach to Nar was over a high pass from Manang. Works had clearly been done however, and the walking was easy though the scenery spectacular. We crossed and recrossed the river, in the bottom of a deep and steep sided gorge, on very solid bridges, some of them new. Parts of the route had been blasted out of the cliffs. Those who wanted their ice axes accessible for this part of the approach may have been disappointed. This trail leads essentially nowhere in economic terms, so I was both surprised and impressed that it had received so much attention.

We camped that night at Dharmasala, a single building best described as a high-class Scottish bothy. It was a new stone built shed with an earth floor but also an upper story and a balcony, unlocked and available to any travellers. Kaji guessed it was built by the government – again a surprise to me as these outlying Tibetan areas used to receive virtually nothing from Kathmandu. There was just enough flat ground for our rather large tents. Our small army of porters disappeared into a series of small caves in the boulders and smoke rose here and there on the hillside. The two young lady porters, in colourful saris and nose jewellery, changed caves frequently as the evening progressed.

Next morning we climbed steeply for several hundred feet and came very suddenly into a Tibetan landscape. The lush forest vegetation of the gorge gave way in a half-mile or less to junipers and barberries widely spaced on a dry hillside. The first chortens appeared. We stopped for a break in an area of disused terraces below a small and very broken-down village. A few houses were still in use, with padlocks on their doors, and an old lady carrying a load of dried plants told us they brought the cows down here in the winter. She herself lived in Nar, high up on the far side of the valley. This pattern was repeated as we went up the valley, with quite large areas of terraced fields, now disused, and villages largely abandoned, used only for storing winter fodder. The glaciers descending from Kang Guru and Gyachi Kang to the east had clearly retreated a long way and this may well have cut off old irrigation systems. Kaji, whose home is Phaphlu in the Dudh Kosi gorge, was so impressed by the amount of unused flat ground that he wanted to build a hotel – and an airport to bring the tourists in.

I watched the lammergeiers, golden eagles and Himalayan griffons soaring around cliffs as impressive as anything in the Dolomites, and traced some very theoretical climbing lines as we waited in the sun for the tea to come. I had forgotten how soft

81 See Postscript at the end of this article.

travel in Nepal could be. Then the sun went down and I was reminded abruptly that it was November. Days were getting short and nights cold.

We continued through more gorges, still on an impressive and newly-cut trail, and reached the old fortifications below Phu. These too were pretty dilapidated but it was clear that the residents had not always welcomed visitors from down the valley. A small fort overlooked the narrowest point in the gorge and competent stone throwers would have made life difficult for an unarmed invader.

Phu and Nar are the only regularly inhabited villages in this valley. They once comprised a significant principality which also ruled over Manang and some points south, but clearly the people of Phu had not always got along with those of Nar.

Phu itself is built on the sides and top of an old moraine terrace at around 13,500 feet. It is a warren of perhaps a hundred thick-walled stone houses with lanes, drains, chortens[82,] firewood and fodder piles all packed into a very small space. The modern world had intruded in the form of Maoist slogans painted on a few walls, and solar panels on the flat roofs. The fields around the village, now bare, showed remains of barley and buckwheat, and somewhere they also grew potatoes as there were plenty for sale.

The gompa[83] was across the river and higher than the village. We had been without beer for days and I had hopes that the lama kept a good chang cellar, but the only occupant was an old lady spinning wool on the sun terrace, who didn't even have a key. The man who had it would come 'later'. This was as close as we got. We followed a well-used trail to the hilltop above and found a flat area strewn with what appeared to be parts of human skulls. Traditional Tibetan funeral customs seem to be still going here. In striking contrast, just below the gompa was the village helipad, with all the works for yet another steel-cable suspension bridge, recently delivered and waiting to be taken down to the new bridge pillars we had passed below.

We were now over 4000m, which made us feel we were getting into the mountains. A reconnaissance day out of Phu showed us some impressive peaks to the east (notably Nemjung, which is a very beautiful pyramid) but we made the mistake of having three parties go in different directions. Kaji came back with very definite ideas about how to climb Pokharkan, as did Martin, Bill and I from a different perspective. We overruled him, and not just because we were the paying customers – his route involved sleep loose-looking rock, pegs and fixed ropes even below the base camp. I had a magnificent view of the east side of Pokharkan from the vultures' roosting ground far above the gompa, and we were fairly sure there was a snow route to the summit from this direction. This would at least give us a new route for our second ascent.

Next morning, as we walked up the valley, we saw some cat-like tracks on the trail They seemed a bit small for a snow leopard, but one lives in hope. A vulture flew in unusually low above us and landed in a depression on the hillside just above – then another, then two more. By the time we had climbed up far enough to see them there were almost 20, tucking in to the corpse of a male bharal, heads and necks red with its blood. It was hard to believe that this big goat had just tripped over and died on such a gentle hillside, so we suspected we had disturbed a predator at its kill, giving the vultures a free lunch. The cat tracks didn't go beyond this point.

---

82 *Ed.* Also known as "stupas"
83 *Ed.* monastery

Two more days took us to a base camp on a meadow at around 4800m where, by some miracle on this dry hillside, there was flowing water. As we all sat around breathing hard and hoping to acclimatise, the Sherpas played football. The meadow was not exactly flat and every few minutes someone would have to chase the ball several hundred feet downhill. The football survived the whole trip, only to succumb to a reversing bus in Pokhara on the way home.

We made a very modest carry to a higher campsite, then it snowed six inches or so overnight. On the south-facing slopes it melted off very quickly, but elsewhere it just stayed. Hoping that winter had not arrived for real, we gave ourselves two more valuable acclimatization days. Unfortunately for me personally, a cold had been going around and it now settled in my chest, reducing me to a serious level of decrepitude.

We went up to the next campsite at around 18,000 feet, still no more than walking on moraines and boulder fields, but by now the Sherpas were running rings around us. John had picked up a copy of *Rum Doodle* at the bar of that name in Kathmandu, and it was beginning to seem too relevant for comfort. Kaji and two others climbed most of the way to the summit this day, ignoring our chosen route, cached some ropes and came down to join us for dinner. The next day they carried our gear up to a camp on the glacier, our only one on permanent snow. They themselves returned to the moraine campsite for a warmer night and a full kitchen: "We'll see you at six am tomorrow. Be ready to go." This was getting embarrassing. There was a time when I reckoned I could keep up with most Sherpas.

Figure 85 "Far, far, the mountain peak". Pokharkan from the distance.
Photo: R. Isherwood

I was now in a bad way and spent a horrible sleepless night, gasping for air and keeping John awake with my coughing. The next morning I just couldn't progress uphill at all and even had trouble getting down. The others, now reduced to five plus three Sherpas, climbed to the rope cache and discovered why Kaji had stopped where he did. The route ahead was not the snow slope he had indicated but a mess of seracs. Dave now took the lead and climbed a steep ice pitch to more snow slopes that led to a summit, but unfortunately not the real one. The route to that was down 150 metres to a saddle and up along another snow ridge. Dave, Martin and Kaji did this bit to finish the job. They all got down to the snow camp that evening after a 12-hour day.

The descent and return were uneventful until we reached the roadhead at Besisahar where the army and police were on alert and shopkeepers were pulling shutters down early. A Maoist attack was rumoured, and we could feel the tension all around, but fortunately it didn't happen that night. I did have the feeling that solo wandering in Nepal, which used to be very safe and lots of fun, is not a good idea these days. Next day we were by the lake in Pokhara.

POSTSCRIPT

Ed. – Dave Wynne Jones wrote to try to clarify this issue.

"*Re Pokharkan, there is a Japanese claim to have made the first ascent from the north. We encountered the guy's sirdar on our walk-in to the peak, who recounted tales of wading through waist deep snow. This really didn't square with our subsequent experience and we saw no signs of any previous presence on the summit when Martin Scott and I reached it with Kaji Sherpa. Our recollections of the appearance of the summit and environs did not match the published Japanese account (in English) either, and the author presumed to mark as "our" summit the foresummit we had crossed en route to the main summit. However, despite our misgivings Martin and I never challenged the claim and were content to record our climb as the first ascent of the South Face, an altogether more technical climb, as the account indicates. Interestingly, Dick noted that Pokharkan was listed as "unclimbed" in a Nepali source only about a year ago (meaning in 2012).*"

KING OF MOUNTAINS[84]
HAIZI SHAN 5833M, SICHUAN

The good mountaineer is never separated from his pit.

Ken Wilson, c 1966

In case you haven't heard, Western Sichuan is the 'in' place. Tamotsu Nakamura publicises it at every opportunity, and very generously gives out his beautifully produced *East of the Himalayas* to all comers. Young hard men and old soft men alike are flocking there.

Geoff Cohen and Martin Scott got a hold of this and recruited two others in the latter category – Bill Thurston and myself. With a mean age of 59 we had a bit of trouble finding anything in Tam's book that we thought we could climb, but we settled for Haizi Shan, a little over 19,000 feet and not too far from the road. It had a bit of a history – the survey expedition of the Baron Szechenyi in 1877 determined its height at 7774m, in a region where there was thought to be at least one peak over 30,000 feet. The Tibetan name, Ja-Ra, apparently translates as 'King of Mountains' and there is a story that the Tibetan King's eldest son preferred to live up there for ever more, despite offers of palaces and concubines down below. He must have had good circulation.

Haizi Shan is a fine peak, mostly snow on the north and rock on the south, well separated from everything else, and looking over the big plain of the Tagong grasslands to the west. We had some pictures from the north, which seemed the way to go, and were pleased to find we could drive to the base camp in a day and a half from Chengdu. We established ourselves in a meadow, with two cooks and two huge propane cylinders to look after the catering and tons of fresh vegetables, noodles and Sichuan red peppers, and immediately found ourselves surrounded by a Tibetan horde. There was a seasonal camp just up the trail, with at least 200 people in it devoted to the collection of worm grass, also known as caterpillar fungus. This slightly mysterious substance is variously described as a worm, a fungus and a grass, and has remarkable properties, in common with most Chinese medicines.

'Make you strong. Make you strong at night.'

'What does it do to women?' Geoff asked.

'Make your woman hot inside.'

Personally, when I saw my first one, I thought it was just a little weed, but at least one website tells me it is in fact a dead caterpillar with a fungal fruiting body growing out of its head. Yet another miracle of the Orient.

The energy expended on the collection of these small things was astonishing – young ladies in bright red headdresses adorned with silver were all over the hillsides, 2,000 feet above the trail. Maybe you need to eat some just to get you going. Perhaps, we thought later, we should have taken a few up the hill.

We had driven to 3800m so we had an excuse for a fester. We walked for two hours to a very fine hot spring and lounged in the pool watching some hyped-up snails moving much faster than you would expect, and speculating about the west face of

---

84 Dick Isherwood, *AJ* 2005 pp 65-70

Figure 86 Gatherers of the sought-after 'worm grass' below Haizi Shan.
'Make you strong at night,' the mature alpinists were told.
Photo: Dick Isherwood

Haizi Shan which would make a good route for someone a little younger. On another day we encountered a yak caravan and I got into the wrong place at the wrong time. A small boy was leading them, waving a little whip in a very photogenic fashion. I pointed the camera at him but he didn't want any, so I put it away. While doing this I was suddenly attacked by a classic Tibetan dog, mustard and black and rather determined. It just popped out from between the legs of the yaks and before I could find a rock to throw it had made a big hole in my jeans and two deep gashes in me. I washed them out as best I could and hoped the dog wasn't rabid. Xiao Mei, our interpreter/ minder, was reassuring:

'I was once bitten by a dog too,' she said, 'but the public health man in Kangding says rabies is very rare here.' I decided to believe her. No frothing at the mouth so far.

Eventually we had to address the hill. It was necessary to move about 60 lb per head of gear and food to a camp about 4,000 feet higher up if we were to have any real chance of getting to the top. In the good old days we would just have put it on our backs and headed up. Now, however, a debate began over whether we should do it in two carries of 30 lb or three of 20 lb. Since most of us weighed around 180 lb with boots and other stuff before even lifting a load, I argued strongly for the former.

I felt that the condition of the lower mountain justified me. Steep rhododendron forest with a metre of soft snow on it, and disintegrating steps of ice with bad snow on top and gurgling water below left us totally exhausted and rather short of our planned camp site, despite a good combined effort in which we all shared the trail breaking. Bill led one of the wettest ice pitches I can remember. The fewer times one did this the better. A moraine crest above was the obvious route and we kept looking at it to see how much snow had thawed off it. Not enough, unfortunately. It was still a soggy mess when we left in early May. If I come back here it will be post-monsoon – though maybe a couple of weeks later in the premonsoon season might work well enough.

With much effort we established a camp at around 4900m in a slightly fraught spot on a cone of old avalanche debris, below a couloir that seemed to have shot its load for the season. A Hong Kong party had climbed the ridge above here as far as the north summit, so we knew it was feasible. We carried a dump of food, gear and fuel another 300m up the hill to a jolly little spot on the bottom lip of a crevasse but lack of acclimatisation prevented us going further that day. The weather now became less than perfect, though far from bad, and by consensus but with some reluctance we went down to the valley for another fester. The theory was that we would return reinvigorated and feeling wonderful.

Three days of beer-drinking and nine hours of serious effort later we were back and I felt awful. The rhododendron forests and soggy ice had got worse, if anything, and we had been forced to do what Geoff called 'real Scottish climbing' – pick in the heather and pulling up on half-attached vegetation. We were all pretty exhausted. However, trying to display the character of Englishmen, we set the alarms early and packed everything up for a shot to carry a camp to the north summit, from which we thought we could surely get there and back.

We were very slow indeed that morning. When we had battled our way up to the dump by the crevasse it was clear that we weren't going to make the north summit even on the best scenario. Geoff then came up with a new plan. Camp here and go for it with minimal gear. Only 600m of vertical to go. Everyone bought in to avoid further load carrying.

Figure 87 North face of Haizi Shan (5833m), western Sichuan,
showing the Isherwood-Cohen route and high point.
Photo: Dick Isherwood

The weather was now good, removing our only excuse. Geoff, who had mostly so far been lingering near the back, moaning about his lack of fitness, suddenly sprang to the front, got out of the tent first and beat a mighty trail up the hill in the dark while the rest of us were still grappling with our porridge. We followed him to the ridge crest and a stunning view of Minya Konka and adjacent peaks to the south and enormous plains to the north.

The ridge was of course a bit steeper than we had anticipated and the cornice needed watching. Here and there were nasty cracks going down rather a long way. I had a theory that there was so much tonnage of nice flat frozen cornice that you could walk on it without your weight making any real difference, but I wasn't quite bold enough to put this to the test. We all agreed we would have been uncomfortable soloing this with full camping gear. After a bit Martin and Bill decided to go down and Geoff and I continued, unroped, to the north summit.

We got there around eleven o'clock and thought we had lots of time. We went on easily to the big saddle before the rise to the main summit where a 30-metre serac cuts across the ridge. Geoff led off round its right side and took a while, though protesting that it was all straightforward. When I followed I was impressed by the view – you stepped a long way to the right, across a big hole, and then found yourself looking straight down a good 6,000 feet to the hot spring valley. The rest of the pitch was steep and distinctly exposed. Somehow this one pitch took us almost two hours and it was now 2pm. The remainder of the ridge was steep on the north side, very steep on the south, and corniced. It was definitely climbable but a bit hard to solo, we thought, and would take four to six more pitches. We had no bivvi gear, having failed to follow Ken's dictum, and didn't fancy a cold night out. Therefore we chickened. We both agreed that 20 years ago we'd have pissed on up it, but what's the use of that?

We returned to the north summit and descended the big glacier below it, which was rather crevassed. Geoff introduced me to snow mushrooms as abseil anchors. The first one worked fine – the second disintegrated when I was two metres above a friendly snow bank. I landed flat on my back and made what I thought was an impressive crater. We saved a sling and I felt no pain – it was probably worth six visits to the chiropractor. We got back to the tent just as dark was falling. I don't wish to tell you about the descent next day through the rhododendron forest.

Figure 88 Dick Isherwood on the NE Ridge
Photo: Geoff Cohen
(*Ed.* **This photo was not in the original *AJ* article**)

We had a bit of time left, though not enough for another attempt on the mountain so we went touring to the north and west through this interesting part of culturally Tibetan China. The villages were all Tibetan, the bigger towns at least half populated by Han Chinese. We visited several monasteries all of which, except the one in Tagong, had been destroyed during the Cultural Revolution and completely rebuilt. They seemed to be flourishing; lots of monks wandered the streets and the official Chinese presence was certainly low profile, apart from a couple of very long PLA convoys on the road which were probably heading for Tibet proper. The only thing you mustn't do, we were told, was display a picture of the Dalai Lama. Construction was going on everywhere – the Tibetan villages looked very prosperous, the roads were being worked on after a fashion and the shops were full of stuff. I replaced my dog-eaten jeans with a far more fashionable pair in Garze. We ate exceptionally well everywhere, though we did leave a few red chillies and pigs' intestines on the table. I never thought I could tire of Sichuan food. Mr Ka, who drove our car (no kidding), stuck to tea during the day but in the evening introduced us to serious 'Chinese Alcohol' in quantity. The old tea-trading town of Kangding, deep in a spectacular gorge, now has a six-figure population and apart from its setting is just like Kowloon, with ten-storey buildings being demolished to make way for thirty-storey ones. See it all soon before the hordes arrive.

SUMMARY

An attempt on Haizi Shan (5833m) in the Daxue Shan of Western Sichuan, April 2004. Geoff Cohen and Dick Isherwood reached around 5800m on the north ridge. Grade AD, as far as we got.

ACKNOWLEDGEMENTS:

The trip was supported by very generous grants from the Mount Everest Foundation and from the UK Sports Council via the British Mountaineering Council, to all of whom we would like to express our thanks and appreciation.

Figure 89 Haizi Shan summit
Photo: Geoff Cohen
(*Ed*. This photo was not in the original *AJ* article)

A CAUTIONARY TALE[85]

We all like Tibetans. They are generally friendly and smiling people, and even drink chang while they are praying, which I have always thought a very civilized habit. We think of them as deeply religious and very pacific people. Some of us associate their behaviour with great and inscrutable wisdom. Some of us even contribute to movements such as Free Tibet, though it is not too obvious how they propose to get the Chinese out. The story that follows is not meant to change this admirable view of things, just to show that it is not always quite like this.

In spring 2004 I was a member of a four-man party that attempted Haizi Shan (5833m) in the Daxue Shan mountains of western Sichuan. At the end of our trip we travelled north as far as Garze where my attention was caught by the twin peaks of the Gongkala group (5992m and 5928m) to the east of the town. Enquiries seemed to indicate there had been only one reconnaissance of these mountains, by a Japanese group in the 1990s, and no real climbing attempts. The only photos we could obtain (from Tom Nakamura) were all taken from on or close to the Sichuan Tibet Highway, which crosses a pass just north of the peaks.

It seemed almost too good to be true that here were two good-looking, unattempted peaks with a base camp within a day's journey of the road. I did not think such things still existed. I had no trouble recruiting three companions for a trip in the autumn of 2005. I knew Toto Gronlund and Dave Wynne-Jones from Steve Town's trip to Pokharkan in Nepal in 2002, while Peter Rowat and I had a climbing association going back to an ascent of Cenotaph Corner in 1965. Peter's wife, Nona, accompanied us to our base camps and also acted as trip doctor.

In two days' travel by road from Chengdu we reached Garze, and spent three interesting days reconnoitring the north and south sides of the Gongkala peaks. There were possible but not easy routes from the north, including a 1000m "grand course" direct to the summit of Kawarani I, but we decided the south side offered better prospects for us.

A good grazing trail led from the village of Khur Chong, in the gorge of the Yalung Jiang river, around the hillside to a hanging valley directly below the southern glaciers of Kawarani I and II. From this it appeared possible to reach the col at about 5500m between the two summits. From the col there seemed to be routes to both.

Below the village were two or three apparently rather inactive monasteries. We stopped at the principal one but found literally no one to talk to, so we continued to the village where the people were very friendly and cooperative.

One young man spoke good Mandarin, which helped as our interpreter had little or no Tibetan. He also told us he was the nephew of the Rinpoche, which made him seem even more useful. We explained our plans and they were very happy to assist us by making horses available to carry to the base camp. On the afternoon of our first visit there was a thunderstorm with lots of large hail; this was not unusual as it seemed that the monsoon was not yet over.

---

85 Dick Isherwood, *AJ* 2006 pp 71-74

Figure 90 The south face of the Gongkala peaks. Kawarani I (5992m) is on the right.
Photo: Dick Isherwood

Two days later we returned with all our gear and had an uneventful journey to a base camp at 4200m. The monastery showed its goodwill by providing a monk leading a very large white yak at the head of our column. We were told he had been sent to bless our climb. It was like being led into battle by a knight on a white charger. We could hardly have got off to a more auspicious start. There was no evidence that any climbers had been in this area before.

We set to work and four days later had just completed carrying to a second camp at 4800m when we heard a commotion in the valley below. Eight young monks came running up the moraines in red robes and plastic shoes at an impressive speed. We did not have a word in common with them but it was immediately clear that this was not a social call. They wanted us off the mountain right away. As we argued in sign language, reinforcements appeared from below and we concluded that resistance was hopeless.

We returned to our base camp and found that the total delegation was around 40 assorted monks and villagers. The monks were from the same monastery that had assisted and blessed us four days earlier. When we pointed this out they simply said that they had changed their minds as a result of two thunderstorms that they believed we had caused. One mature and corpulent gentleman was introduced as their leader and for a few minutes I thought he might prove reasonable to deal with, but he was soon pushed aside by a younger and much more aggressive individual who said that *he* was in charge. As our meeting progressed it became apparent that this was a mob with no one in charge. They had no respect at all for our permit from the Sichuan Mountaineering Association. They were very confrontational and thoroughly unpleasant to deal with. After a long and unproductive discussion, during which distinctly un-pacifist attitudes were repeatedly displayed, we decided we had no alternative but to go down. Toto began to swear in Finnish, which I have come to recognize as a bad sign.

By now it was past 5pm and there was not nearly enough horse and yak transport to clear the base camp that night. The mob was, however, adamant that as many of us and as much gear as possible should go down right away. Dave and I stayed up, with a posse of monks to keep an eye on us, while the others suffered a chaotic descent, largely in the dark. The gear that went down with them was taken to the monastery and we spent much of the following day retrieving it, not without cost. They claimed money for injury to the horses in the dark, which if it happened at all was entirely their own fault. Once this was handed over every one, even the most aggressive of them, became all sweetness and light. They waved us farewell like lifelong friends. While all this was going on we were told that the helpful young man and his family were being banished from the village for assisting us.

A telephone protest by our outfitter, Sichuan Adventure Travel, to the civil administrator of the Garze Tibetan Ethnic Group Autonomous Prefecture, which governs this area from Kangding, drew only the comment that these monasteries can be difficult to deal with (this gentleman himself is apparently a reincarnate Lama.) As it was now 6pm on a Friday and the following week was one long national holiday we gave up on any further protest through the government, but I cannot believe it would have done any good for our immediate situation.

We were able to get our permit switched, with amazing speed, to Haizi Shan and spent our last ten days attempting to complete the route which Geoff Cohen, Martin Scott, Bill Thurston and I had tried on the North face in spring 2004 . Unfortunately the weather was poor and we expended a lot of energy getting nowhere. We retreated from the bottom of the northern glaciers at 4800m in a foot of new snow on 10 October.

So what does one make of all this? Firstly, if we had been a bit faster up the hill rather than allowing time for acclimatisation, rest days, etc, we would have been in the snow and ice and well out of plastic shoe country before the monastery took umbrage. The eventual consequences might not have been pleasant, but we might have climbed the mountain.

Secondly, we are not the only climbing party to have run into this sort of problem in recent years. See, for instance, the *American Alpine Journal* 2001 p.408 and 2003 p.410. The latter, though in Yunnan rather than Sichuan, describes a very similar experience in that the villagers welcomed the climbers, but the monks told them not to co-operate and threatened punishment if they did.

Third, the Chinese Government seems to have a "hands off" approach to this area, in striking contrast to what goes on in Tibet proper. The Garze Autonomous Prefecture was established in November 1950 within a few months of the invasion of Tibet. This is perhaps more than coincidence. The Khampas of Sikong, as this western slice of Sichuan was formerly known, have clearly been given freedom of religion, and also considerable economic assistance, just possibly in return for making no trouble. Their communities certainly look prosperous today. How this squares with the well-known Khampa resistance to the Chinese occupation of Tibet in later years I do not know. In trying to find out a bit more about this I got as far as a Khampa website which seemed to be dominated by different tribal subgroups trading insults. I guess there are Khampas and Khampas.

The monastery's stated reasons for their actions have little credibility, since thunderstorms and hail were regular events in the area. Perhaps the simple fact that we were the first outsiders to go onto the mountains was enough to spook them, but it seems more likely that we got into the middle of a feud between monastery and village, which we could hardly have foreseen.

There is also, as ever, the question of money. It is possible that a sufficiently large donation to the monastery up front might have averted what happened, but on our arrival there seemed to be no one suitable to give it to, even if we had thought it necessary. Certainly a number of previously hostile monks became remarkably friendly once we had paid $250 for the return of our gear.

We did not have a liaison officer. It did not seem to be a requirement in this area and was not a condition of our permit. Possibly if we had had one of suitable stature the outcome might have been different, but I suspect that even if we had asked for one we would have been given someone too junior to be effective in this situation. You would have needed a general in the PLA to make an impression on these people. Besides, who would want to go down in history as the first expedition to have *insisted* on having a liaison officer? Our interpreter was a pleasant but very young Han Chinese lady from Chengdu who was clearly and understandably intimidated by the situation and not very effective as a negotiator. Perhaps a different individual in this role could have achieved a better outcome, but I doubt it.

I guess it is a matter of opinion how much of this really relates to religion, or superstition, or local politics, or plain greed. I do not have any answers – it is just a cautionary tale.

SHALULI SHAN, 2007[86]

Dave Wynne-Jones

Figure 91 Walking around the range on the south-eastern approach to Dangchezhengla (left, 5830m) and the central summit of Yangmolong (6066m)

Photo: Dave Wynne-Jones

Steve Hune, Dick Isherwood, Peter Rowat, and I (*David Wynne-Jones*) spent October in Western Sichuan, exploring the northern approaches to Yangmolong (6066m) and attempting to climb it. In good, though never totally clear, weather we entered the Sanchu River valley and stayed with villagers, before establishing base camp at 4400m in a tributary valley. From there we stocked an advance base camp at 4900m at the foot of the western-most glacier descending from the northern side of Yangmolong. Dick found himself suffering from breathing problems, which meant that he was unable to climb above 5000m. To acclimatize, the rest of us made the first ascent of a fine 5600m snow peak to the south-west of ABC and south of Peak 5850m, at about PD in difficulty. After a day's rest, we climbed a new route on the north side of Dangchezhengla, first climbed by a Japanese team in 2002. Our ascent climbed through a rocky buttress to the south of the main glacier to gain a snow ridge leading to a steep fore summit, where we joined the Japanese route up the difficult summit ridge. After a steep 70m pitch of deep unconsolidated snow to a shoulder, climbed largely via my burrowing efforts, we flanked the corniced ridge on unconsolidated snow, sometimes crusted over but hollow to a depth of a foot. At one point we tiptoed along the cornice break-line with axes planted in the ridge crest for support. Estimated grade: D. (Dangchezhengla is referred to locally as Bongonzhong – Ed. of *AAJ*)

The weather then became very cold and windy, with frequent snow showers, which put a stop to climbing for about a week. Peter managed a reconnaissance of the shattered saddle to the north-east of the main summit, and we established a camp at 5100m on the eastern-most glacier descending north on Yangmolong. Steve and I attempted the steep north spur, which falls almost directly from the main summit, but were forced to turn back at 5400m. It was extremely cold, and snow conditions were difficult, with an inch or two of crust over unconsolidated snow. A threatening storm finally blew in around 2pm and lasted until after dark.

Figure 92 From the south-west, Dangchezhengla (5830m)
is on the left, Yangmolong (6066m) on the far right
Photo: Dave Wynne-Jones

With just a few days left, we decided to pack up, descend to the valley, and walk around the mountain to reach Dangba, while the base camp team supervised the return of equipment by the original route in from the north. We believe ours was the first Western party to make this trek through beautiful and varied country. So it was a good trip despite not climbing Yangmolong.

SUMMARY

Peak 5600m (First ascent); Dangchezhengla (Bongonzhong, 5830m), N side (New Route).

Figure 93 High on Dangchezhengla (5830m)
Photo: Dave Wynne-Jones

YANGMOLONG (6066M), ATTEMPT[87]

Dave Wynne-Jones

In 2007 Dick Isherwood, Peter Rowat, and I attempted Yangmolong (*AAJ* 2008) In September-October 2009 we returned with Derek Buckle to explore the northern approaches. We traveled up the Sanchu River valley and stayed at lower Sanglong Xi, before setting up base camp on the riverside east of Yangmolong, at an altitude of 4000m. The local people identified the expedition as a suitable target for extortion which became more serious following several thefts; binoculars, food, a stove, trekking poles, etc were stolen. The binoculars were eventually "ransomed." The police were summoned but tacitly admitted they were unlikely to obtain statements from the local community. For the duration of our time at base camp the support team slept virtually on top of remaining stores and was forced to hire "camp guards" from among the more law-abiding locals.

Figure 94 Yangmolong (6066m, left) and Makara (a.k.a. Central Peak, 6033m) from the north. Highest point of Yangmolong is just above left arm of seracs/hanging glacier left of center. Dangchezhangla (5830m) is off picture to right.
Photo: Dave Wynne-Jones

After several reconnaissance walks, we realized there was nothing for it but an arduous 1000m ascent to an advanced base camp on glacial moraine below the east ridge of Yangmolong. A period of prolonged bad weather followed the establishment of this camp, during which we kicked our heels at base camp listening to rain hammering flysheets. When the weather finally cleared, we made several forays onto the flanks of the east ridge. However, we found no line that would offer a safe route to the crest. With time running out, Derek and I established a camp on a col at the head of the glacier cirque and prepared to tackle the shallow ridge and steep face above. However, more unstable weather rolled in, and after two days of abortive alpine starts we decamped to advanced base.

---

87 *AAJ* 2010, Dave Wynne-Jones pp 335-336

On the one remaining day available for climbing, Derek and I attempted the 5700m satellite peak to the north, but the upper part of the route proved too difficult in the deteriorating weather. The team evacuated the valley amid more tension and unpleasantness from the locals, including theft of money from the bus driver at the roadhead.

Something had changed significantly in this valley. In 2007 it had been populated by friendly, helpful people, but in 2009 we encountered only a few whom we recognized from the earlier visit. Perhaps the 2008 disturbances, which resulted in a police house being burned down in a neighboring valley, had some influence. However, there seemed to be only two observable material changes: the illegal logging of virgin forest, which started in 2007, had been shut down by the government, although a new road and electricity pylons had been built to the village as compensation. And during 2007 there had not been a single monk or nun in evidence in the valley, while in 2009 there was a significant presence. No one on the team has any inclination to return. We wish to acknowledge the support given by the Mount Everest Foundation.

Figure 95 Broad summit ridge of Yangmolong (6066m) from north-east.
Highest point is right of center.
Photo: Dave Wynne-Jones

NO BLENDS![88]

"Whichever way you want to go, he will lead you up it."

I have been interested in Himalayan rhododendrons for a long time. I worked long ago in East Nepal, which has a much greater variety than areas of the Himalaya further west, but I knew that the real place to see them was Sikkim. Hence when Geoff Cohen got interested in doing a trip there I signed on.

One of the problems with climbing in Sikkim is that permission for foreigners to go to the really exciting stuff is almost impossible to obtain. Unless you have some very good connections in Delhi you are practically limited to a little list of "Alpine Peaks" only five in number and all climbed already. This didn't bother me too much, as I didn't really expect to get to the top of anything, but I did want to see the rhododendrons and in May we were going at the right time.

Geoff put the team together; I hadn't met any of the other four though I had corresponded with Steve Kennedy about the hip problems we both had experienced Steve, Bob Hamilton and Dave Ritchie are all Highland Scots, being respectively an Advocate (Scottish for lawyer), a prawn fisherman, and a fix-it-all welder/plumber/ mechanic. The other member of the team was Paul Swienton, an American engineer and one of Geoff's climbing mates from his time in the Washington DC area. I was slightly surprised to find that I was the only totally retired person in the group, though I was the oldest by a few years.

These days in the Himalaya you don't just go on the trains and buses as far as they go, then hire a bunch of unknown and usually unwashed locals at the trailhead You use an outfitter who quotes you an all-inclusive price from meeting you at the airport to putting you back on the plane at the end. It is all very much simpler than it used to be, though sometimes more expensive. Geoff found us a good outfitter through Roger Payne, who has made Sikkim a bit of a speciality in recent years, and who was extremely helpful.

Barap Namgyal, who runs Sikkim Holidays, is I believe a distant relative of the former Sikkim royal family, who hailed from Tibet long ago. The last Chogyal, or king, married a New York socialite, who doesn't seem to have been terribly popular with his subjects. The royals were booted out unceremoniously in 1975, when Sikkim ceased to be a semi-independent entity and became a state of India. Barap, however clearly knew his way around Gangtok, and permits were not a problem. We went for Jopuno (5936m) which seemed to have had one or two previous ascents, but with plenty of scope left for new routes. It did also seem that you could do a few other things on the sly on neighbouring peaks.

Planning was quite simple as far as climbing gear went – the Scots had lots of it and Paul had as much as them all put together. Nobody wanted my 30 year old rope or old ice screws. Food planning was more interesting however. Barap told us everything was

88 Dick Isherwood CCJ 2011 pp 28-34

The Ed. of this issue of the *CCJ* added the following comment under the title: *"When not out collecting his crab pots biologist Dick Isherwood's long interest in rhododendrons has taken him to some of the more remote places in the world. In this tale his quest takes him to the less travelled eastern Himalayan region of Sikkim, where his outfitter is a descendant of royalty and his Highland accomplices have strict rules about the choice of alcoholic beverage."*

available in Sikkim but we might bring some "highly protein chocolates" for which we searched the western world in vain. I did bring a load of good strong tea bags as I think Darjeeling tea is pretty feeble stuff. Steve felt the same way so we were well supplied on that front.

We all met in Bagdogra, which is the airport for both Sikkim and Darjeeling. My plane from Delhi was late and I was a bit knackered after coming straight through from Seattle, but Barap and his right hand man, Sanjeev, revived me with a couple of beers and we were on our way, across the Tista plain and then up, down and up again, mostly in the dark, to Gangtok. I was not looking forward to this journey but was impressed by the quality of the roads, at least compared to Nepal, or Western China. We had filled out endless forms and sent passport copies and photos in advance but when we reached the Sikkim frontier, or whatever they call it where you leave West Bengal, we had to do it all again anyway. Fortunately there was cold beer there too.

Figure 96 The West Face of Jopuno, showing the route attempted.
The peak on the left is Tinchenkang, another Alpine Peak
Photo: Dick Isherwood

I had been struck by a repeating phrase in emails from Steve – "No Blends!" I hadn't been sure what this was about, but I soon caught up. These Scots were serious about whisky. They had made a fair attempt to clean out the Glasgow Airport duty free shop. One whopping bottle of very good malt had already gone in a long night in Calcutta – "Waiting for Paul" – but there was a lot left. Personally I am less particular, and tend to judge my whisky on volume per unit of currency, so I was looking forward to sampling the local Scotch of Sikkim, which has extremely low duty and tax rates on most things.

After various temple tours and shopping excursions we got on the road to the real hills
The geography of Sikkim is not simple – a series of rivers come down from the Himalaya
sometimes north to south but quite often sideways , following geological weaknesses, just
like the rivers of Nepal next door. We were going west, to the ancient capital of Sikkim
at Yoksum, and this involved crossing two major river gorges. With stops for a very good
lunch in an unprepossessing roadside hut, and a few more temple tours, this took the
whole day. The roads really were in very good shape compared to Nepal.

We found ourselves in a very attractive honeymoon-type hotel, with beautiful
gardens, which seemed surprisingly luxurious until the electricity went off, the
hot water ran cold, and the plumbing turned out to be leaky. Still, you can't have
everything, and the beer was cold enough.

We still had to pay Barap and he wasn't even there. We had all sent him half
payment in advance, by normal bank transfers, but he seemed to want the rest in
hard currency on the spot, so we were carrying rather a lot of dollars and Euros -
more than I generally like to have in my pockets in new places. We tried to give it all
to him in Gangtok and he kept putting us off. Finally he showed up, just before we
were due to set off with the yak train, and rather reluctantly agreed to take payment
This was done over the open air breakfast table in the garden, with a variety of
strangers watching. Barap, being of royal lineage, found counting money to be a bit
beneath him so he tossed the whole great wad to Sanjeev who did the needful. Barap
then stuck the whole lot in his back pocket and wandered off. This is not how I deal
with large amounts of cash, but then he is a relative of royalty.

We got on the trail, with ten porters, ten horses and ten yaks. There was no need
to carry much ourselves. It was a rather wet trail, but it was good and wide. Steve
was suffering from intestinal distress – either too much malt or not enough Sikkim
blended. But we all made it to a decrepit forest lodge at 9,000 feet or so, where you had
to position your sleeping bag out of the drips, and take care which floorboards you
stepped on. The next day we got up into the serious rhododendrons, and they were
very fine. This, as much as anything, was what I had come for. Red, yellow, orange
white, in all sizes, with lots of other flowers under them too and with a great variety of
birds – if you can spot them. There were great pale green rosettes of the blue poppies
but you need to come in the monsoon, and brave the leeches to see them flowering.

On day two we got to 12,000 feet in a meadow from which there were said to
be mountain views. It was, of course, socked in with cloud by the time we arrived
but we had a good camp. Barap had provided a very grand base camp tent, or really
two tents within one outer skin. It was enormous and came from Norway. Putting it
up was quite an operation – with the combined expertise of an advanced degree in
engineering, much knowledge of statistics, a qualification from the Scottish Bar and
thirty five years of prawn fishing experience it still took most of the afternoon. I kept
out of it and just took photos.

In the morning it was clear, so we were roused in the dark to climb a thousand
feet or so to a viewpoint. At this point I realized how many other trekkers there were
around here: friendly and mostly young folks from Europe, the US and not least India
There were at least forty of us up there. I'm not sure where they had all been hiding.
The sunrise on Kangchenjunga was terrific and we could see, closer to hand, the peaks
we had come for.

Jopuno (5936m) was our stated objective. It had no obvious easy way up, and an interesting history. The first recorded ascent was by William Woodman Graham, a member of the Alpine Club, in September 1883. Graham has the great distinction, in my mind at least, of having been the first Westerner to go climbing in the Himalaya for fun. Everyone prior to him was there for diplomatic, military, religious or commercial reasons.

He was a man of some means, and took two Swiss guides with him on a year long trip which included the Nanda Devi area as well as Sikkim. One of them was the redoubtable Ulrich Kauffmann, thought to be the fastest step cutter in the Alps at the time – a sort of nineteenth century Tom Patey.

Graham climbed Jopuno by its West Face, which was the side we were looking at. His account doesn't seem to fit perfectly with the terrain we saw, and it is just possible that he actually climbed one of the other summits close by, but I personally am happy to give him the benefit of the doubt, since he was doing it for pleasure, not money or personal gain. Herr Kauffmann excelled himself and Graham described the climb as 'incomparably the hardest ascent we had in the Himalaya, owing to the great steepness of the glacier work"

Figure 97 Paul Swienton climbing on Lama Lamani.
Photo: Steve Kennedy

Graham became a controversial figure back at home, as he also claimed an ascent of the south summit of Kabru, at around 7200m, which would have been an altitude record at the time. He was disbelieved by various pundits but supported by

Tom Longstaff, who knew more about the Himalaya than most people at that time He later lost his fortune and emigrated to the USA where he became a cowboy. As I now live in the Western US I keep meaning to track him down – he was, to say the least, a colourful individual.

Many other climbers visited Sikkim after this. Douglas Freshfield made a celebrated circuit of Kangchenjunga in 1899, which has seldom if ever been repeated. Many great names made ascents, or attempts, particularly in the 1930s and climbing especially on the eastern flanks of Kangchenjunga. After the independence of India in 1947 however, access for foreigners became very difficult.

Sikkim then retreated into the mists, as Roger Payne has put it, for rather a long time. Political upheaval and tensions between India and China put it off limits to foreign climbers for many years.

There was another reported ascent of Jopuno in 2002 by a pair of Sikkimese climbers, up its rather steep, long and gendarme studded South Ridge. There is some doubt about this, not least because one of them was a relative of Barap, who says they didn't get to the top. A confirmed ascent was made in 2008 by an American party, up the West Ridge at about an Alpine Difficile standard.

We were hoping to do something new and we realized that the east side of the mountain, above the Talung Chu valley, had never been attempted. We thought we were really on to something here, but as tends to happen, when you think you have found your own little untouched corner of the Himalaya, we discovered that Bill Tilman had been there seventy years ago. His account of the Talung Chu was enough to put anyone off, and he had merely gone down it, after a failed attempt to cross the Zemu Gap.

"The third day gave us a ten hour bush crawl along the right bank, with midges, tree ticks and leeches doing their best to enliven the proceedings. The tree ticks were in the minority but by far the most troublesome. They were strategists. When they dropped, one by one, instead of attaching themselves at once to the first handy bit of skin, they invariably sought out the soft underbelly before burying their heads deep in the flesh."

Figure 98 Kabru (left) and Kangchenjunga (far right) from below
Photo: Dick Isherwood

After reading this we decided to skip the Talung Chu and take the easy approach on the trekking route.

Sanjeev, a witty and very engaging fellow from Assam via Darjeeling, was looking after us, together with a very good cook, several young lads, and an interesting and clearly strong Sherpa character called Karma. It was said that Karma had climbed Jopuno before, but conversations with him about it were far from clear. The quote at the head of this article is what Sanjeev had to say about him. Geoff had tried hard to tell Barap and Sanjeev that we wanted to do our own climbing and routefinding, so Karma was for a while relegated to digging the toilet holes with his high tech ice tool.

Base camp was established at about 4000m in another large meadow known as Thansing. Several very decrepit huts didn't promise much but lo and behold, in one of them was a government servant – the Chowkidar, or caretaker. He proved to be a very amiable fellow from the Limbu tribe, which I knew well from my time in East Nepal. The Limbus are known, among other things, for their hospitality and their large scale consumption of hot millet beer, drunk through a bamboo tube and known as Tumba. Our host seemed to have an endless supply of this, at a very modest price.

The meadow was quite large, though not exactly flat, and a group of New Zealand trekkers organized a cricket match – Sikkim vs the Rest of the World. Here Sanjeev showed the value of his Darjeeling education with some very stylish bowling. Sikkim won, after several improvised bats were broken.

After a bit of pottering, justified as acclimatization, we set off up the hill. This was a rather steep 900m or so, initially on a grazing trail but later just up very steep grass. Sanjeev had not been up here before, but Karma had, so we looked to him to find the way in the cloud, fog and increasing snow. For a while we thought he was just as lost as us, but eventually he found the way to a little recess with flat ground and a bit of water drainage through it. "A wee glen" as one of the Scots called it.

It had snowed quite a lot and we scraped out tent sites – then next day it thawed rather rapidly and there was suddenly a river in the glen. After re-pitching the tents we set off to see what lay above. We stumbled up a lot of glaciated rocks in the dark and met dawn at the snow line on a nice clear morning. The West Face of Jopuno was right above us and the views were great. At about 5200m I decided that age was taking a sufficient toll and sat in the sunshine watching the others poking around the face of Lama Lamani (5650m), just to the south, which Geoff had chosen as a good initial climb.

A route was found, probably new, and four set off up it the next morning. I had opted out and Dave was struggling with the altitude. I again sat in the sun and took photos. Steve and Bob soloed happily up the face while Geoff and Paul climbed in pitches. They reached the North Summit of the mountain in six hours or so, over steepish mixed ground followed by a fine snow arête, and descended with a couple of long abseils to get back just before dark. The route was maybe AD or D by traditional Alpine standards.

Dave recovered enough to climb a wee peak with Bob, at the very head of the glacier and on the watershed between Jopuno and Lama Lamani, from which they had some fine views.

After a bit of a rest, the A team set out for Jopuno. Again I pleaded age and opted out – I would have slowed them down, at the very least – and Dave was again having altitude problems, so they were two ropes of two.

Dave and I descended to Tansing, passing en route a torpid figure in the bushes who turned out to be Karma, distinctly drunk. Maybe we should have made him lead us up it, to keep him out of trouble – after all we were paying for him.

The others considered the unclimbed steep ridges on the West Face of Jopuno pretty good objectives – but eventually settled for a repeat of the American route on the West Ridge. Geoff's account follows:

"At 2.45am on May 18th the four of us left camp to climb the W ridge. Bob was still not well, but decided to accompany us. Above the point reached the previous morning was a short icy section where a belay on ice screws was taken. We then climbed unroped up snow for several hours to a height of perhaps 5450m. Here the ridge became quite icy and it was necessary to rope up again and belay on screws. After two quite time-consuming pitches, with a traverse right under the next rocks, we got established on the firm brown rock mentioned by the previous American party that first climbed this ridge in 2008. The rocks had a fair bit of snow on them and though broken up gave climbing of about Scottish grade III standard. Steve and Bob reached the foot of the looser black rock that forms the summit of the mountain at about 11am, with Geoff and Paul a pitch behind.

The black rock section is easier angled than the brown section that we had climbed, but it is longer (maybe 300m) and likely to take quite a lot of time. The party was climbing quite slowly and it appeared unlikely that we could reach the summit and descend safely before evening. So it was decided to turn around. A succession of 60m abseils, including two from abalakov threads, got us down the rocks and the icy section."

It made a 15 hour day. As their average age was about 25 years older than the American team, this was a pretty good effort. At least I thought so as a spectator.

We took various walks before going home. One took us to the high altitude lake of Lam Pokhari (Long Pond) above which was a very fine Crag X, which has already featured in the CC Newsletter. It is like a large scale Esk Buttress, and untouched by human hand or rock boot. It does, however, start around 4500m so your breathing would need to be OK.

Our other outing was north toward the Goecha La, sometimes spelt Gotcha La below one of the east ridges of Kangchenjunga. We had some great early morning views before the cloud came in, but the highlight of the day was an encounter with a very large male yak, who took offense at the two stray dogs following us, which had been pestering him no end, and charged us while we were sitting happily eating our sandwiches. Gotcha indeed. We abandoned lunch and ran in all directions, thus removing his objective. I could sympathise with him.

The rest of the trip was basically tourism, including a surfeit of interesting Buddhist temples, and ending in Darjeeling, where the Scottish contingent were delighted to find that the steam engines on the little railway were still the originals, made in Glasgow around 1910.

I would recommend Sikkim to anyone wanting an enjoyable and culturally interesting Himalayan trip, provided you are not hung up about virgin summits It is in many ways like Nepal was thirty years ago. People are very friendly and costs are reasonable.

THE FOLLOWING REFERENCES GIVE MORE BACKGROUND:

- Sublime Sikkim. Roger Payne. *AJ* 2009 147
- Kabru, 1883 – a reassessment. Willy Blaser and Glyn Hughes. *AJ* 2009 219
- Jopuno, West Ridge. Jason Halladay. *AAJ* 2009 213
- *When Men and Mountains Meet*, Bill Tilman. p 312 of the Seven Mountain Travel Books (Diadem 1983)
- Barap Namgyal can be found at barap14@hotmail.com

BIFE DE CHORIZO[89]

"The average intake of beef is around 70 kg per person per year, though in the past Argentines ate even more."

Lonely Planet

I have had a general interest in climbing in South America for some time, but had never done anything about it till last year, when I saw an offer from Simon Yates in the Alpine Club newsletter. His objective was Monte Bove in Tierra del Fuego 2150 metres or maybe a bit more, just north of the Beagle Channel, first climbed by Eric Shipton in 1962 and not often done since. The trip offered an interesting boat approach in a totally new part of the world, but nothing too hard on the climbing front, which suited me well, I thought.

We were a party of six – Simon, whom everyone knows by repute, Hugh Alexander a fellow Alpine Club member, and three Australians, Geoff and Sue Robb and Steve Shrimpton. Sue does not climb and came for the ride, about which she may at times have had second thoughts. Geoff has the Seven Summits under his belt, and a few more big peaks besides, while Steve revealed that he had never done a roped climb before.

Figure 99 Simon Yates and Geoff Robb near the summit of Monte Bove
Photo: Isherwood collection

We met in Ushuaia, at the very bottom end of Argentina and the jumping off point, as you might say, for tours to Antarctica. These have become very popular in recent years and Ushuaia is accordingly a boom town. You might expect it to be expensive but the Argentine government in its wisdom has made it a duty free place, so you can buy whisky at ten dollars a litre, even for known Scottish brands (admittedly blended!) The bife de chorizo (rump steak) and red wine are good value too.

Simon introduced us to the Belgian boat captain and owner, Marcel de Letter. He has been down in the far south since 1994 in his steel hulled 39-foot boat which he built himself apart from the basic hull. He has a piratical air about him and clearly knows the best and most economical watering and eating holes in Ushuaia. His boat, Iorana, had an astonishing capacity for food and, perhaps more important, drink.

Figure 100 Camp on Monte Bove
Photo: Isherwood collection

One of the problems with climbing in the Cordillera Darwin from Ushuaia is that the mountains are in Chile. The Chileans do not get on too well with the Argentinians, in this area at least, as the Argies, around 1980, tried to seize a Chilean island of distinctly limited economic potential in the Beagle Channel. The Chileans chased them off but have been suspicious ever since, so the border formalities are a little prolonged. (After failing in the Beagle Channel the then Argentine government had a go at the Falklands).

Having imagined that all was peace and harmony down here I was a little surprised when it took us almost three hours just to check out of Argentina. Since no one starts work before ten am it was then lunchtime. Marcel, who is well used to this, took us off for a bit of bife de chorizo, washed down with more than a little Malbec. He knew that there was no way we could reach the Chilean immigration port of Puerto Williams, 25 miles east – that is, in the opposite direction to the mountains – before they shut their doors for the night.

We proceeded to Puerto Williams, mostly downwind, and actually sailed quite a bit of it till the wind died. We saw an albatross or two and some spectacularly unimpressive little penguins. We arrived just before dark and tied up with a host of other boats at the Club Yates, not named for Simon, and distinctly informal – it is an old motor vessel, firmly attached to the bottom of a creek, and offering toilets, showers, and if you're lucky hot water. We rafted up to a large catamaran owned by a homely Dutch couple, who had been living on board for over 20 years, and had just sailed around Cape Horn. Chatting to the wife, a plump and sociable lady, it was hard to believe that she had spent most of her adult life doing this. Sailors are a different breed.

Figure 101 Approaching Monte Bove across the Glacier Frances
Photo: Isherwood collection

By the time we were organised, dinner beckoned and Marcel's friend down the road had assembled a massive asado (barbecue). No one, apparently, minds you walking about town before you have dealt with the immigration and customs. There never seems to be any shortage of meat in this part of the world, or of charcoal to grill it on. I do not know how you would survive down here as a vegetarian.

Next morning we had to deal with the Chilean bureaucracy. Again they don't start till ten am, and it takes a few hours. Again Marcel was master of the situation, and after signing our names a few times, and looking respectfully at photos of Chilean admirals, we left it to him and wandered the dusty streets of Puerto Williams till he had the papers organised. Then – guess what – lunch before we depart. Again it was past 2 pm before we got moving. This time the wind, which typically blows from west to east in the Beagle Channel (and in lots of other places too) was against us. We motored into it till progress became a bit futile, then Monsieur le Capitain said, with a wicked grin, "We will not make it. We must wait" He hove too, put the boat sideways across the wind in the middle of the channel, heeling at 25 degrees or so in three foot sloppy waves, tied off the wheel and went below to peel potatoes for the dinner. Sue was seasick and I barely escaped myself. The wind abated after a couple of hours and we bashed on. The Chilean navy was dying to know where we were all the time, and eventually as it got dark we anchored in a bay short of where we told them we would be. Marcel made various excuses and they seemed happy enough. By now, after thirty hours or so, we were just about back opposite Ushuaia.

Figure 102 High on Monte Bove
Photo: Isherwood collection

The following day we motored west up the Beagle Channel in calm weather and anchored in a beautiful sheltered bay, Calleta Olla. It was 5 pm and more or less opening time, so I was a little surprised when Simon said "Let's carry the first loads this evening."

This, we had been told, was Wellie country. It is indeed very boggy in the lower parts, and some of the bogs are quite steep. I was impressed by Simon's routefinding. We tried to avoid peeling too much vertical sodden grass off the wet rock below, and in only an hour and a half we were at the "base camp", a sheltered spot in the beech forest which Simon and others had used before.

I abdicated after three carries, feeling I had done my share, but the others did several more. I found out why so much was needed when we got established. Simon had definite ideas about food, which for the base camp included tinned peaches and large quantities of raw potatoes and carrots. The logic of this was that you might have to sit out a week's bad weather here, though as it was less than an hour down to the fleshpots of the boat one would be tempted to retreat there.

The following morning was fine, so it was time to go, leaving the potatoes for later. We battled past a beaver dam and its associated swamp (the beavers were introduced by some clever person and are wreaking havoc), climbed some bald slabs, still in Wellies, and at last put our boots on by a striking glacial lake below a large and obviously retreating glacier.

Figure 103 Lenticular cloud formation above Monte Bove
Photo: Isherwood collection

We were carrying over 40 lb, and I felt the weight just on the steep grass above the tree line, but then we got to the rock. Two short pitches, nothing more than severe, Simon said, and I'm sure he was right, but it was nearly too much for me. I realised I hadn't done a roped rock climb for a good long time, and hadn't done one with a pack this size for maybe 30 years. Hugh led both pitches with ease but I struggled mightily. The scree and snow slopes above seemed to go on forever, but we made a camp on a nice flat shoulder, all of 1000m above sea level. Two huge Andean Condors came to have a close look at us, claws hanging down, perhaps thinking some of us were no longer fully alive.

We were now on serious mountain rations, very different from down below, so dinner comprised instant mash, flavoured with – well, nothing, as our leader doesn't believe in salt. At least we had enough tea bags, and as an admirer of Shipton and Tilman I had brought plenty of sugar.

The next morning, again in perfect weather, we climbed easy frozen snow, over the shoulder of Monte Frances and on for over two horizontal miles, above the impressive icefalls of the Frances Glacier, to the foot of Monte Bove. The obvious route led up a ramp below some rather threatening seracs, but nothing seemed to have come down for a few days at least. We went up to a large flat shoulder in a very striking position below the rime covered summit block. Steve had opted out lower down, and Hugh and I decided we had done enough too at this point, so we watched Simon and Geoff work their way up the steep bits to the top. The views were magnificent – there really is a big area of snowy mountains down here, many of them untouched and rather inaccessible, and the glaciers are more extensive than I, at least, had imagined.

It was a thirteen hour day by the time we got back to our camp, and I for one was beat. The next day we descended slowly to the base camp, abseiling the two rock sections, and changing back into Wellies for the swamps below. We had been very lucky indeed with the weather. At this point I developed a rather nasty bronchitis, which at least gave me an excuse to minimize my role in the reverse load carrying back to the boat.

The rest of the trip was essentially tourism. A 147-foot "super-yacht" anchored by us and we were invited aboard for cocktails and canapés, served by two young ladies in short black dresses. It had a full time crew of seven to look after the owner and her five guests, each bedroom with attached bathroom and shower, all powered sail controls, two desalinators, two washers and dryers, bow and stern thrusters – in short, the lot. Since they were over a hundred feet in length they had paid the same port fees in Ushuaia as the Antarctic cruise ships, but this didn't seem to be a concern. The owner and guests were very nice people, and seemed quite intrigued by a group of unwashed climbers. Seven of us in a 39-foot boat was distinctly cozy by comparison.

We went a bit further west up the Beagle Channel, past the impressive sea level snout of the large Roncagli Glacier, watched Marcel catch a few large and very tasty spiny crabs, then returned, via friends of his at the Estancia Yendegaia and a lot more bife, before sailing past Ushuaia to repeat the leisurely Chilean immigration routine, and to restock with beer. The following evening we got back to Ushuaia just in time, at dusk and barely ahead of a strong westerly. The Argentine immigration officer looked at our passports the next morning and said "Ho Ho! You left Chile before you entered it!" The Chileans had forgotten to advance their rubber stamp from February to March. No one seemed to care.

REFLECTIONS ON TREKKING IN NEPAL[90]

I have been visiting Nepal since 1970 – I lived and worked there for five years in the seventies and eighties, and trekked and climbed fairly extensively during that period, and in the years before and after. I recently completed two 25-day treks in the hills of central Nepal, which gave me time to think about the changes that have occurred in the hills and the living situations of the local people.

I worked on an agricultural programme, funded by the British Government, in 1976-7, at a place called Pakhribas, above Dhankuta in the eastern hills of Nepal which in those relatively road-free days was on the trekking routes to both Makalu and Kangchenjunga. The work was not too demanding and I had plenty of time to look around the countryside, think and try to learn. I soon subscribed, by and large, to the prevailing view that everything in the Nepalese hills was going downhill, economically and environmentally – and sometimes literally, as with the many landslides and obvious topsoil erosion, particularly in the monsoon. Many expert reports were being written to that effect and Mike Thompson has summarized some of them very effectively, and critically, in this Journal (AJ 2000, p.153). Many highly respected people, watching the baskets of firewood and fodder coming down the footpaths, thought that the Nepalese hills would be completely devoid of trees within ten years, and life would become untenable. History has now shown that these supposed experts were way off the mark, and this article is, to some degree, a confirmation of Mike's observations.

The extent of the forest around the rim of the Kathmandu Valley is virtually the same now as it was in 1970. Admittedly some areas, such as Sheopuri, have been put under more effective protection, but it is remarkable nevertheless. I first visited the Langtang Valley in 1976 and apart from minor clearings for trekking lodges the extent of the forest, and the subalpine vegetation above it, were again unchanged in 2012. There are a few small sawmills within the Langtang National Park, which would not, in theory at least, be allowed in an American national park, but whose counterparts operate fairly happily, I believe, in the English Lake District. They just don't take too much at once. In 2009 I revisited the area in East Nepal where I worked in the seventies, and there is now more forest rather than less, due to considerable planting of pines. The forest cover in the Marsyandi Valley too is as good now as in 1974.

At Pakhribas, we were concerned about the amount of forage and firewood we saw being carried down from the forests, so we put someone on to study it – a British volunteer who was fluent in Nepali. He went out with the woodcutters, talked at length to them and realized that they knew just how much they could take off a tree without killing it, or even reducing its productivity in subsequent years. All my observations on the trekking trails tend to confirm that this is generally true. Some of these trees seem to have been brutalized – "Hardly a tree at all any more" was one comment from a fellow trekker, but I think this too is deliberate. What your cattle want is soft stuff – first year growth with leaves on it – so you prune your forest trees to give plenty of that. It makes a tree which is not conventionally beautiful, but think

90 By Dick Isherwood
Ed. This article was clearly intended for publication in the *Alpine Journal*. It was kindly retrieved by Dick's son, Sam Isherwood

of the pollarded willows in East Anglia which were treated the way they were for very similar reasons. I just read Oliver Rackham's well known book on the history of the English countryside, and the parallels between his account of traditional management of village woodlands and what you see at the mid elevations in Nepal is striking – Rackham even points it out himself a couple of times. Some of our environmental experts perhaps overlook the fact that trees grow.

I now have a few fruit trees in my own garden and it is amazing to the novice how much you can cut out in the winter and how much grows back next year. It is really quite difficult to kill a tree once it has got its root system going. The prunings, once dried out, make good firewood too.

Food in the hills has been, of course, largely produced from crops grown on terraces – rice low down, maize and finger millet further up, then wheat, barley, potatoes and buckwheat at the higher altitudes. I have never seen, anywhere in the hills of Nepal, significant recent extensions of terraced agriculture. One of the reasons for this may be that in the short term it doesn't work too well. We had a project at Pakhribas to "improve" the maize terraces which provided the staple food for most people, and which sloped outwards and were essentially fed by rain during the monsoon. To reduce soil runoff we changed the angle so that the terraces sloped slightly inward. Great agricultural practice, you would think, but unfortunately the re-terracing removed the topsoil, which was very thin to start with. The result was that nothing much would grow in these improved terraces for several years, and only after a lot of fertilizing and ploughing in of nitrogen fixing legumes. If your family is short of food this year, how are you going to deal with that? How all the terraced agriculture ever got going in the first place is an interesting question, but there were a lot fewer people around then.

Thus there has been a situation of increasing population, constant crop area, and rather low soil fertility. So what to do? – an expression the Nepalese often use about any problem with no obvious answer.

I met a young British lady in the Langtang and happened to tell her that I had worked on an agricultural programme in Nepal. Her immediate question was "Were you teaching them organic farming?" No way, I said, but the real answer was that organic farming was what they had been practicing for centuries and that was one of the reasons they are short of food. Nutrient levels in the soils on upland terraces are very low indeed, and manure from livestock really can't contribute much. A very small amount of concentrated nitrogen fertilizer produces dramatic yield improvements on these hill terraces. A man and his two sons can carry up, in one journey, enough urea or ammonium sulphate to boost yields on an average farm by around fifty percent. This never seems to have got through, to any extent, to the government or the major aid agencies. Given that the cultivated area is constant while the population continues to increase, you might think that it deserved some attention.

Roads in the hills of Nepal have been the subject of some controversy in the past. Some have considered them "counter-developmental", arguing that the newly connected villagers use them to buy consumer goods they can't afford, rather than to increase local production of cash goods. This certainly did not seem to be the case in East Nepal where the road to Dhankuta and beyond has facilitated production of cabbages and other crops for sale to the Terai. On both my latest trips we crossed and re-crossed many half completed roads. There was conspicuously little activity to finish them once they had become barely jeep-passable, leading me to wonder whether the labour gangs are only called out when the aid donors are coming to inspect. One of the few things the Nepalese government is really good at is exploiting the big foreign aid agencies.

I met several people who were concerned at the impact of their own trekking activities. "These people are cutting down trees to cook our noodles," etc. I think this is simply not true – most of the lodges we stayed in used both a propane stove and a wood fire – the former for the basic boiling and frying and the latter for warmth, cosiness and the essential activity of finishing off the Tibetan bread. The wood comes from pruning rather than felling whole trees, just as in Olde England. You now see mule trains carrying propane cylinders up and down. Trekking is bringing in substantial income to these areas. It is becoming rather less concentrated than it was – we walked along what is now called the Tamang Heritage Trail, between Langtang and the Ankhu Khola, and it was very enjoyable.

Solar power and small-scale hydro schemes have been taken up with enthusiasm. It is impressive to look out over a hillside after dark and see the number of lights in areas that would have been totally dark thirty years ago. Everywhere on the regular trekking routes, at least, you can recharge your cellphone, camera or Kindle, usually for a moderate fee. Cell-phone coverage is astonishingly good, given the geography. On my last trip it seemed to be a lot better in the depths of the Buri Gandaki than in Borrowdale, five miles out of Keswick. There is electric light in the lodges in the evenings, which is nice in all sorts of ways, but especially in one.

Even in my prime, long ago, I found rural Nepalese sanitation a bit hard to take – two wobbly logs over a black hole in the pitch dark – but the trekking lodges, and even many basic hostelries off the tourist routes, have really got the message about this side of life. There are now clean toilets everywhere where any degree of tourism has arrived, and even in some places where it hasn't. Electric light, no paper, but plenty of water, and a brush to clean up with. Some even have pedestals to sit on. As one western lady said, the only thing they still lack is a hand-basin in there. It would then be at least as good as France. They are also very good indeed at disposing of the waste – you can never see where it goes and there are no bad smells. To one who has become used to American "suburbia" with its individual and frequently leaking septic systems, this is remarkable.

There are other sources of income too. Many Nepalis now work in the Gulf, as demonstrated by the number of Gulf airlines flying into Kathmandu. Bazaar towns now have signs out for Western Union and other money transfer agencies. Kathmandu itself has grown enormously and while this is creating all sorts of problems – traffic, air pollution, sanitation, electricity, etc – it does at the same time provide work opportunities.

In the spring of 2012, at the end of our trek, we managed to get spectacularly lost while trying to follow the Tiru Danda, a ridge south of the Ganesh Himal. At 4000 metres in the cloud I made the elementary error of trusting the judgment of our porter who had been there once before, rather than the compass, which told us we were way off course. We were rescued by a delightful old lady (probably twenty years younger than yours truly) who took time off from herding her cows and led us downhill, talking nonstop in the Tamang language – she didn't speak any Nepali.

She told us she had three sons who were all in Kathmandu, in the jewellery trade – but she didn't like Kathmandu, she preferred to stay up with the cattle.

Many things, at least to the eye of the passing foreigner, are getting better in the Nepalese hills, and not only on the trekking routes. A traditional indicator of relative wealth, in the seventies, was a corrugated iron roof on your house. Typically, off the major trade and tourist trails, only one or two houses in a village would have them – the homes of the big shots. Now everyone has them. Even the cattle sheds are often metal roofed. As you fly into Kathmandu you typically come in low from the south, over the outer ridges of the valley. You get a good view of what I have always thought is one of the poorer bits of the Nepalese hills – very dry, narrow little terraces, miles to walk for water, largely out of range of the cash income available in the valley. Even these people now have metal roofs. The same is true of villages way up the hillsides of the Marsyandi, way off the road and main trail. Something is going in the right direction.

And then there is global warming. It is clearly real and will have an impact, though the distinguished Indian professor who predicted that all the Himalayan glaciers would be gone in thirty years was rightly pilloried for his statement. (Not dissimilar to the "ten-years-to-deforestation" brigade). I have a photo of Langtang Lirung, taken in 2009 from a viewpoint close to the Gosainkund Lakes, which just happens to be virtually identical to one in John Cleare's *Collins Guide to Mountains*, published in 1979. There is no difference whatever in the extent of the glaciers, size of the rock outcrops, etc, above 6000 metres. This is not to say there won't be in the future, just that it doesn't seem to have started yet. Lower down the glaciers are obviously retreating, as they have been for well over a hundred years – the lateral and terminal moraines were already huge when the first western climbers got to Nepal around 1950. There will certainly be spectacular and disastrous moraine dam bursts and floods, but they will equally certainly not be the first. There will also, of course, be some very significant positive effects on people's ability to grow more food, particularly at the higher elevations.

THE CANOE DIARIES[91]

Priscilla Kaufman

FISH HEAD SOUP

My love affair with canoeing began after a bowl of curried fish head soup in a small open air restaurant on the far north-eastern corner of Singapore sometime in January 1997. I had been traveling around Asia on business and met up with an old colleague, Dick Isherwood, who just happened to be in Singapore on business, too. When Dick asked me whether I wanted to have lunch and then go hiking on an abandoned plantation somewhere in the middle of the Straits of Johor over the weekend, I should have realized what I might be getting into. Years back when Dick and I worked for the same company, everyone had a Dick Isherwood story – How he convinced another colleague to bushwhack up the side of an unexplored volcano in Indonesia or how he swam to Ellis Island when a freighter heading out of Manhattan swamped his sea kayak.

Dick started with the company years before I did, but took a hiatus for 10 years to trek and work in Nepal. It wasn't until he found himself married and the father of a Bengali girl and a Nepali boy that he returned to resume his corporate existence somewhere in his late 40s. By the time I met Dick, he and his family had worked and traveled across the world. But, he had settled in northern New Jersey with his kids in middle school and photographs of the Himalayas filling his office walls.

After we finished our curried fish head soup, Dick led me to a rickety dock, to an even more rickety wooden boat which took us, along with about 10 local residents, across the rolling sea to an island several miles distant.

"If only" said Dick looking longingly across the swells, "I had my sea kayak".

"Ummm", I replied, thinking "If only I had taken two Dramamine."

The sky was warm and blue and the breeze finally convinced me that eating fish head soap was not such a bad idea after all. We landed at another old wooden dock at the edge of a ramshackle village. As we disembarked, I was struck by how different this place was from Singapore, with its rusty old cars and chickens and dogs roaming freely.

Dick and I wandered through the streets of the town to the far side of the island with its white sand beaches and unidentifiable rusty machine carcasses. The weather was warm and clear, and I asked Dick a million questions about his adventures. Even if Dick were by nature a boring or stogy person, which he is not, his adventures are so enthralling, I could listen to him for hours. I was not his captive audience. Rather, he was my captive storyteller.

Somewhere after Dick reentered corporate life, he started taking his family canoe tripping, a term I had never even heard of. I wasn't interested in canoeing, but I found vicarious pleasure listening to Dick's adventures. As we walked along he told me how the summer before his family paddled a river up in Canada all the way to a place

---

91 *Ed.* Found via Google at http://canoedreams.blogspot.co.uk/2007/03/canoe-diaries-chapter-1.html It is signed "PK" from New York and Janet Isherwood informs me that the writer is Priscilla Kaufman who was a colleague of Richard when he worked with Cyanamid (in Asia).

called Moosonee on the St. James Bay. His kids had flipped paddling through one of the rapids and they had a fire sale of wet gear floating down the river. After paddling north for nearly two weeks without meeting a soul, they arrived in Moosonee – a town filled with tourists who had traveled North by train on the Polar Bear Express.

As we were walking along, Dick told me that in the coming summer he was heading to a place I'd never heard of called Algonquin Park. To get there, he would have to drive from his home in New Jersey, through Toronto and on up into Ontario Province. When I realized that he would be driving through my hometown of Rochester, I invited him to stop on his way north. We made our way back across the Straits of Johor, Dick looking longingly at the occasional sea kayak that we would pass and me looking longingly at shore. On the taxi ride home, Dick explained that the old cars littering the abandoned plantation were exported from Singapore where driving rusty or damaged cars was illegal. As the taxi sped on, we passed Changi Prison.

"You know why crime is so low in Singapore, don't you?" he asked.

I raised my eyebrows in a blank response.

"Well", he said "they hang all the criminals."

A PROPER UPBRINGING

I grew up in Utah and like most local residents only went to the Great Salt Lake under duress – usually entertaining out of town relatives – who were simply dying to say they'd floated in the salt waters – or who had just overstayed their welcome so long that there was absolutely nothing else to do with them. Wilderness wasn't foreign to me. Fresh water was.

In Salt Lake City in the 70s, the most accessible alternatives to Church activities were smoking pot and hiking. You either fell in with a Good crowd or a Bad one because there weren't any other options, like, for instance, band camp. I had my first marijuana brownie, spelunking somewhere in the Uinta Mountains on a school outing in Eighth Grade.

As a teenager, I would walk out the front door of my house, up the foothills of the Watch Front and into the canyons and ridges of the surrounding Mountains. Neither of my parents went camping, but they were happy to let me backpack in Southern Utah with any family friends that would take me. Routinely, they let me hike off into the Wasatch Mountains to camp unsupervised with several boys I knew from high school. I spent one summer working for the forest service and another at wilderness survival school. By the time I graduated high school I had hiked all over the Rockies, wandered the canyons of Southern Utah, backpacked in the Uintas, smoked a little marijuana and somehow managed to maintain my virginity.

All that changed my freshman year in college.

When I turned 18, I made a beeline for the Utah border and headed for the east coast. By my junior year, I had transferred to school in Boston to study Chinese, and from there I went Shanghai and then to New York City. Perhaps with a broader range of social options, I went outside a little less. Don't get me wrong, I always loved to be outside, but I got distracted. By the time I first met up with Dick Isherwood in Singapore, 20 years had passed since I'd spent a night outside under the stars.

WHY NOT?

Several months after Dick and I made it safely back to the shores of Singapore, I called Dick in New Jersey, to see if he and his wife, Janet, would indeed like to stop for a night on their way to Algonquin Park.

Dick said instead, "Why don't you just come with us?"

Twenty years is a long time to be inside. And my sole canoe experience at the age of 17 had been less than stellar. For hours my mother and I fumed at each other's incompetence as we paddled in circles down the Delaware River. I wasn't sure a week long canoe trip was for me.

"Well", I said, "I'd love, too, but I don't think my husband, Brian, will go for it."

I know. I know. I can't always be expected to own up to my own shit, can I? Besides, Brian is a nice Jewish guy, born in Miami and raised in the suburbs of New Jersey. I wasn't expecting a whole lot of enthusiasm about this one from him either.

But I called Brian at work because I told Dick I would.

When I explained to Brian what Dick and his family had invited us to do with them, he paused and said "Sure, why not?"

"Why not?"

Next time you are at the edge of a quiet pond, drop a pebble in and watch the water ripple. See how the minute waves stir up the silt at the edge of the pond. Maybe a seed pod resting at the shore is pushed over just a little, so that the sunlight and the warm earth take hold and the magic that is encased within the seed swells up. Over the next week a small sprout pushes through and then, the first leaves unfurl. Return each year in spring and look again as the sapling takes root. Over time you will watch the trunk strengthen and the branches open to the sky. Remember this.

"Why not?" These two words changed everything.

Figure 104 Dick "looking for orcas" in Johnstone Strait, NW Vancouver Island, May 2007
Photo: Rob Collister

Ed. Dick was also interested in sailing although he never considered this worthy of writing about. He had two boats, a 23-foot Catalina and later a 28-foot San Juan, which he sailed singlehanded to the San Juan Islands near his home in Port Townsend and the Gulf Islands in BC, Canada.

Figure 105 Dick sailing with Tim, his son-in-law and two grandchildren
Photo: Janet Isherwood

RICHARD (DICK) ISHERWOOD 1943-2013[92]

Geoff Cohen

lthough he had not lived in the UK for over 40 years, Dick Isherwood was
an active and loyal member of the Alpine Club and a regular contributor to
the *Journal*. Dick was born in Lancashire in 1943 and attended Manchester
Grammar School, where he excelled, both academically and as a cross-country runner.
In a class several years below his I well recall our chemistry teacher one day going
into rhapsodies about a brilliant student in the sixth form, the finest he had ever
taught – none other than Dick! At Cambridge Dick studied Natural Sciences and did
a postgraduate diploma in agronomy. Perhaps more importantly, he discovered rock
climbing. His first job on leaving university gave him a company car and had him
visiting agricultural test plots around the country. Conveniently, he could arrange
for Friday's test plot to be on the road to Wales or the Lakes, regular visits that gave
him the chance to reach the top levels of climbing ability. As related in his excellent
Climbers' Club Journal article 'Climbs of My Youth' [p.1] he quickly progressed to the
leading edge, with early ascents of Cloggy's Great Wall and Anglesey's Big Groove
[p.50], plus pioneering routes such as Carnmore's The Sword [p.245]. His Alpine career
progressed too. A summer trip to the Dolomites was frustrated by bad weather, but
succeeded on one quality route, the Aste Diedre on the Crozzon di Brenta, and in
1968, with Mike Kosterlitz, he climbed an important new route on the north-east face
of the Piz Badile [p.245]. They had intended to follow the existing Corti-Battaglia route
but ended up doing a direttissima. Many years later Dick was delighted to discover
that their route was number 100 (i.e. the hardest) in the Rebuffat-style book *Hundred
Best Climbs in the Bregaglia* [p.249].

Dick's career in exploratory mountaineering began in 1964 when he joined an overland
expedition to Swat Kohistan led by Henry Day [p.17]. They managed to lose all their ice axes
on the journey out, but nevertheless proceeded to the mountains, and accomplished some
respectable ascents (the ice axes were eventually replaced through the good offices of
Buster Goodwin) [p.17]. In 1969 Dick returned to Pakistan to lead an expedition to Thui II
in the Hindu Raj range [p.81]. This signalled the start of a decade of activity in the Greater
Ranges. Dick moved to Bangkok in 1969 and to Hong Kong in 1972. From Hong Kong
he organised, together with Jack Baines and Leo Murray, an expedition to the Carstensz
Pyramide in New Guinea. Not only did they succeed in an early reascent of this then
remote peak, but Dick also soloed a new route on the north face of Sunday Peak, of which
he gave a typically hair-raising account in *AJ* 1973 [p.93]. The following year Dick joined
Rob Collister on the first ascent of Parbati South (6227m) by a very impressive rock route.
On the return from this expedition, in which John Cardy and I also participated, Dick
was in a hurry to get back to work in Hong Kong. With his huge sack he got well ahead
of us on the walk down the Parbati Valley, and as we were unable to cross a river it ended
up with Dick having all the cooking equipment and no food while our situation was the
reverse. We did not see him again for several years!

92 Geoff Cohen, *AJ* 2013 pp 392-396
Ed. A few minor details have been updated from the published version and photos reproduced elsewhere in this book
have not been duplicated in this article.

In 1974 Dick took part in a joint services expedition that made the first ascent of Lamjung (6983m) in central Nepal [p.113]; and in 1976 accompanied by Ron Giddy and Dave Holdroyd he succeeded in gaining access to Kanjiroba via the difficult Jagdula Khola and reached the virgin summit (6883m) with only sherpa Pemba for company [p.131]. In 1978 Dick and Rob Collister made a bold two-man attempt on Annapurna II but were beaten back by weather and snow conditions [p.143].

*Figure 106 Dick Isherwood in 1974 on a Joint Services expedition
that made the first ascent of Lamjung (6983m), central Nepal*
Photo: Phil Neame

Having worked in Hong Kong since the early 70's as an agricultural representative of Cyanamid, with a brief to support research and trials of pesticides in a variety of Asian countries, in about 1977 Dick took up a post offered by the Overseas Development Administration to manage a UK-aided agricultural project based at Pakhribas in eastern Nepal p.219. This gave him a hugely enjoyable two years in which he enlarged his knowledge of Nepali, did a vast amount of solo and accompanied trekking in the Arun & Barun valleys, as well as enhancing his appreciation of all things Nepali, especially raksi and chang. The agricultural project developed very successfully under his leadership, but at the end of two years, feeling the need of a change, he tried his hand at leading treks for the burgeoning American trekking company Mountain Travel. Although he was clearly a popular and highly competent trek leader, Dick was too interested in exploring byways for this to become a career choice. Having enjoyed a solo cycle tour of southern India in early 1979 he wrote to me suggesting teaming up for a year of Himalayan climbing combined with a winter tour of India's archaeological sites, bird sanctuaries and *chai* shacks. Dave Broadhead had recently proposed a similar venture, so it came about that the three of us, together with Anne Macintyre, went to Dorje Lakpa (7007m)[93] in late 1979, followed by further sorties in Rowaling, the Garhwal and the Hushe valley in 1980 (described in his article in *AJ* 2012). p.155

With a need to change career Dick self-funded an M.Sc. in Community Medicine at the London School of Hygiene and Tropical Medicine in 1980-81, and then took a post back in Asia with Save the Children. He had married Janet in 1981 and in Bangladesh they adopted their daughter Marion, followed by Sam, adopted in Nepal a couple of years later. On being posted to Dhaka Dick commented that the Overseas Development Administration classed it as a hardship post because booze was cheaper than anywhere else in the world and hence a risk to health. While in Nepal Dick joined Henry Day and Rob Collister on a reconnaissance expedition to Shisha Pangma, and more typically he enhanced family holidays by trekking on the flanks of Dhaulagiri and penetrating to Hagen's Col at the far end of the Langsisa glacier where he climbed a couple of 'easy' 19,000 foot peaks.

A serendipitous meeting with a former colleague, plus the need for a stable income for bringing up his new family, resulted in Dick rejoining Cyanamid in 1985. After a spell in Singapore (allowing an ascent of Mt Kinabalu) he and Janet relocated to New Jersey in 1987, though he kept a foothold in UK by purchasing a house (for a short time) in the Duddon Valley that was very conveniently situated right next to a pub! Over the next decade Dick's work still took him regularly all over the world supervising agricultural field research trials, but his family responsibilities allowed less opportunity for climbing expeditions. The family went on camping/canoeing trips every summer in the Adirondacks and to various Canadian lakes and rivers; trips which got progressively hairier until the teenage kids called a halt. They lived next to a small lake and having taught himself to roll a kayak he took up sea kayaking on the east coast of the US, allowing him to pursue his bird-watching interests while seeking out remote places nearer home.

---

93 *Ed.* The height quoted here as 7007m represents yet another possibility. Notice the comments of John Cleare in Footnote 71 on p 156

Having retired at only 55, in 1999 Dick entered a new phase of his adventurous life. The family relocated to Port Townsend on the Olympic Peninsula of north-west USA, where remote mountain and sea kayaking trips were on the doorstep. He twice teamed up with Rob Collister for multi-day kayaking adventures among the Gulf Islands north of Vancouver. The most recent was in 2012, to visit Tremble Island set amidst the fearsome Nawakto Rapids, when Dick's energy and his meticulous planning and attention to detail were still much in evidence. Dick made ascents of important 'local' peaks such as Mounts Rainier, Baker and Shuksan, and took to making winter canoeing trips in Baja California, although he also canoed in the Arctic, making a fascinating attempt to circumnavigate Bylot Island in two-man kayaks. They got halfway round before being driven back by adverse weather. Later he acquired a sailing boat and indulged in exploration of the San Juans and other nearby islands. He also returned many times to the Himalaya. In 2000 he joined a party making a winter traverse of the frozen Zanskar river p.171; in 2002 he was on an Alpine Club expedition to Pokharkan in Nepal p.177 and between 2004 and 2009 he made four expeditions to Sichuan p.199 and 203 ; in 2010 he joined us for an expedition to Sikkim p.205. There were also frequent treks in Nepal, often with Sam.

On our 2004 trip to Haizi Shan he survived a savaging by an uncontrolled Tibetan mastiff and later came within a few hundred feet of this virgin summit p.189. On the descent over unknown ground I was embarrassed when a snow mushroom that I had prepared for an abseil over a bergschrund collapsed when Dick was on his way down and left him deposited in a heap of soft snow. Characteristically he was unfazed and later commented that it was worth six visits to the chiropractor.

Throughout his life Dick was a keen naturalist, and on treks was rarely to be seen without his binoculars. He was particularly interested in birds and an abortive climbing trip in the Gilgit area in 1975 was put to good use when he wrote an article for the *Himalayan Journal* on the birds of Swat and Gilgit p.121. To trek in his company was a privilege; it felt like having a personal wildlife handbook. Even if he couldn't identify a plant or animal he could usually have a good stab at the family it was related to; and of course he noticed far more birds and interesting plants than most of us.

Dick had a wonderfully dry sense of humour, employed to great effect in his many articles for the *Alpine Journal*. In 2005 he took on the task of compiling the Nepal section of 'Area Notes' in the *AJ*, the annual summary of principal mountaineering achievements, and in 2009 he added the Pakistan Notes to his portfolio. With his vast experience of exploratory trekking in both countries, and ability to quickly grasp the essentials of complex mountain terrain, he was an ideal person for this task. When I commented that it must be a huge amount of work he replied, "Doing the Nepal (and Pakistan) notes for the *AJ* is fun, and I get to correspond with all today's Himalayan hard men. They are generally very helpful as basically, like politicians, they think all publicity is good."

A slightly strange feature of Dick's climbing life was how he changed from being a top class rock climber in the 1960's to lacking confidence on technical ground once he moved to the Far East and had no opportunity to climb regularly at a high standard. But he was always amazingly strong when it came to carrying heavy sacks for long days over difficult ground, and my diaries of our trips together frequently stress that he 'made 95 percent of the steps' and 'I would never have made it without his steps'.

He was quite highly strung in the sense of having a huge amount of wound up energy which could occasionally be released in flares of temper. These bouts were never in my experience directed at fellow climbers; obstructive porters or bureaucrats were the targets of his rage. In 1973 on my first Himalayan trip we hired about 20 porters to take us from Gosheini to the Sainj Nala. We first needed to cross a grassy ridge at about 12,000 feet but when we reached a high point on the ridge from which we had to descend several thousand feet the porters announced that they were going no further. Disingenuously they said they had thought we only wanted to go as far as this high pasture. We had no liaison officer as the authorities had been too dilatory in dealing with our application. It appeared that the expedition was going to fail at the outset. But by sheer force of character, and with very little linguistic competence at his disposal, Dick managed to persuade the column to continue. We still had to do several days of load ferrying from the Sainj Nala to base camp, but without Dick's controlled rage we would probably never have got to the mountain.

Long years of working and travelling throughout the developing world, but especially in south Asia, induced in Dick strong emotions regarding the incompetence of bureaucracies – not that he was much more patient with the European variety. Despite his occasional rants his attitude was always leavened with humour and his lack of self-regard meant that his impatience could be taken at face value – the wish of a highly intelligent and competent man that things should be managed better for the sake of everyone, rather than the selfish desire that things should be organised better for his own benefit. In this way I came to understand how he could make disparaging comments about lazy and duplicitous locals and yet be extremely caring about the poor in the villages we passed through. His knowledge of Nepali and his ability to make comparisons between the state of affairs in remote Himalayan villages 40 years ago and now made him a fascinating travelling companion. Added to this was his immense gusto for Asian food and drink. Perhaps this contributed to his untimely demise, but I cannot think he would have wished to forego his tumba and raksi even if he had been told that it would finally do for him. He just took enormous pleasure in being among Himalayan hill people, and with his great white beard and his sense of fun they took to him too.

Dick brought to his enthusiasm for travel to remote places a formidable intelligence and an eclectic range of interests. When holed up in a tent in bad weather he might be well into a serious book on English history, or he might engage in thoughtful and wide ranging discussion of politics and economics, as well as touching on his agronomic areas of expertise. He was really a delightful companion. The climbing world has lost a splendid character and a very fine mountaineer.

APPENDICES

BIBLIOGRAPHY

Note: All articles were authored by Dick Isherwood unless otherwise accredited

CAMBRIDGE MOUNTAINEERING (THE CUMC JOURNAL)

Cambridge Mountaineering 1963
- (Dick was Journal Treasurer but wrote nothing in this one)

Cambridge Mountaineering 1964
- Editorial pp.45-46 (Dick was Journal Editor)
- Book review (Lionel Terray) pp 48-49
- Climbing Notes Lakes, Gritstone and Limestone pp 52-55
- New Route p.56 (Forget-Me-Not, White Ghyll, Langdale) (see page 242)

Cambridge Mountaineering 1965
- Cambridge Chitral Expedition 1964 pp 20-25 (see page 11)
- Climbing Notes Ben Nevis pp 51-52
- Climbing Notes Gritstone p 54

Cambridge Mountaineering 1966
- Routes done on Alpine Meet p 54.

Cambridge Mountaineering 1967
- Extol pp 32-35 (see page 55)
- A glimpse of pre-Cambria pp 18-22 (by R.A.B. [Bob] Keates) (see page 49)
- Frontispiece: – Photo of Dick on Big Groove, Anglesey (by Bob Keates) (see page 50)

Cambridge Mountaineering 1968
- Carnmore pp 13-19 (see page 59)

Cambridge Mountaineering 1968
- New Routes pp 58-61 includes: The Sword, Penny Lane, The Cracks (Carnmore); Compensation (A'Mhaighdean); The Mushroom, The Sewer (Craig-y-Rhaedr, Wales); The Curatess's Egg (Clogwyn-y-Ddysgl); The Cracks (Gogarth); Hydra (Esk Buttress) (see page 242)

Cambridge Mountaineering 1969
- A Visit to Scotland pp 22-25 (see page 65)
- New Route: Piz Badile NE Face (Bregaglia) p 63 (see page 245)

ALPINE JOURNAL

AJ 1965	More Climbs in Swat pp 205-212 (see page 17)
AJ 1968	Technical Note Piz Badile p 254
AJ 1969	Direttissima on the Piz Badile pp 1-6 (see page 68)
AJ 1973	The Dugundugoo pp 188-194 (see page 96)
AJ 1975	Lamjung Himal pp 37-42 (see page 115)
AJ 1977	A summer in Gilgit (1975) Pt I pp 158-164 (by Rob Collister) (see page 125)
AJ 1978	Kanjiroba 1976 pp 37-42 (see page 133)
AJ 1979	Regional Notes 1978 (by Tom Connor): Annapurna II p 231 (see page 144)
AJ 1980	Buni Zom pp 147-150 (see page 149)
AJ 2000	Of Jimmy and the Tchador pp 63-67 (see page 171)
AJ 2004	Pokharkan South Face pp 24-28 (by Dave Wynne-Jones) (see page 177)
AJ 2005	King of Mountains: Haizi Shan, Sichuan pp 65-70 (see page 188)
AJ 2006	A Cautionary Tale pp 71-74 (see page 195)
AJ 2008	Cambridge in the late Sixties pp 181-190 (by Rob Collister) (see page 31)
AJ 2010/11	A Year off Work pp 168-177 (see page 155)
AJ 2013	Richard (Dick) Isherwood pp 392-396 (see page 226) (by Geoff Cohen) *Also intended for the 2013 edition but never submitted:* – Reflections on trekking in Nepal (see page 218)
AJ 2005-2013:	Area Notes Nepal (*Ed.* The Nepal and Pakistan Notes for 2013 were completed just shortly before his death)
AJ 2009-2013:	Area Notes Pakistan

HIMALAYAN JOURNAL

HJ Vol XXX 1970	Attempt on Thui II from Shetor Glacier, 1969 pp 278-281 (see page 91) (Stated to be "by permission of the AC" but it was never published in the *AJ* in the end)
HJ Vol XXXIII 1973-4	Lamjung Himal, 1974 pp 42-45 (a shortened version of the *AJ* article, so not included in this book)
HJ Vol XXXV 1976-77-78	The Hong Kong Kanjiroba Expedition, 1976. pp 160-165 (Article almost identical to *AJ* 1978 article, but *HJ* includes a photo of the route on the mountain, which was not published in *AJ*) (see page 139)
HJ Vol 69 2013	Richard (Dick) Isherwood 1943-2013 (by Rob Collister, submitted October 2013)

CLIMBERS CLUB JOURNAL

CCJ 1968   Weekend pp 378-383 (see page 79)
CCJ 1969   Hindu Raj (by Colin Taylor) pp 11-19 (see page 84)
CCJ 2002-03   Bhaje Expedition pp 15-20 (see page 182)
CCJ 2008   Climbs of My Youth pp 15-23 (see page 1)
CCJ 2011   No Blends! pp 28-34 (see page 204)
CCJ 2012   Bife de Chorizo pp 22-27 (see page 84)

AMERICAN ALPINE JOURNAL

AAJ 2008   Shaluli Shan pp 420-422 (see page 199)
                  (by Dave Wynne-Jones)
AAJ 2010   Yangmolong (6066m), attempt pp 335-336 (see page 202)
                  (by Dave Wynne-Jones)

HARD ROCK

Big Groove p.121
Dwm p.167

EXPEDITION REPORTS

Cambridge Chitral Expedition Report (1964)
Cambridge Hindu Raj Expedition Report (1969)
The Hong Kong Mountaineering Club Expedition to the Snow Mountains of New Guinea (1972)
The Hong Kong Mountaineering Expedition to Lamjung Himal Spring 1974
Kanjiroba Expedition report (1976)

KAYAKING

Canoe Dreams (2007) *The Canoe Diaries Chapter 1* (see page 222) (by Priscilla Kaufman)

BIRDS

HJ Vol XXXIV 1974-5 Birds of Swat and Gilgit pp130-131 (see page 144)

CLIMBING EXPEDITIONS
Compiled by Geoff Cohen and John Ashburner

1964   **Where:**   Siri Dara, Swat Kohistan

   Articles: *How to be a greater Mountaineer* (see page 11) and
   More climbs in Swat (see page 17)

   Team: M.W.H. Day (Leader), J.F.S. Peck, H.R. Samuel,
   R.J.Isherwood

   Outcome: 7 peaks including **Mankial (5718m)** and
   Swat Breithorn (ca. 19,000 feet)

1969   **Where:**   Hindu Raj

   Articles: *Hindu Raj 1969* (see page 84) and
   Attempt on Thui II from Shetor glacier (see page 91)

   Team: R.J. Isherwood (Leader), Colin Taylor, R.J. (Rob) Collister,
   Chris Wood, Major Manowar Khan (Liason Officer)

   Outcome: *Attempt on Thui II (6524m)*

1972   **Where:**   Carstensz Pyramide (New Guinea)

   Article: *Dugundugoo* (see page 96)

   Team: R. J. Isherwood; L. Murray; J. Baines

   Outcome: **Carstensz Pyramide (4884m)** by the N face (**New Route**).
   Traverse of Sunday Peak and Ngga Poloe (4861m).
   N face of Sunday P eak - R. J. Isherwood (solo).

   The Carstensz Pyramide was first ascended in 1962 by
   Heinrich Harrer *et al*. This was the 3rd ascent but a new route.

1973   **Where:**   South Parbati, Kulu

   Articles: *Parbati '73* (see page 103) and
   Himalayan Grande-Course (see page 109)

   See also: *Parbati South 1973* (*AJ* 1974 - Collister)

   Team: Rob Collister, Dick Isherwood, Geoff Cohen, John Cardy

   Outcome: **Parbati South (6128m), South Face (First Ascent)**
   - Collister and Isherwood)

   Ed. This route appears not to have been repeated to date.

   Ridge Peak (5791m)

   Ed. The height of Ridge Peak is taken from the map
   in *AJ* 1978 p120

1974   **Where:**   Lamjung Himal

            Article: *Lamjung Himal* (see page 115)

            Team: Mike Burgess (Leader), Dick Isherwood, John Scott, Derrick
                            Chamberlain, Frank Fonfe, Phil Neame, Jeff Barker and
                            two Gurkhas, Angphurba Sherpa and Sange Tamang.

            Outcome: Lamjung (6983m)

1975   **Where:**   Swat, Chitral and Gilgit

            Article: *Birds of Swat* (see page 123)
                            A summer in Gilgit (see page 125)

            Team: Dick Isherwood, Rob Collister.

            Outcome: Trekking from Matiltan, in Northern Swat, via the Kachikani
                            An to Sor Laspur, thence via the Shandur Pass to Gilgit

1976   **Where:**   Kanjiroba Himal

            Article: *Kanjiroba 1976* (see page 133)

            Team: Dick Isherwood, Ron Giddy, Dave Holdroyd, Pemba (Sirdar)

            Outcome: Kanjiroba (6883m)

1978   **Where:**   Annapurna

            Article: *Annapurna II* (see page 144)

            Team: Rob Collister, Dick Isherwood

            Outcome: *Turned back by bad weather at about 7000m
                            on Annapurna IV (7525m)*

1979   **Where:**   Hindu Kush, Karakoram, Jugal Himal and Rolwaling Himal

            Article: *Buni Zom* (see page 149) and
                            A Year off Work (see page 155)

            Team: Various at different times including Joe Reinhard,
                            Geoff Cohen, Dave Broadhead, Anne Macintyre and several
                            trekking parties

            Outcome: Buni Zom (6551m) – Dick Isherwood, Joe Reinhard;

                            Dorje Lakpa (7007m) – Dick Isherwood, Geoff Cohen,
                            Dave Broadhead

                            Bauddha Peak (Urkinmang, 6151m) – Dick Isherwood
                            and Geoff Cohen

                            Chulu East (6584m) – Dick Isherwood leading a commercial
                            trekking party (see page 238)
                            Attempt on Tsoboje (6689m)

Figure 107 Chulu East (6584m). Dick led a commercial trekking party there in 1979
Photo: John Cleare

1980	**Where:**	Garhwal Himalaya
	Article:	*A fortnight in Garhwal* (see page 166)
	Team:	Geoff Cohen, Dick Isherwood
	Outcome:	Rataban (6166m) Nilgiri Parbat (6474m)
also:	**Where:**	Karakoram
	Article:	*A Year off Work* (see page 155)
	Team:	Geoff Cohen, Dick Isherwood, Des Rubens
	Outcome:	*Attempt on K7 West (6858m).* Drifika (6447m) - Geoff Cohen, Dick Isherwood, Des Rubens
1984	**Where:**	Jugal Himal
	Article:	None
	Team:	None
	Outcome:	Solo ascent of Hagen's Col (c.6000m) from the Langsisa (Nepal) side

also *in 1984:*	**Where:**	Jugal Himal
	Article:	None
	Team:	Henry Day, Dick Isherwood, Dave Nicholls, Rob Collister
	Outcome:	*Attempt on Goldun (6447m)* – Dick Isherwood, Rob Collister Reconnasance of Shisha Pangma – decided to plan for an attempt via the East Face
2000	**Where:**	Ladakh
	Article:	*Of Jimmy and the Tchador* (see page 171)
	Team:	Leo Murray, Dick Isherwood, Terence Lam, Mike Whelan and Steve Hale, guided by "Jimmy"
	Outcome:	A walk up the Zanskar river gorge from a roadhead near Leh to Padam and back
2002	**Where:**	Damodar Himal
	Article:	*Pokharkan South face, Nepal* (see page 177) and *Bhaje Expedition* (see page 182)
	Team:	Dave Wynne-Jones, Steve Town, Dick Isherwood, Toto Gronlund, Martin Scott, Bill Thurston (plus others who descended before the summit assault).
	Outcome:	**Pokharkan South face (6350m) – First ascent** and **Pokharkan 2 (6250m) – First ascent**
2004	**Where:**	Daxue Shan, Western Sichuan
	Article:	*King of mountains – Haizi Shan* (see page 188)
	Team:	Geoff Cohen, Martin Scott, Dick Isherwood, Bill Thurston
	Outcome:	*Attempt on Haizi Shan (5833m)* Cohen and Isherwood reached around 5800m on the north ridge. Grade AD, as far as they got.
2005	**Where:**	Gongkala Group & Daxue Shan, Western Sichuan
	Article:	*A cautionary tale* (see page 195)
	Team:	Dick Isherwood, Toto Gronlund, Dave Wynne-Jones, Peter Rowat, Nona Rowat (Trip Doctor)
	Outcome:	*Attempt on the twin peaks of the Gongkala group (5992m and 5928m) to the E of the town of Garze. Another attempt on Haizi Shan (5833m)* Defeated by local problems.

2007   Where: Western Sichuan
        Article: *Shaluli Shan, 2007* (see page 199)
        Team: Dave Wynne-Jones, Steve Hune, Dick Isherwood, Peter Rowat,
        Outcome: Peak 5600m – Wynne-Jones, Hune, Rowat;
                    **Dangchezhengla (Bongonzhong, 5830m), N side
                    (New Route)** – Wynne-Jones, Hune, Rowat
                    Attempt on Yangmolong (6066m).

2008   Where: Southern Everest
        Article: None (but see *Figure 105* below)
        Team: Dick Isherwood with his son, Sam
        Outcome: Trek to Everest Base Camp (one of a number of treks
                    over the years with Sam)

Figure 108 Dick and Sam Isherwood above Kamjung village on the Everest trek November, 2008
Photo: The Isherwood Family collection

2009	**Where:**	Western Sichuan
	Article:	*Yangmolong (6066m) attempt* (see page 202)
	Team:	Dave Wynne-Jones, Dick Isherwood, Peter Rowat, Derek Buckle
	Outcome:	*Second but still unsuccessful attempt on Yangmolong (6066m)*
2010	**Where:**	Sikkim
	Article:	*No Blends!* (see page 204)
	Team:	Geoff Cohen, Dick Isherwood, Steve Kennedy, Bob Hamilton, Dave Ritchie, Paul Swienton
	Outcome:	**Lama Lamani (5650m)** – Cohen, Kennedy, Hamilton, Swienton **(possible New Route)** and *Attempt on Jopuno* W Ridge (5936m)
2011	**Where:**	Patagonia
	Article:	*Bife de chorizo* (see page 212)
	Team:	Simon Yates, Dick Isherwood, Hugh Alexander, Geoff Robb, Steve Shrimpton and Sue Robb (non-climber)
	Outcome:	Monte Bove (c. 2150m – *"or maybe a bit more"*[94]) - Simon Yates, Geoff Robb

Ed. – The above list has been compiled from a number of sources and probably contains the most note-worthy expeditions, most of which have been more fully described in the pages of this book. It will be noticed that there are very few years where something has not been recorded but this by no means indicates inactivity.

To give an example, his wife Janet recently commented: –

"*His many trips culminated in an expedition to circumnavigate Bylot Island, off the north-east corner of Baffin Island. Since retirement he returned to Nepal several times, participated in three expeditions in Sichuan (Yangmolong and Haizi Shan), took two birding trips to Costa Rica, visited Arizona and Baja California in Mexico twice, birding and kayaking; apart from many forays into the Olympics, and summiting Mounts Baker and Rainier in the Cascades.*

He also learned to sail and had two boats, a 23-foot Catalina and later a 28-foot San Juan, which he sailed singlehanded to the San Juan Islands here and the Gulf Islands in BC, Canada".

His last big expedition was an attempt (Sic – He climbed it! – see above, p 213) on Monte Bove in Chile: Tierra del Fuego. Last year, 2012, he took two trekking trips to Nepal, and managed to squeeze in a kayaking trip with an old friend Rob Collister, in BC.

---

94 *Ed.* This is Dick's figure in his article. Wikipedia has 2300m from the *AAJ* and "Mountain Dream" quote 2400m on their Website

NEW ROUTES

LAKE DISTRICT

LANGDALE - WHITE GHYLL[95]

FORGET-ME-NOT   220 FT   VERY SEVERE

Start: about 15 feet right of Route 1 on White Ghyll Slabs, a fine first pitch[96].

1.   80 ft: Straight up, passing a few feet right of a prominent small overhang, and up two thin flake cracks to a bulge. Move up to a small spike (crux) and pull onto the traverse line (junction with White Ghyll Traverse). Go up diagonally left to a large spike belay, almost on Route 1.

2.   60 ft.   Up a short crack behind the belay and over a bulge to the mossy upper regions of the slabs. Belay on a grass ledge.

3.   80 ft.   Scrambling to the top.

M. (*Martin*) R. Sinker, R. J. Isherwood, 8th September, 1963,

No signs of a previous ascent were seen, although the line is fairly obvious.

SCOTLAND

CARNMORE CRAG[97]

THE SWORD   330 FT   VERY SEVERE

On the upper crag, 50 ft. right of Dragon, is a groove starting from a deep cave. Start below this.

1.   50 ft.   Up the dirty groove on the left to belay at the top of Dragon slab.

2.   140 ft.   Climb the wall to a spike at 30 ft. Descend 15 ft. to a ledge on the arête and use the rope to move down and right onto a steep slab. Go diagonally right across this to reach the main groove above the cave Climb the groove to a small stance and peg belay below the roof (junction with Gob).

3.   60 ft.   Climb up and right into a break in the roof (sling and peg for aid). Move right onto the rib and go up to a stance.

4.   80 ft.   Up the shallow groove above to the top.

First ascent: R. J. Isherwood, E. (*Eddie*) Birch. June, 1967.

---

95 This from: New Climb, *Cambridge Mountaineering* 1964
96 *Ed.* Bob Courtier said in May 2013...
"*I have established that it should be (number) 1 and not (capital) I in the route description for Forget-Me-Not where it refers to Route 1. The current editor of the guide has traced Route 1 back to its original forms of record. Forget-Me-Not apparently has a colourful history in the log book at Raw Head, with perjorative comments about folk who claimed first ascents on their first visit to the crag and wasn't put in Alan Austin's guide in 1966. It is now recognised however.*"
97 All these from: New Climbs, *Cambridge Mountaineering* 1968

PENNY LANE   290 FT   VERY SEVERE

The right hand part of the lower tier is composed of overlapping slabs.
Between the two main overlaps is a grassy groove.

1.   60 ft.   Grassy slabs to a long ledge below the main crag. Belay high up this on the left.
2.   100 ft.   Traverse right along a big flake and continue traversing between the two overhangs, round the comer into the central groove
3.   80 ft   Go diagonally left under the top overlap and climb over it into a groove.
4.   50 ft.   Rightwards up slabs to the gangway.

First ascent: E. Birch, R. J. Isherwood. Alternate leads. June, 1967.

THE CRACKS   140 FT   VERY SEVERE

On the left side on the steep grey wall is a steep red groove. There are some cracks in its right hand edge

1.   70 ft.   Up the cracks to a ledge on the right.
2.   70 ft   Up the crack above to ledges.

First ascent: E, Birch, R. J. Isherwood. Alternate leads. June, 1967.

A'MHAIGHDEAN - GRITSTONE BUTTRESS

COMPENSATION   180 FT   SEVERE

The central chimney of the Gritstone Buttress.

1.   100 ft.   Climb the corner to the left of the chimney for 40 ft and traverse right on ledges to a wobbly block. Bridge across the chimney and go up it to a cave.
2.   80 ft.   Up the chimney to the top.

First ascent: R. J. Isherwood, E. Birch. Alternate leads. June, 1967.

WALES

CRAIG-Y-RHAEADR

THE MUSHROOM   250 FT   VERY SEVERE

Climbs the buttress just right of the Waterfall Direct Start.

1.   30 ft.   Cracks lead up right to a grass ledge.
2.   70 ft.   Climb diagonally left up a steep wall on big holds to another ledge. Belay below big spikes 20 ft. higher.
3.   150 ft.   Climb the groove above to the triangular overhang and move left Continue easily to the top.

First ascent: M. R. Sinker, R. J. Isherwood. Alternate leads. May, 1967.

THE SEWER   290 FT   HARD VERY SEVERE

Climb up where the water comes down. A good route for a heat-wave.
Start 15 ft left of Waterfall Direct Start.

1.   80 ft   Climb the buttress right of the big wet flake, to reach a long ledge.
                Belay on the left

2.   30 ft.   Up a little groove at the left end of the ledge to reach the big terrace
                on Waterfall Climb.

3.   60 ft   Move right and climb the shallow slimy groove which leads up to the
                right end of the roofs. Sling and peg for aid. Small stance and peg belay.

4.   120 ft   Move right and climb the rib on the edge of the overhangs to the top.

First ascent: M. Boysen, R. J. Isherwood. Alternate leads. June, 1967.

CLOGWYN-Y-DDYSGL

THE CURATE'S EGG   220 FT   VERY SEVERE

The next real buttress left of the Rosy Crucifixion, across a wide gully.
It has a narrow bilberry ledge halfway up.

1.   80 ft   Easily up to big spikes at the foot of a 30 ft. groove, leading
                to the bilberry ledge.

2.   40 ft.   Up the groove on dubious rock to the ledge. Move right to belay
                below a comer crack,

3.   100 ft.   Up the comer and move left onto a slab. Up this and a rib above
                to easy ground.

First ascent: R. J. Isherwood, C. H. Taylor. Alternate leads. July, 1967.

ANGLESEY—CRAIG GOGARTH. UPPER TIER

THE CRACKS   160 FT   MILD VERY SEVERE

More or less on the left hand arête of the Amphitheatre are some prominent cracks
in two tiers. Scramble desperately up to below them. The bottom tier has two wide
cracks with a narrow one on their left.

1.   80 ft   Climb the narrow crack to a ledge.

2.   80 ft.   Just right of the arête is a wide crack. Climb this and move left where
                it narrows. Up the arête to the top.

First ascent: J. M. Kosterlitz, R. J. Isherwood. Alternate leads. September, 1967.

LAKE DISTRICT

ESK BUTTRESS

HYDRA   300 FT   VERY SEVERE

On the wall right of the Red Edge is a shallow groove line starting about 30 ft. above the foot of the steep section. The route climbs this.

1.   80 ft.   Scramble up to the foot of the steep wall and belay just right of the arête (peg).

2.   140 ft.   Move diagonally left onto the arête (very close to Red Edge) then go up right past a block to a good ledge level with the foot of the shallow groove. Swing down right to a flake, and move up into the groove (sling for aid). Climb the groove (sling and peg at the top) and the wall above to a juniper ledge. Step right and up another groove to the belay on Red Edge.

3.   80 ft   Up to the top.

First ascent: R. J. Isherwood, C. H. Taylor. Alternate leads. July, 1967.

THE ALPS[98]

PIZ BADILE, NORTH-EAST FACE

The climb takes the most obvious crack on the face which starts about 500 ft. up the glacier from the start of the Cassin route and ends in a very clean dièdre topped by a roof. 2,000 ft ED. The first pitch was very difficult (VI and Al) and there was another hard pitch (VI) in a loose chimney after about 700 ft. Otherwise it was straightforward climbing dièdre for the first 1,000 ft., which took about 4 h. The last 500 ft. to the shoulder was all artificial (Al-2) with four stances in étriers. Jammed nuts very useful. Bivouac on the last étrier stance before the shoulder. Climbing up the shoulder was not hard - one pitch of V - but it could be difficult in snowy conditions. Total climbing time, 16 h. About 80 pegs: 4 left in place.

The climb was done in mistake for the Corti-Battaglia route, which apparently started up this line but then branched off to join the next crack system on the left, practically all pegging.

First ascent: R. J. Isherwood, J. M. Kosterlitz. July 8-9th. 1968.

INDEX

Alexander, Hugh, 212-217
Annapurna II, 144-148
Ashburner, John, 28
  Book Keeping, 141-143
  Reflections on the CUMC Minutes, 41-48
  Climbing Expeditions, 236-241
Aste Diedre, Crozzon di Brenta, 226
Baines, Jack, 1, 96-102, 226
Baldock, David, 177
Banks, Mike, 46
Banner, Hugh, 44
Barker, Jeff, 115-120
Barton, Bob, 31
Bauddha Peak, Jugal Himal, 157-158
Big Groove, Gogarth, 6, 8, 50, 54, 226, 233, 235
Birch, Eddie, 59-64, 242-243
Biven, Barrie, 46
Biven, Peter, 44
Black Cleft, Clogwyn du'r Arddu, 5
Bloody Slab, Clogwyn du'r Arddu, 32, 34
Blum, Arlene, 144
Boardman, Peter, 145
Bongonzhong; See Dangchezhengla
Bonington, Chris, 1, 41
Boysen, Martin, 35, 49, 244
Braham, Trevor, 11, 13, 16-20
Brant, Clogwyn y Grochan, 2
Breithorn, Siri Dara, 13, 14, 19,20, 23, 236
Bridge, Alf, 42
Broadhead, Dave, 156-158, 228, 237
Brown, Joe, 5-7, 9, 27, 43, 49, 82
Buckle, Derek, 202-203, 241
Buhl, Hermann, 1
Buni Zom, Hindu Kush, 149-154, 234, 237
Burgess, Mike, 115-122, 237
Cardy, John, 32, 34, 103-114, 226, 236
Carnivore, Carnmore, 5, 65-67
Carstensz Pyramide, New Guinea, 91-102, 226, 236
Cemetery Gates, Dinas Cromlech, 32
Cenotaph Corner, Dinas Cromlech, 4, 49, 196

Central Peak, Siri Dara; See Mankial
Chamberlain, Derek, 115-122
Chase, Brian, 2, 45
Cheney, Mike, 133, 137, 156, 158
Chulu East, 177, 238, 237
Cima Ovest, Dolomites, 6
Cleare, John, Front and back covers, Frontispiece, 119, 155, 156, 221, 228, 238
Clements, John, 41
Clough, Ian, 41
Cohen, Geoff, 33, 103, 108-114, 156-165
  A fortnight in Garhwal, 166-170
  Obituary, 226-230
  Climbing Expeditions, 236-241
Collister, Rob, 84-95, 103-108, 123, 224, 226-229, 234, 236-237, 239, 241
  Annapurna II, 144-148
  A summer in Gilgit, 125-132
  Cambridge in the late sixties, 31-40
  Himalayan Grande-Course, 109-114
Compensation, A'Mhaighdean, 64, 233, 243
Confusion Peak, Swat, 16, 19, 24
Cormack, Alan, 34
Courtier, Bob, 1, 3, 5, 45, 141, 242
  Translation of Pizzo Badile, 74-78
Cox, David, 41
Cram, Geoff, 5, 7, 60, 65-67
Crew, Pete, 6, 7, 35, 41, 44, 51, 53, 55
CUMC, 1, 2, 3, 6, 17, 26, 34, 38, 141, 233
  Club Minutes, 41-48
Dangchezhengla, 200
Day, Henry, 3, 16-25, 35, 42, 226, 228, 239
Devenish, Robin, 2 , 27
Direttissima, Piz Badile, 68-78, 226, 233-234, 245
Distaghil Sar, 125
Dixon, Mike, 41
Dorje Lakpa, Jugal Himal, 155-158, 228, 237
Dovedale Groove, Dove Crag, 5, 55
Dream of White Horses, Gogarth, 31
Drifika, Karakoram, 61-165
Drummond, Ed, 6, 7

Dubey, Suman, 42
Owm, Castell Cidwm, 51, 235
Edmundson, Henry, 41, 47
Estcourt, Nick, 2, 31, 41, 51, 55-57
Evans, Denise, 42
Extol, Dove Crag, 5, 55-57, 233
Fairley, John, 178
Falak Ser, Siri Dara, 15, 16, 22-25
Ferguson, Rob, 33, 132
Fonfe, Frank, 115-122
Fox, Paul, 41, 43, 48, 141
Giddy, Ron, 133-140
Gob, Carnmore, 60
Gongkala, Sichuan, 195-198
Goodfellow, Terence, 1
Goodwin, Buster, 17, 18, 85, 226
Gray, Dennis, 44
Great Wall, Clogwyn du'r Arddu, 6-7,
    57, 68, 226
Greenbank, Tony, 2, 45
    Night Climbers Beware!, 26-30
Gronlund, Toto, 177-187, 195-198
Guilliard, Mick, 9, 31, 39
Gundry, David, 35, 38
Gurung, Harka, 46
Hagen's Col, Jugal Himal, 228, 238
Haizi Shan, Daxue Shan, Sichuan,
    188-194, 195, 197, 229, 234, 239, 241
Hale, Steve, 171-176, 239
Hamilton, Bob, 204-211, 241
Hand Traverse, Clogwyn du'r Arddu,
    5, 81-82
Hartley, John, 43
Hiraeth, Dove Crag, 5, 55-56
Holdroyd, Dave, 133-140, 227, 237
Howell, Ian, 41
Hune, Steve, 199-201, 240
Jones, John, 66
Jones, Trevor, 43-44
Jopuno, Sikkim, 204-211, 241
K7 West, Karakoram, 155-165, 238
Kachikani Pass, Chitral, 123, 126, 128,
    149-150, 237
Kanjiroba, Kanjiroba Himal, 42,
    133-140, 142, 227, 234-235, 237

Kaufman, Priscilla, 235
    The Canoe Diaries, 222-225
Keates, Bob, 6, 8, 55, 57-59, 233
    A glimpse of Pre-Cambria, 49-54
Kennedy, Steve, 204-211, 241
Kinabalu, Borneo Island, Sabah, 97, 228
King's Chapel, 2, 27, 39
Kosterlitz, Mike, 5, 45, 65-67, 68-73, 75,
    77, 79-83, 226, 244-245
Lama Lamani, Sikkim, 204-211, 241
Lamjung, Lamjung Himal, 115-122,
    142, 227, 234-235, 237
Lam, Terence, 171-181, 239
Left Unconquerable, Dinas Cromlech, 2
Lewis, Tim, 49
Llithrig, Clogwyn du'r Arddu, 32
Longstaff, Tom, 109, 155, 165, 208
Machapuchare, 41, 145, 147
Macintyre, Anne, 155, 228, 237
Macnair, Gordon, 33, 60-64
Maden, Ted, 4, 57
Makara, 202
Mankial, Siri Dara, 13-25, 126, 236
Martin, Steve, 6, 55, 57
Master's Wall, Clogwyn du'r Arddu, 6, 57
McCormick, John, 2, 29
McNaught-Davis, Ian, 49
Messner, Reinhold, 97, 99, 100, 144
Metcalfe, Dick, 34
Miotti, Giuseppe (Popi)
    Pizzo Badile 3308m, 74-78
Monte Bove, Cordillera Darwin, 212-217,
    241
Mortlock, Colin, 44
Murray, Leo, 96-102, 171-176, 226, 236,
    239
Mynydd, Clogwyn du'r Arddu, 7, 10
Nakamura, Tamotsu, 188, 195
Namgyal, Barap, 204-211
Neame, Phil, 116-122, 142, 227, 237
Ngga Poloe, New Guinea, 96, 100, 236
Nilgiri Parbat, Garhwal Himalaya,
    166-170, 238
Odell, Noel, 39-40, 145
Overstall, Olly, 31

Pakhribas, 218-219, 228
Parbati South, Kulu, 103-114, 226, 236
Patey, Tom, 31, 33, 207
Payne, Roger, 204, 208, 211
Peck, John, 4, 13-25, 34-36, 42, 236
Peck's Dièdre, Swat, 15, 21, 23
Peck, Trevor, 44
Penny Lane, Carnmore, 61, 233, 243
Peuterey Ridge, Mont Blanc, 2
Phantom Rib, Clogwyn y Grochan, 2
Pinnacle Arête, Clogwyn du'r Arddu, 5, 81
Pinnacle Flake, Clogwyn du'r Arddu, 79
Piz Palu, 2, 109
Point 20,101; *See Parbati South*
Point 21,700; *See K7 West, Karakoram*
Point Five, Ben Nevis, 3
Pokharkan 2, Damodar Himal, 180, 181, 239
Pokharkan, Damodar Himal, 177-187, 195, 229, 234, 239
Pyramid Peak, Swat, 21, 23
Rataban, Garhwal Himalaya, 166-170, 238
Reinhard, Joe, 149-154, 237
Ritchie, Dave, 204-211, 241
Robb, Geoff, 212-217, 241
Roschnik, Rupert, 1, 41
Roscoe, Don, 41
Rouse, Alan, 31
Rowat, Peter, 4, 51, 55-58, 59-60, 195-198, 199-201, 203, 239-241
Rubens, Des, 159-161, 238
Samuel, Hugh, 11-25, 236
Scott, Doug, 31
Scott, John, 115-122, 237
Scott, Martin, 177-187, 197, 239
Senate House Leap, 39
Seven Summits, 96, 212
Shipton, Eric, 31, 143, 212, 217
Shisha Pangma, Jugal Himal, 228, 239
Shrike, Clogwyn du'r Arddu, 5, 83
Sinker, Martin, 242-243
Siri Dara, 11-16, 17-25, 236
Slanting Slab, Clogwyn du'r Arddu, 9, 66
Smythe, Tony, 46
St John's Chapel, 2, 26-29

Sunday Peak, New Guinea, 98-102, 226, 236
Swallow, Jim, 7, 9, 10, 43
Swienton, Paul, 204-211, 241
Taurus, Clogwyn du'r Arddu, 5, 9, 79-82
Taylor, Colin, 35, 91-95, 235-6, 244-245
    Hindu Raj 1969, 84-90
The Cracks, Carnmore, 243
The Crucible, Craig Yr Ogof, 58
The Grasper, Tremadoc, 54
The Grooves, Cyrn Las, 4
The Ramp, Gogarth, 182
The Sword, Carnmore, 226, 233, 242
Thompson, Mike, 183, 218
Thui II, Hindu Raj, 35, 37, 84-95, 226, 234, 236
Thurston, Bill, 177-181, 182-187, 188-194, 197, 239
Tilman, Bill, 41, 143, 156, 158, 177, 178, 182, 183, 208, 211, 217
Town, Steve, 177-181, 182-187, 195, 239
Troach, Clogwyn du'r Arddu, 44
Tsoboje, Jugal Himal, 159, 164, 237
Tyson, John, 42, 133, 135, 136
Urkinmang; *See Bauddha Peak*
Vember, Clogwyn du'r Arddu, 4, 9
Watershed Peak, Siri Dara, 13
Whelan, Mike, 171-176, 239
Wherry Library, 141
Whillans, Don, 1, 5, 6, 9, 43, 64, 66, 67
White Slab, Clogwyn du'r Arddu, 4, 7, 31
Whortleberry Wall. Glencoe, 65
Wilson, Ken, 31, 49, 80, 188
Wood, Chris, 73, 84-90, 91-95, 236
Woubits, Clogwyn du'r Arddu, 9, 63, 79
Wynne-Jones, Dave, 177, 195, 234, 235, 239-241
    Pokharkan South Face, 177-181
    Shaluli Shan, 199-201
    Yangmolung attempt , 202-203
Yangmolung, Western Sichuan, 199-203, 235, 240, 241
Yates, Simon, 212, 241
Zanskar Gorge, 171-176